THE
FARM COOK & RULE BOOK

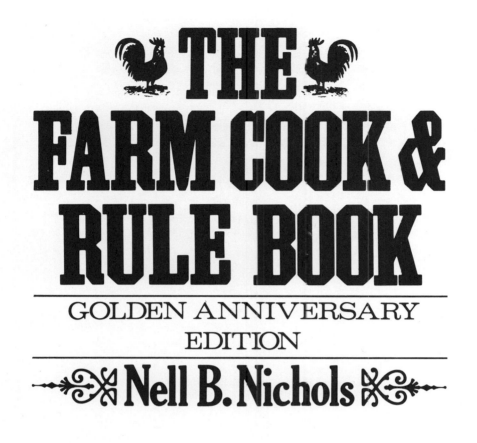

THE FARM COOK & RULE BOOK

GOLDEN ANNIVERSARY
EDITION

Nell B. Nichols

Harcourt Brace Jovanovich
New York and London

Printed in the United States of America

Library of Congress Cataloging in Publication Data

Nichols, Nell Beaubien.
The farm cook and rule book.

Includes index.
1. Cookery. 2. Receipts. I. Title.
TX715.N58 1976   641.5'973   76-932
ISBN 0-15-130406-8

ISBN 0-15-130407-6 (paperback)

First edition

B C D E

The use of ingredients and recipes recommended in this
book are based on personal knowledge. If any ideas or
ingredients are new to you, you might want to approach
the recipe or formula with caution.

Use safety glasses or safety masks when doing work that
might shatter or chip.

Be sure that all work done with cleaning solvents is done
in an area that is fireproof and where there is plenty of ventilation.

When dyeing or using chemicals of any kind, wear rubber gloves
and avoid skin contact with chemical or herbal concentrates.

Do not use any cosmetics or unguents without consulting your
own doctor.

The first _Farm Cook and Rule Book_
was dedicated to my mother,
Rachel Curtis Beaubien.
This revised edition, 53 years later,
is for my daughter, Betsy McCracken
and granddaughter, Janet McCracken.

CONTENTS

PART II

PREFACE

Aromas of baked country ham, clove-studded and glistening with glaze . . . plump, homemade doughnuts rolled in sugar . . . true-butter-flavored layer cakes and quivering wild plum jelly—these returned with many other memories during my review of *The Farm Cook and Rule Book*. The aftermath of the two world wars brought many changes to country living, and these contrasts, too, swirled in my thoughts.

When I wrote the book more than 50 years ago, I wanted to record both the best of the new and the old recipes and rules, as we called them, for successful homemaking. My inspiration evolved from interviews I was having with farm women in the Midwest and my observations of what they were doing for their families and themselves.

I was contributing food stories regularly to the *Capper Farm Press* in Kansas, which had a wide circulation throughout the Midwest, and to *Farm and Fireside*, one of the oldest farm publications, for which I was the corresponding food editor. My sources of information were first-hand and widespread, and I came to know the substance and feeling of living on the land.

In comparing the old recipes and rules with those of today, I relied heavily on experiences during the past 20 years as a member of the food staff of *Farm Journal*, the national farm magazine. Home visits with many readers over the years gave me a wonderful backdrop.

It was revealing and thought-provoking to balance today's carefully tested recipes against those of a half-century ago. Then, as today, country recipes were regarded as the ultimate in flavorful cooking; one can't help wondering how such superb results were frequently attained with so many variables and sketchy directions.

Old recipes give no pan sizes, for instance, because there was no standardization of kitchen utensils. They varied from one kitchen to another. The friendly wood- and coal-burning range, supplemented in summer by the kerosene stove and fireless cooker, still existed in most kitchens. Oven heat regulators were unknown and cooking thermometers rarely were used. There were no blenders, electric mixers, oven timers—so many of the aids we take for granted today.

Not all families, especially those living in remote areas, had ice-boxes, the common name for refrigerators. That is why some of the old recipes merely suggest keeping the food in a cold place. Freezers, which revolutionized country cooking, were not yet on the drawing board. I mention these background factors because they're important to keep in mind in reading the old recipes in this book.

Poultry was from the barnyard and it varied greatly in quality. Lazy, fat hens, good for little else, were almost always culled from flocks and converted into broth and a fricassee with puffed-up dumplings or homemade noodles. The meal on the table, I might add, seldom reflected dishonor on the hen.

Farm animals were slaughtered and butchered on the farm, and part of the meat was cured and canned to use in the months ahead. There was lard, too, rendered to use in pies for flaky crusts that never have been surpassed and are certainly worth duplicating today.

Commercial flours were not as reliable as those available now. They differed in hardness, or the amount of gluten. Homemade vinegars were seldom uniform in their acid content. How, then, could such marvelous pickles and relishes sometimes be made with them? Were the failures concealed?

Cooking with the old-time recipes by a woman without considerable experience always must have been a game of chance. With the differences in ingredients and equipment used today, it is an adventure that may lead to success or to occasional failure. It is a test of cooking skill.

Even with their lack of modern conveniences, old-time country kitchens enjoyed many advantages pleasant to recall. Milk was plentiful, although the cows had to be milked by hand and cream skimmed from crocks. Almost all farms had orchards, at least a few trees, and berry patches. Some seasons the crops were bountiful and there followed a tempting array of pies and fruit desserts.

Eggs and poultry were home productions. Fish came from nearby streams and lakes, nuts and wild fruit from the woods, and wild game from the fields and pastures. Perhaps the greatest charm of old-time country living was the feeling of self-sufficiency city people can never know.

Good food was abundant, but it did not arrive in the country kitchen in convenient packages. Cooking 50 years ago was the true from-scratch type, with much time and work required in preparing it. The home repairman was the farmer, with his wife and children as able assistants. Running the home was a whole-family affair.

When I was writing *The Farm Cook and Rule Book,* I frequently consulted my mother, a Colorado ranchwoman who was a superior cook. For a start on this revised edition, I prevailed upon my daughter, a home economist, and my granddaughter to read the original book and give me their reactions. The margin notes largely are the answers to their questions and reflect changes and the requirements of later generations.

This edition pictures the tremendous improvements the last half-century brought to country homes and the women who live in them. In predicting the future, my guess is that today's recipes and rules will, by the end of the twentieth century, appear as quaint and old-fashioned to readers as do those of 1923 to today's woman. Some of the echoes of yesterday will fascinate and amuse, as do "Grandmother's Beauty Secrets" in the first *Farm Cook and Rule Book.* But, overall, this book will take you on a visit to friendly country kitchens in the era we think of as "the good old days."

Nell B. Nichols

January, 1976

PART I

Metric Equivalents

Volume

1 tsp. = 4.9 ml.
1 tblsp. = 14.8 ml.
1 fluid ounce = 29.6 ml.
1 cup = 236.6 ml.
1 pint = 473 ml.
1 quart = 946 ml.
1 gallon = 3.78 liters
1 peck = 8.8 liters

Weight

1 ounce = 28 grams
1 pound = 454 grams

Temperature

200° F. = 93° C.
250° F. = 121° C.
300° F. = 149° C.
350° F. = 177° C.
400° F. = 204° C.
450° F. = 232° C.
500° F. = 260° C.

THE FARM
COOK AND RULE BOOK

CHAPTER 1

MEASURING FOODS

BEST results are obtained from the recipes in this book by using level measurements. A spoonful of any dry ingredient is measured by leveling the surface with the straight edge of a knife.

Half a spoonful is a spoonful divided lengthwise with the point of a knife. One-fourth of a spoonful is a half-spoonful divided crosswise a little nearer the handle end of the bowl. One-eighth of a spoonful is a fourth-spoonful divided lengthwise. Measuring spoons, which consist of spoons holding one, one-half, one-fourth and one-eighth spoonfuls fastened together on a ring, do away with the necessity of dividing the spoonful.

A cupful is a cup level full. To take this measurement pile the dry ingredient lightly in the cup with a spoon and then level it off with the straight edge of a knife.

In measuring dry food materials, such as flour, baking powder and soda, care should be taken not to press or pack them down. Flour is sifted once before being measured. Fats, such as butter or lard, are packed tightly before being leveled. To measure less than a cupful, time is saved by using a tablespoon instead of a cup. A cupful or a spoonful of liquid is all that the cup or spoon will hold.

Table of Equivalents

3 teaspoonfuls—1 tablespoonful	2 cupfuls—1 pint
16 tablespoonfuls—1 cupful	2 pints—1 quart

Additional Equivalents

2 tblsp. — 1 fluid ounce

4 tblsp. — 1/4 cup

5 tblsp. plus 1 tsp. — 1/3 cup

8 tblsp. — 1/2 cup

10 tblsp. plus 2 tsp. — 2/3 cup

12 tblsp. — 3/4 cup

1 cup — 8 fluid ounces

4 quarts — 1 gallon

8 quarts — 1 peck

4 ounces — 1/4 pound

16 ounces — 1 pound

Not all temperatures recommended in 1923 are indicated on today's oven heat regulators. Here is an up-to-date list.

Very slow—250 to 275° F.
Slow— 300 to 325° F.
Moderate—350 to 375° F.
Hot—400 to 425° F.
Very hot—450 to 475° F.
Extremely hot—500 to 525° F.

Temperatures are given for foods cooked in the oven with many of the recipes that follow.

Oven Temperatures

Slow Oven—250 to 365 degrees Fahrenheit
Moderate Oven—365 to 410 degrees F.
Hot Oven—410 to 450 degrees F.
Very Hot Oven—450 to 550 degrees F.

These temperatures are to be used with ovens having direct heat, such as gas and kerosene. If oven door "thermostats," like those on many wood and coal ranges, are registering the heat, subtract from 50 to 60 degrees from the temperatures in the above table. The following tabulation of temperatures for baking in the ordinary household range has been made by the United States Department of Agriculture.

Biscuits—400 to 500 degrees F.
Bread—350 to 425 degrees F.
Angel Food Cake—300 to 375 degrees F.
Cookies—350 to 400 degrees F.
Cup Cakes—300 to 400 degrees F.
Gingerbread—350 to 400 degrees F.
Layer Cake—300 to 400 degrees F.
Loaf Cake—280 to 400 degrees F.
Sponge Cake—300 to 375 degrees F.
Custard—250 to 350 degrees F.
Meat, roasted—450 to 550 degrees F. for searing, then reduce to 350 and on to 250 degrees F.
Muffins—375 to 425 degrees F.
Pastry, no filling—450 to 400 degrees F.
Pies, uncooked filling—500 to 400 degrees F., gradually reducing to the lower temperature.
Popovers—450 to 350 degrees F.

Flour helped in judging oven temperatures in wood- and coal-burning and kerosene stoves when a portable oven thermometer was not available. About 1 tsp. flour was sprinkled on brown paper and placed in oven. The degree of browning in 5 minutes was the guide.

Slow oven — light brown
Moderate oven — medium golden brown
Hot oven — dark brown
Very hot oven — very dark brown

CHAPTER 2

BEVERAGES

THE most common beverages are water, milk, coffee, tea, chocolate, cocoa and the fruit juices. Water, the natural beverage, forms a large part of all others. Although milk is a drink, it also is a food. It contains the substances needed for the growth, development and upkeep of the body in better proportions than any other food. For this reason it should have an important place in the diet of everyone, especially of the child.

Coffee and tea have a better flavor and are more wholesome if not allowed to stand on the grounds and leaves after being made. If they cannot be served at once, they may be poured in a warm china, silver or earthenware pot or pitcher.

Cocoa and chocolate are cooked in a small amount of water until smooth and glossy before being combined with milk. This cooks the starch and therefore prevents the beverage from having a raw taste. Since sugar does not dissolve quickly in cold liquids, it is advisable to boil it with water to form a syrup, which is cooled before being added to the fruit drink.

Percolated Coffee

For a rather strong beverage, use from 1½ to 2 tablespoonfuls of coffee ground medium fine to every cup of water. The water may be hot or cold; place it in the bottom part of the percolator and do not pour it over the grounds. Let the water percolate slowly for 10 minutes, but do not let it reach the boiling point.

If a small amount of coffee is being made in a large percolator, set the percolator back on the range where there is sufficient heat to make the water bubble over the grounds without boiling.

Boiled Coffee with Egg

1 cupful coffee	2½ cupfuls cold water
1 egg or 3 egg shells	6 cupfuls boiling water

5

Grinding coffee beans frequently was the countrywoman's first step in getting breakfast. She never dreamed that someday antique dealers would seek grinders like hers. Nor did she imagine the market ever would offer for sale a wide variety of coffee grinds.

The directions were for use with wood- and coal-burning stoves.

Heat coffee with egg and cold water just to the simmering point, add boiling water, stir and again heat to simmering, never letting the brew boil.

Mix coffee, egg and 2 cupfuls of cold water together. Boil 3 minutes. Add boiling water and allow to boil up at once. Draw to the back of the range, add the ½ cupful of cold water and let stand a minute to settle. Add the egg or egg shells to clear the decoction.

Drip or Filtered Coffee

½ cupful finely ground coffee   4 cupfuls boiling water

Put coffee into strainer or pot. Gradually pour in the water, a half cupful at a time, keeping the pot covered between times. The coffee may be poured through the grounds a second time if desired. Another way to make this coffee is to place the grounds in an unbleached muslin bag and pour hot water through this steadily, letting this drain into a pitcher from which it may be served.

After-dinner Coffee

Make coffee double strength and serve it clear in small cups.

Steeped Coffee

Use 1 tablespoonful of medium fine ground coffee for every cupful of water. Add 1 extra tablespoonful of coffee. Place the coffee in the pot and pour the boiling water over it. Steep 5 minutes or longer, according to taste, over a slow fire. Settle with a dash of cold water and serve at once.

Iced Coffee

Make a strong coffee infusion, using the recipe for Percolated or Boiled Coffee. Pour the beverage into a pitcher and allow to cool. Serve iced with cream and sugar. A tablespoonful of whipped cream or vanilla ice cream may be added to every glass filled with iced coffee.

Tea

6 teaspoonfuls tea   6 cupfuls water

Scald the earthenware utensil or pot, put in the tea leaves and pour over them the fresh water just brought to the boiling point. Cover and steep 3 minutes. Strain and serve at once.

Modern drip coffee pots banished the daily chore of washing the muslin coffee bag and hanging it on the clothesline to dry.

Not good enough to last.

Iced Tea

Use one-fourth more tea than is used in making hot tea and prepare in the same way, only steep 5 minutes instead of 3. Pour off from the leaves and let cool. When cool, dilute with ice water if a weaker beverage is desired and add ice. For special occasions a tablespoonful of lemon ice may be added to every glass filled with iced tea, or orange ice may be used instead. A few sprigs of crushed mint and slices of lemon provide other variations.

Cocoa

6 tablespoonfuls cocoa	4½ cupfuls milk
5 tablespoonfuls sugar	1½ cupfuls water
¼ teaspoonful salt	½ teaspoonful vanilla

Mix cocoa, sugar and salt. Add the boiling water and boil until the mixture is smooth and glossy. Add milk and heat to the scalding point. Beat with a Dover egg beater if one is available and add the vanilla just before serving. A marshmallow or spoonfuls of whipped cream may be added to every cupful of the hot cocoa.

Breakfast Cocoa with Egg

1½ teaspoonfuls cocoa	⅔ cupful milk
1½ teaspoonfuls sugar	⅛ teaspoonful salt
2 tablespoonfuls boiling water	1 egg

Mix the cocoa, sugar and salt and add the water. Bring to the boiling point, stirring constantly, and boil 2 minutes. Turn into the scalded milk and beat. Beat an egg to a light froth and add the cocoa gradually, beating constantly. This makes a nutritious beverage for a child or a person who is ill.

Chocolate

1½ squares chocolate	1½ cupfuls boiling water
6 tablespoonfuls sugar	4½ cupfuls scalded milk
	¼ teaspoonful salt

Melt chocolate over hot water. Add sugar and salt. Add the water gradually, stirring constantly, and boil until smooth and glossy. Pour into the milk, reheat and beat with a Dover egg beater just before serving.

Mothers were concerned about providing their children with nourishing foods. Including egg in cocoa is one example of their efforts.

Chocolate contains more fat than cocoa and was considered a special-occasion drink. Calorie-counting had made little headway along country lanes. The chocolate used was the unsweetened kind.

Keep syrup in refrigerator.

While lemonade and iced tea were the social summer drinks in the early twenties, they also were the refreshing beverages toted at midafternoon to men working in the field on hot and sultry days.

Use canned, unsweetened pineapple juice. It had not been introduced to markets when this recipe was invented.

Cocoa Syrup

½ cupful cocoa	4 cupfuls boiling water
½ cupful sugar	1 teaspoonful vanilla
4 tablespoonfuls flour	¼ teaspoonful salt

Combine the dry ingredients and add the boiling water gradually, stirring all the time. Cook slowly 10 or 15 minutes. Then add vanilla and salt. Cool and keep in a cool place until used.

Iced Cocoa

Add 4 cupfuls of milk to the Cocoa Syrup. Either heat the milk and beat in the syrup and chill before adding the ice or combine the cold syrup with the cold milk and beat with an egg beater until the two mixtures are blended. After filling glasses with iced cocoa, place a tablespoonful of whipped cream or stiffly beaten egg white on top of every glass.

Lemonade

4 cupfuls water	3 lemons
	¾ cupful sugar

Make a syrup by boiling the sugar with ½ cupful of the water and a slice of lemon. Cool, add lemon juice and the remainder of the water. Ice and serve garnished with a thin slice of lemon or a sprig of mint.

Honey Lemonade

To 1 quart of lemonade add 1 cupful of strained pineapple juice and 1 cupful of strawberry or red raspberry juice. Add 4 tablespoonfuls of strained honey and a few drops of vanilla. Serve ice cold.

Grape Lemonade

To every glass of lemonade add 1 tablespoonful of grape juice, a thin slice of lemon and crushed ice.

Russian Tea

To 1 pint of tea infusion add 1 pint of lemonade. Ice and serve.

Grandmother's Lemonade

4 cupfuls sugar	1½ cupfuls lemon juice
grated rind 3 lemons	6 cupfuls water

Boil water, sugar and rind together 10 minutes. Add the lemon juice while hot. Cool and dilute with ice water, using 1 cupful of the lemon syrup to 3½ cupfuls of water. Add chopped ice. The syrup may be bottled and kept for future use if one wishes.

Fruit Foundation Drink

2 oranges	6 tablespoonfuls sugar
1 lemon	3 cupfuls water

Squeeze the juice from the fruit and strain. Make a syrup by cooking the sugar with 1 cupful of the water 5 minutes. Cool, add the fruit juice and the rest of the water. Add ice to chill and serve very cold. To vary this, add other fruit juices which have been sweetened to taste.

Raspberry Juice

Use 1 part of the Foundation Fruit Drink to 3 parts of sweetened raspberry juice.

Pineapple Juice

Use 3 parts of the Foundation Fruit Drink to 1 part of pineapple juice.

Cherry Juice

Combine 1 part of sweetened cherry juice with 3 parts of the Foundation Fruit Drink.

Grape Juice Delicious

Use equal parts of the Foundation Fruit Drink and sweetened grape juice.

Tea Punch

Use 1 part of the Foundation Fruit Drink to 3 parts of Russian Tea.

One lemon, medium-sized, yields about 3 tblsp. juice and 1 tblsp. grated peel. Use only yellow part of peel and reduce amount of it to 1 tblsp. for a less pronounced flavor. When making the syrup, boil sugar, peel and water. Cool before stirring in lemon juice. Refrigerate.

Milk was abundant in country kitchens. Drinks made with it rated high. Shaking milk with flavorings in a glass fruit jar gave milk shakes their name. Since cookie jars were replenished every few days, there almost always were crumbs to garnish milk drinks.

Eggnog

1 egg	⅔ cupful milk
2 teaspoonfuls sugar	¼ teaspoonful flavoring
	speck of salt

Beat the egg slightly, add the sugar, salt and flavoring. Beat a little and then add the milk gradually. Strain and serve.

Milk Shake

Place 1 cupful of milk in a glass fruit jar, add 1 egg or 1 egg white, 2 teaspoonfuls of sugar and ¼ teaspoonful of vanilla. Add a little ice or use very cold ingredients. Screw on the top of the can and shake vigorously. Pour into a tumbler and sprinkle a few cooky crumbs over the top.

Café au Lait

Make 1½ cupfuls of strong coffee, using 5 tablespoonfuls of coffee to 1½ cupfuls of water. Heat 5 cupfuls of milk and pour the coffee in this. Serve for breakfast.

Flavored Milks

Place a few drops of any good flavoring extract in a glass of milk and add 2 teaspoonfuls of sugar. Sprinkle a little nutmeg or cinnamon over the top. A spoonful of whipped cream on top of every glass of flavored milk improves its appearance and taste.

Spiced Milk

Heat 2 cupfuls of sweet milk but do not let it boil. Add 2 teaspoonfuls of sugar, a speck of salt and ⅛ teaspoonful of nutmeg, ⅛ teaspoonful of cloves and ⅛ teaspoonful of cinnamon. Beat until the spices are blended with the milk and serve warm.

Cocoa for a Party

½ cupful cocoa	¼ teaspoonful salt
½ cupful sugar	4 cupfuls cold water
¼ cupful flour	4 cupfuls milk
	½ teaspoonful vanilla

Mix the cocoa, sugar, flour and salt together; add the water; stir to remove the lumps and cook 20 minutes, stirring the mixture constantly until the boiling point is reached and occasionally afterward. Add milk, bring to the boiling point and add vanilla. Beat 1 minute and serve with marshmallows or stiffly beaten cream. This cocoa will stand for hours and improve with the standing. There will be no settlings in the bottom of the utensil in which it is placed. This serves 10 persons.

Hot cocoa was served at practically all parties for youngsters, including the teen-age crowd. During the Christmas season, mothers frequently entertained at chocolate parties to honor their daughters of high school age. Delicate, slender, tall chocolate pots with small cups and saucers to match, now prized antiques, on the tray, contributed a festive air.

Sometimes whipped cream, sweetened and flavored with vanilla, was spooned from a bowl and dropped into every cup filled with the hot beverage. And some mothers forced whipped cream through a paper funnel to form a rose on top of the first cup of cocoa, which was served to each guest from the kitchen. Seconds were poured from the pretty pot.

The bonus in cutting a hot loaf as a test for doneness is the slice of warm bread to spread with butter and eat. Another method is to tap the top crust with the fingers. A hollow sound indicates doneness.

Compressed yeast is not easily found. Substitute 1 package of active dry yeast for 1 cake of compressed yeast, following package directions for using.

CHAPTER 3

YEAST BREADS

Good bread may be obtained by the use and careful manipulation of wholesome materials. The flour should be creamy white and free from contamination by molds, bacteria and insects. The yeast must be fresh with the well-known yeasty odor. Of course, it must not be sour. The shortening should have a good flavor.

What is the Ideal Loaf?

In making bread for exhibits at fairs and for use at home quite frequently the question is asked: What is the ideal loaf? The appearance of the loaf is the first factor of importance. The crust should be of an even golden brown color on the top, bottom and sides. The sides are straight and the top is slightly rounded. The surface is free from cracks and creases.

One of the necessary requirements of the ideal loaf is a pleasing fresh or nutty flavor with no trace of a sour or acid taste. Thoroughness of baking influences both the flavor and the appearance of the loaf. A way to determine whether the baking is thorough is to cut a slice from a newly baked loaf and then press the two crusts together. If the loaf springs back in shape again with no injury to the crumb, the baking is thorough.

The crumb should be of a creamy white color and feathery in appearance; the openings in it should be small and of a uniform size.

Yeasts for Bread Making

If compressed yeast is used, one should be certain that it is fresh. The cakes which have patches or streaks of black on them should be discarded. Since very high or low temperatures destroy the yeast plant, only lukewarm liquids are used in bread making. When liquid yeast is the form used, it should be kept covered and in a cool place from one baking day to another. It produces best results when used frequently. Water, potato water, whey, whole milk and skim milk are liquids suitable for use in bread. Milk should always be scalded and cooled until lukewarm before being added to the dough.

Caring for the Sponge and Dough

Bread sponge should be kept at ordinary room temperature, around 70 degrees Fahrenheit, unless one uses the straight dough method and does not let the sponge stand overnight. In such cases a warmer temperature, one from 80 to 88 degrees Fahrenheit, is more satisfactory.

The dough should be covered tightly with a lid or clean towel to keep a crust from forming on top due to surface evaporation. Sponge standing overnight may be kept in the oven of the range, the well of a fireless cooker with the radiator slightly heated or in a sponge-box; the directions for making this device are found elsewhere in this book.

After bread dough is kneaded, it is allowed to rise until double in bulk. Then it is kneaded lightly, cut in divisions, shaped into loaves and placed in the pans, taking care that it is pushed well into the corners. Individual bread tins produce a loaf with a uniform crust on all surfaces. If they are used, the tins, not the bread, are greased. When more than one loaf is baked in a tin, the bread is greased so that the loaves can be separated when baked. The loaves should rise double their bulk before being baked.

Temperature Needs Attention

A hot oven is desirable for the first 15 minutes of baking, but after that the temperature is reduced gradually so that the loaves will not be browned too much and too thick a crust will not be formed. If an oven thermometer is used, it should register at 400 to 420 degrees Fahrenheit during the first 15 minutes and then the temperature should be reduced to 365 degrees Fahrenheit. These temperatures are for use with the gas and kerosene heated oven. Reduce the heat from 50 to 70 degrees in the range oven with a thermostat in the door. When a thermometer is not available for judging the temperature, one can tell when the

Fireless cookers and sponge boxes have given way to any warm place, 75 to 85° F., that is free of drafts.

Bake bread in gas and electric ovens with automatic heat control at 400° F., 40 to 45 minutes.

oven heat is right by spreading 1 teaspoonful of flour one-fourth inch thick on a small tin, like a lid to a jelly glass, and setting this in the oven. If it is browned throughout in 5 minutes, the temperature is right for inserting the bread to be baked. If a tender crust is desired, brush the dough with melted butter, and if a crisp crust is wanted, brush the tops of the loaves with slightly beaten egg white. It requires from 50 to 60 minutes to bake bread.

Storing Bread

After the bread is removed from the oven, it is taken out of the pans and placed on a wire rack or across the edges of the pans to cool. Bread is not covered while cooling unless the covering is necessary for protection from flies, dirt or insects. When the loaves are thoroughly cool, they are placed in a clean, well ventilated and covered tin or aluminum box or in a stone crock.

YEASTS

Dry Yeast

Place 2 cupfuls of strong hops or peach leaves in 2 quarts of water and let this boil 30 minutes. Sift 4 cupfuls of flour into an earthenware crock or jar and pour the boiling hop water into it, stirring constantly. Set the mixture in a cool place. When lukewarm add 1 cupful of dry yeast which has been moistened in lukewarm water. Set in a warm place until the batter rises, then stir down. Continue this process until the fermentation ceases, which will be about 2 days.

Then pour the yeast into a quart of sifted cornmeal. Add sufficient meal to make a dough stiff enough for kneading. Knead well, roll 1 inch thick, cut in squares, place on a cloth. Cover with another cloth and set aside to dry in a room where there is no danger of freezing. Turn frequently until these yeast cakes are thoroughly dry.

Buttermilk Yeast

Scald 2 cupfuls of buttermilk, add ½ cupful of sugar, 2 tablespoonfuls of salt and stir in sufficient flour to thicken. When

---

Look in antique shops for an old stone crock. It is ideal for storing a single loaf of bread. Cooled loaves, well-wrapped, keep up to a year in the freezer.

Pioneer women learned by experience how to make yeast. It takes the spirit of adventure to try to follow in their footsteps.

cool add 1 yeast cake which has been dissolved in ¼ cupful of lukewarm water. Stir in cornmeal to make a stiff dough, shape into cakes with the hands and dry in a moderately warm room.

Potato Yeast

4 medium-sized potatoes	4 tablespoonfuls sugar
4 cupfuls boiling water	2 teaspoonfuls salt
	1 cake dry yeast

Grate the pared potatoes into the boiling water and boil until the starch is cooked, stirring constantly. Stir in the sugar and salt while the mixture is hot, cool to lukewarm, then add the yeast cake which has been broken up and soaked in a little lukewarm water. Put into a clean jar and allow to ferment 24 hours, then set in a cool, dark place. This will keep 2 weeks, and the last cupful may be used in place of a dry yeast cake in making a new supply.

White Bread (Straight Dough Method)

4 cupfuls liquid	4 teaspoonfuls salt
3 tablespoonfuls sugar	½ to 1 cupful potato yeast or
2 tablespoonfuls shortening	1 cake compressed yeast
	14 to 16 cupfuls flour

Mix the sugar, shortening and salt in a large mixing bowl or a bread mixer and add the liquid. Milk, whey, potato water or water may be used. Milk is always scalded before being added to the other ingredients. Cool the mixture, stirring occasionally. When lukewarm, add the yeast. If potato yeast is used, shake it thoroughly before adding and use 3½ cupfuls of liquid instead of 4 cupfuls. When compressed yeast is used, it is softened by being soaked in ¼ cupful of lukewarm water. If one is in a hurry, the amount of compressed yeast may be increased to 1½ or 2 cakes. After the yeast is added, stir in the flour gradually, beating thoroughly after every addition.

Add flour until the dough can be lifted in a mass on a spoon, leaving the bowl or bread mixer free from dough. Turn on a floured board, if a bread mixer is not used, and knead lightly, keeping a small amount of flour on the board, until the dough is smooth, elastic to touch and stiff enough that it will not stick to a clean board or to the hands. It takes about 10 minutes to knead bread by hand and from 3 to 4 minutes in a bread mixer.

Potatoes give bread a characteristic taste some people enjoyed. It needs to be used two or three times a week.

Bread mixers commonly were used when this book was written. Even children could knead the dough with it. See the description of the helper in the chapter on labor-saving devices.

Directions are not complete. Beat sponge in the morning to break it up. Add remaining flour, 8 to 10 cups, or just enough to make a soft dough that may be handled. Knead, let rise, shape in loaves, let rise again and bake.

The sponge is set in the morning instead of in the evening.

After kneading the dough, place it in a clean bowl or leave it in the bread mixer, cover to prevent the formation of a crust on top and let rise until double in bulk. Set in a place of uniform temperature and away from drafts. When light, knead on the unfloured board or in the bread mixer long enough to distribute the gas bubbles evenly. This takes only a few minutes. Shape into 4 loaves and place in oiled pans, pressing well into the corners. Let rise again until double in bulk and bake in a hot oven, decreasing the heat somewhat after the first 15 minutes of baking.

White Bread (Sponge Method)

4 cupfuls liquid	½ cupful potato yeast or
3 tablespoonfuls sugar	1 cake of dry yeast
2 tablespoonfuls shortening	14 to 16 cupfuls flour
4 teaspoonfuls salt	1 cupful mashed potato (if desired)

Soak the dry yeast 30 minutes in lukewarm liquid. Add the potato and salt to the scalded milk or to any liquid, such as potato water, water or whey, which one wishes to use. If mashed potatoes are added, use 3½ cupfuls of liquid instead of the 4 cupfuls. When this mixture is lukewarm, add the yeast.

In case potato yeast is used, the amount of liquid is decreased because the yeast is in liquid form. When liquid yeast and potatoes are used, the total amount of milk, whey, water or potato water added should be 3 cupfuls. If the liquid yeast is used without the addition of potatoes, 3½ cupfuls of the liquid are added.

Add 6 cupfuls of flour, beat until the mixture is smooth, cover and set to rise overnight in a place having a temperature of from 60 to 70 degrees Fahrenheit. Shape into 4 loaves and place in oiled pans, pressing well into the corners. Let rise again until double in bulk and bake.

White Bread (Quick Sponge Method)

2¾ cupfuls liquid	2 tablespoonfuls shortening
4 teaspoonfuls salt	¾ cupful potato yeast
2 tablespoonfuls sugar	1 cupful mashed potato
12 to 16 cupfuls flour	

Scald the milk or add the other liquids such as whey, water and potato water, if they are used instead, and stir in the sugar, salt and shortening. When the mixture is lukewarm, add the yeast, potato and 6 cupfuls of flour, beating until smooth. Cover and let rise in a warm place. When quite light and full of bubbles, which will be in about 1½ hours, break up the sponge with a spoon and add sufficient flour that the dough may be kneaded. Knead and follow the directions for making bread by the sponge method.

If one wishes to use compressed yeast instead of the potato yeast, from 1½ to 2 cakes will give good results. This is dissolved in a small amount of the lukewarm liquid and instead of using 2¾ cupfuls of the liquid, as is the case with potato yeast, use 3½ cupfuls.

Graham Bread

Use the same ingredients as for White Bread, only substitute Graham or whole wheat flour for one-half of the flour. Mix either by the Straight Dough or Sponge Method.

Rye Bread

A simple and easy way to make a couple of loaves of rye bread when the dough for white bread is mixed stiff and is ready to be made into loaves is to take 6 cupfuls of the dough and add to it ½ cupful of molasses, ¾ teaspoonful of salt and 2 cupfuls of rye meal. Work in the hands until the ingredients are mixed in the dough. If the mixture is not stiff enough to mold into loaves, add just enough wheat flour so it can be shaped properly. Let rise until light and bake.

Parkerhouse Rolls (Quick Method)

1 cupful milk	1 teaspoonful salt
2 tablespoonfuls sugar	¼ to ½ cake compressed yeast or
2 tablespoonfuls butter	2 to 4 tablespoonfuls potato yeast
3 to 4 cupfuls sifted flour	

Add the sugar, salt and butter to the scalded milk. When lukewarm, add the compressed yeast which has been soaked in ¼ cupful of lukewarm water or the potato yeast. Add flour until no more can be worked in with a spoon. Cover tightly and let rise until three times its bulk. Turn on a floured board, knead lightly and roll ¾ inch thick. Cut with an oval or round floured cutter. Crease in the middle with a floured knife han-

The rolls were less sweet and rich than most rolls today, but everyone added his own sweetening with honey or a fruity spread and plenty of butter.

dle, rub one half with melted butter and fold over. Place the rolls one inch apart in an oiled tin and let rise until light. Bake in a hot oven 20 minutes.

Parkerhouse Rolls (Sponge Method)

1 cupful milk	¼ cake dry yeast or
1 teaspoonful salt	2 tablespoonfuls potato yeast
2 tablespoonfuls sugar	1 egg
2 tablespoonfuls shortening	3 or 4 cupfuls flour

Scald the milk and cool. When lukewarm add the potato yeast or the dry yeast, which has been soaked 30 minutes in ¼ cupful of lukewarm water. Add the salt and 1½ cupfuls of flour. Beat until smooth, cover and set to rise overnight. In the morning break up the sponge with a spoon, add the sugar, shortening, well beaten egg and enough flour to make a dough that may be kneaded. Knead until the dough is smooth, elastic and no longer sticks to the board or the fingers. Cover and let rise. Then turn on a board, knead lightly and roll ¾ inch thick. Cut with an oval or round floured cutter. Crease in the middle with a floured knife handle, rub one half with melted butter and fold over. Place the rolls one inch apart in an oiled tin and let rise until double in size. Bake in a hot oven 20 minutes.

Cinnamon Rolls

Roll Parkerhouse roll dough ½ inch thick. Spread with melted butter and sprinkle liberally with a mixture of 5 parts of sugar to 1 part of ground cinnamon. Roll as a jelly roll, cut in ¾ inch slices. Put closely in a buttered tin after rubbing the surface of the rolls with melted butter. Have the cut side up. Cover and let rise until double in bulk. Bake in a moderate oven 35 minutes.

Dinner Rolls

Use the same ingredients as for Parkerhouse rolls. Shape the dough in small biscuits, place in rows on a floured board, cover with a cloth and let rise until very light. Flour the handle of a knife and make a deep crease in the middle of each roll. Take up and press the edges together. Place closely in a

Baking sheets, now used, were not a part of country kitchens' equipment. Women baked rolls in pans, commonly made of tin. They called practically all pans "tins."

Women shaped dough with their hands instead of rolling and cutting it. Another busy-day specialty.

buttered tin, after rubbing the surface of the rolls with melted butter, cover, let rise until light and bake 15 or 20 minutes in a hot oven.

Crescents

When the dough for Parkerhouse rolls is light, roll in a sheet ⅛ of an inch in thickness and cut strips about 4 inches wide; cut these in sharp pointed triangles, then beginning at the base, roll them up, bringing the ends toward each other, keeping the point in the middle of the roll to give the shape of a crescent. Place some distance apart on an oiled tin and let rise until light. Bake from 15 to 20 minutes.

Brush rolls with melted butter before baking. Use a moderate oven (375° F.) and bake 15 to 20 minutes.

Clover Leaf Rolls

Oil muffin tins. Take small bits of Parkerhouse rolls dough, knead until smooth and shape into balls. Fit three of these in each muffin tin. Let rise and bake.

Braids

When the dough for Parkerhouse rolls is light, roll in a sheet ¼ inch in thickness, cut in strips ½ inch wide and then braid them in 3 or 4 strands, having the braids wider in the center than at the ends. When light bake 15 or 20 minutes in a hot oven.

Raisin Coffee Bread

2 cupfuls bread dough	¼ teaspoonful nutmeg
1 beaten egg	½ teaspoonful cinnamon
2 tablespoonfuls butter	½ cupful chopped raisins
½ cupful sugar	2 tablespoonfuls powdered sugar

Work the egg, melted butter, sugar, ¼ teaspoonful of the cinnamon and the floured raisins into the dough. If additional flour is needed to make a soft dough, add it and work it in with the fingers. Place the loaf in an oiled round pan and sprinkle the top with the rest of the cinnamon which is mixed with the powdered sugar. Let rise until light and bake from 30 to 40 minutes. Chopped dates or currants may be used instead of the raisins.

A much-praised coffee-break special. Bake at 400° F., 30 to 35 minutes.

Countrywomen used to brush the loaves with an egg white beaten with 2 tsp. cold water and sprinkle on a little rolled oats just before baking. This produced an attractive, crisp, textured crust. Quick-cooking rolled oats were not yet on the market.

Coffee Bread

¼ cupful scalded milk	¼ cake compressed yeast or
¼ cupful strong coffee	2 tablespoonfuls potato yeast
2 tablespoonfuls butter	¼ cupful currants
2 tablespoonfuls sugar	1 teaspoonful cinnamon
½ teaspoonful salt	½ teaspoonful nutmeg
	flour

Scald milk and add to the coffee. When lukewarm, add the yeast, salt and sufficient flour to make a drop batter. Let rise; then add sugar, butter, egg, spices, currants and flour to make a soft dough. Put in an oiled tin, let rise and bake in a hot oven.

Oatmeal Bread

2 cupfuls oat cereal	1½ teaspoonfuls salt
1 yeast cake	1 cupful sugar
4 cupfuls boiling water	4 tablespoonfuls butter
¼ cupful lukewarm water	2 quarts wheat flour

Pour the boiling water on the oat cereal and let stand until lukewarm. Then add the yeast which has been dissolved in the lukewarm water. Add the other ingredients, stirring together with a spoon. Knead until the dough is elastic, smooth, and no longer sticks to an unfloured board or to the fingers. Use more flour if necessary. Let rise until light, shape into loaves, let rise and bake in a moderate oven.

Raisin Bread

2 cakes compressed yeast or	4 eggs
¾ to 1 cupful potato yeast	2 teaspoonfuls salt
2½ cupfuls milk	2 teaspoonfuls cinnamon
½ cupful sugar	9 cupfuls flour
½ cupful shortening	3 cupfuls raisins

Scald the milk and cool. Add the compressed yeast, which has been dissolved in a little lukewarm liquid, or the potato yeast when the milk is lukewarm. Stir in 1½ cupfuls of flour. Beat well and let stand until light. Then add the other ingredients and knead thoroughly. Add more flour if the dough is not stiff enough to knead. Let rise until double in size. Divide in six parts, let rise and bake.

Eggless Raisin Bread

3½ cupfuls milk	½ cupful potato yeast or
4 teaspoonfuls salt	1 cake dry yeast
½ cupful sugar	3 cupfuls raisins
½ cupful shortening	12 to 16 cupfuls flour

If dry yeast is used, increase the amount of liquid to 4 cupfuls. Scald the milk and add the salt. When lukewarm add the potato yeast or the yeast cake which has been soaked in a little lukewarm water for at least 30 minutes. Stir in one-half of the flour, beating the mixture until smooth. Cover and let rise overnight in a warm place. In the morning stir with a spoon, add the sugar and melted shortening and the rest of the flour, kneading the dough until it becomes smooth and elastic and no longer sticks to the fingers or a clean board. Cover and let rise until double in bulk. Toss on a board, knead long enough to distribute the gas bubbles, dredge the raisins with flour and knead them into the dough. Form into 4 loaves, place in oiled tins, let rise until light and bake 50 minutes in a moderate oven.

Rye Bread

2 cupfuls milk	¼ cake yeast or
3 tablespoonfuls shortening	2 tablespoonfuls potato yeast
5 tablespoonfuls brown sugar	3 cupfuls flour
1½ teaspoonfuls salt	rye meal

Scald the milk and add the salt. When lukewarm add the yeast and beat in sufficient flour to make a thick batter. Cover and let stand overnight in a warm place. Add the melted shortening and the butter in the morning. Stir in the remainder of the flour and sufficient rye meal to make a dough stiff enough to knead. Knead until the dough becomes smooth, elastic and no longer sticks to the hands or a clean board. Let rise, shape into loaves, let rise again and bake.

Ever-ready Biscuit Dough

1 quart milk	1 cake yeast
1 cupful mashed potatoes	½ cupful lukewarm water
2½ teaspoonfuls salt	2 teaspoonfuls baking powder
1 cupful melted fat	1 teaspoonful soda
	flour

Scald the milk and let cool. When lukewarm add the potatoes, salt, baking powder, soda, fat and the yeast, either the compressed or dry, which has been softened in the lukewarm water. Phosphate baking powders give better results than others in this recipe. Add sufficient flour, about 5 cupfuls, to make a soft sponge. Let stand until small bubbles appear on the surface.

Correct directions to read:
Add the melted shortening and brown sugar [not butter] in the morning.

The forerunner of refrigerator rolls, introduced around 1920 at a meeting for farmers' wives at the University of Wisconsin. The keeping qualities of the dough never faced a real test. Hot biscuits or rolls were served once or twice daily in many country homes. People now prefer yeast-leavened refrigerator rolls.

Usually this takes about 1½ hours. Then add sufficient flour to make a dough which may be kneaded. Knead until the dough is elastic and smooth, then place it in a covered mixing bowl and set in the refrigerator or some equally cool place. Do not let freeze, for very low temperatures destroy yeast. This dough may be used any time after standing 24 hours. The amount for biscuits or rolls is pinched off, shaped, allowed to rise and when light, the dough is baked in a hot oven. To prevent the formation of a crust on the dough, it should be kept covered, and it will spoil if not kept in a cool place.

Kolaches

1 cupful milk	3 tablespoonfuls butter
¼ cupful water	1 egg
½ cake yeast	3 cupfuls flour
1 cupful flour	1 cupful cooked prune pulp
4 tablespoonfuls sugar	⅓ cupful sugar
1 teaspoonful salt	1 teaspoonful cinnamon

Make a sponge by adding the yeast which has been dissolved in the ¼ cupful of lukewarm water and 1 cupful of flour to the milk. When light add the 4 tablespoonfuls of sugar, the butter, well beaten egg, salt and sufficient flour to knead, about 3 cupfuls. Let rise until double in bulk, then stir down, roll out and shape into biscuits. Arrange in an oiled bread pan and let rise. When these biscuits are light, press down the centers. Mix the cooked and chopped prune pulp with the ⅓ cupful of sugar and add the cinnamon. Place 1 teaspoonful of this mixture on the center of every biscuit. Bake in a moderate oven. This makes from 30 to 36 biscuits.

English Toasted Muffins

When mixing and kneading bread dough, pinch off a few biscuits and let rise 30 minutes. Then roll to about ¼ inch in thickness and bake these biscuits on a hot, slightly greased griddle, browning on both sides. When the toasted muffin is desired, split open these biscuits, brown and butter generously.

Bread Strips

Cut the bread dough in strips, let rise and fry in deep fat. Serve with maple or some other syrup.

The custom in country kitchens 50 years ago was to use bread dough in many ways to introduce variety in meals. When making bread, it was easy to pinch off dough to make muffins to bake on top of the range while loaves of bread baked in the oven.

They were fried in deep fat like Raised Doughnuts.

Raised Doughnuts

2 cupfuls bread dough	½ teaspoonful nutmeg
1 cupful sugar	2 eggs
1 tablespoonful melted butter	flour

When the dough for the bread rises the last time in the pan and is kneaded on the board to be shaped into loaves, put 2 cupfuls of it in a mixing bowl and add the other ingredients, using the flour necessary to enable one to roll the dough ¾ inch thick. Cut into rings or strips and leave on a floured board to rise. When light, fry in hot fat, browning on both sides. Dip in sugar when taken from the kettle.

Bread Sponge Cake

Mix together 2 cupfuls of bread sponge, ¾ cupful butter, 1½ cupfuls sugar, 1 cupful flour, 3 egg yolks, 1 teaspoonful ginger, 1 teaspoonful cinnamon, 1 teaspoonful cocoa, 1 teaspoonful soda dissolved in ½ cupful of warm water, 1 cupful of chopped and floured raisins, ¼ teaspoonful of salt and 3 stiffly beaten egg whites. Pour mixture into a floured pan and bake at once in a moderate oven. Cover with a caramel or other icing when the cake is cool.

Mincemeat Rolls

Roll out bread dough, spread with butter and a layer of mincemeat. Roll up like a jelly roll and cut off ½ inch pieces. Place these cut side up in an oiled pan, let rise until very light and bake in a moderate oven.

The old way to determine when fat was ready for frying was to drop a 1-inch cube of bread, cut from the soft part of the loaf, into the heated fat. If it browned in 40 seconds, the temperature was right. A fat thermometer registers 375° F.

This is a cake in name only. It generally was made on busy, bread-baking days when there was no time for baking a cake.

Many a country hostess treated guests to fragrant hot Mincemeat Rolls. The aroma of the warm rolls, mingled with that of coffee, greeted the company at the door. Most everyone considered such a welcome with delight. Usually the mincemeat was homemade.

Fill greased muffin pans 2/3 full with batter. The recipe makes about 24 muffins. For a smaller yield, it is easy to cut all ingredients in half. Shortening may be substituted for butter. Bake in hot oven (400° F.) 20 to 25 minutes.

CHAPTER 4

QUICK BREADS

Muffins

½ cupful butter	6 teaspoonfuls baking powder
½ cupful sugar	2 eggs
½ teaspoonful salt	2 cupfuls milk
	4 cupfuls flour

CREAM the butter, add the sugar and beat the mixture until light and creamy. Add the well beaten eggs, sift the dry ingredients together and add them alternately with the milk. Bake in buttered muffin tins 25 minutes. This serves 7 or 8 persons.

Fruit Muffins

To the muffin batter add 1 cupful of chopped and floured raisins, currants or dates. If one wishes, ½ cupful of nut meats and ½ cupful of raisins may be added.

Graham Muffins

Make as muffins, using equal parts of white and Graham or whole wheat flour.

Cornmeal Muffins

Make as muffins, using ⅓ cornmeal and ⅔ white flour.

Berry Muffins

Add 1 cupful of blueberries, huckleberries or chopped cranberries to muffin batter just before baking.

Apple Muffins

Stir 1 cupful of chopped apples into the muffin batter and bake.

24

Squash Muffins

2 cupfuls flour	2 tablespoonfuls sugar
5 teaspoonfuls baking powder	1 egg
1 teaspoonful salt	½ cupful cooked squash
2 tablespoonfuls molasses	1 cupful milk
2 tablespoonfuls melted butter	

Sift the dry ingredients together, beat the egg and add to it the milk and the steamed squash which has been put through a sieve. Add the melted shortening and combine the two mixtures. Bake in oiled muffin tins 25 minutes.

Add molasses to egg and milk. Use Hubbard or other winter squash.

Oatmeal Muffins

1 cupful cooked oatmeal	¾ teaspoonful salt
1½ cupfuls flour	½ cupful milk
4 teaspoonfuls baking powder	1 egg
2 tablespoonfuls sugar	2 tablespoonfuls melted butter
½ cupful raisins	

Mix and sift the dry ingredients. Add the milk, well beaten eggs and oatmeal. Beat thoroughly. Add the melted butter and the slightly floured raisins. Bake in oiled muffin pans.

Buttermilk Muffins

4 cupfuls cornmeal	2 eggs
1 teaspoonful salt	3 cupfuls buttermilk
3 tablespoonfuls fat	1¼ teaspoonfuls soda

Sift the meal, add the salt and melted shortening. Beat the eggs thoroughly and then add the buttermilk. Dissolve the soda in a little water and add it. Pour into hot, well greased muffin or gem pans and bake in a hot oven.

These muffins originally were baked in heavy iron gem or muffin pans. They were made with white cornmeal and make good Southern-style corn sticks. Bake in a hot oven (425° F.) 15 to 20 minutes.

Baking Powder Biscuits

2 cupfuls flour	¾ to 1 cupful milk
½ teaspoonful salt	4 teaspoonfuls baking powder
2 tablespoonfuls fat	

Sift the dry ingredients together and work in the fat with the tips of the fingers. Gradually add the milk, mixing it in with a knife. The dough should be as soft as can be handled without sticking. Turn on to a lightly floured board, roll lightly ¾ inch thick and cut with a floured cutter. Bake in a hot oven from 12 to 15 minutes.

The fat used most frequently for hot biscuits was home-rendered lard, which has greater shortening properties than many fats. Shortening may be used, but increase the measurement to ¼ cup. Bake in very hot oven (450° F.) 10 to 12 minutes, or until golden brown.

Skip flouring raisins before adding them to the dough. The old theory that tossing raisins and nuts in flour prevented them from sinking to the bottom of doughs and batters has been proven a myth.

Parisian Biscuits

Use the ingredients for Baking Powder Biscuits, only add an additional tablespoonful of fat and ½ cupful of chopped raisins. Mix the raisins with a little of the flour and work them into the biscuit dough the last thing before rolling it. Roll about ½ inch in thickness and cut or drop by spoonfuls into a pan. Brush the top with milk and bake.

Cheese Biscuits

Use the Baking Powder Biscuit dough, only add 1 well beaten egg to it. Roll out, cut biscuits and sprinkle one-half of these with grated cheese. Cover with other biscuits and bake in a quick oven.

Quick Coffee Cake

Use the Baking Powder Biscuit dough, adding 1 extra tablespoonful of fat to it. Place the dough in a pan; a round one about 4 inches deep is desirable. Spread a mixture made by combining 1 tablespoonful of butter, 1 tablespoonful of flour, 1 tablespoonful of sugar and ½ teaspoonful of cinnamon on top. Bake in a hot oven.

Fancy Biscuits

Add 2 tablespoonfuls of fat to the Baking Powder Biscuit mixture, roll out and cut in tiny circles. Place 3 raisins or 1 nut meat on top of every circle and brush the tops with melted butter. Bake in a hot oven.

Pinwheels

Use the same ingredients as for Baking Powder Biscuits, only add 1 tablespoonful of fat, making 3 in all. Roll the dough about ½ inch thick. Sprinkle it with 2 tablespoonfuls of sugar mixed with ½ teaspoonful of cinnamon. Dot with butter and then distribute ½ cupful of chopped raisins and 1 tablespoonful of citron evenly over the top. Roll like a jelly roll, cut off ½ inch slices and place them, the cut side down, in a greased pan. Bake 15 minutes in a hot oven.

Jam Rolls

Add 1 tablespoonful of fat to the Baking Powder Biscuit dough, roll ¼ inch thick and spread with strawberry, raspberry or blackberry jam. Roll like a jelly roll, cut off ½ inch slices and place cut side down in a greased pan. Bake in a hot oven. Serve with a pudding sauce.

Fruit Dumplings

Make biscuit dough, using 3 tablespoonfuls of fat. Cut rather large biscuits and in the center of them place well cooked dried fruit or canned fruit and sprinkle with a little sugar and a dash of spice. Bring the edges of the biscuit together with a twist, covering the fruit. Bake in a hot oven and serve with a sauce made from sweetened fruit juice thickened with a little cornstarch.

Steamed Dumplings

Roll out biscuit dough, cut in six parts and pat every one into a square. Place a small pared and cored apple in the center of every piece, sprinkle with brown sugar and a dash of nutmeg and fold the corners of the dough about it, pressing them together tightly. Steam 45 minutes and serve hot with a pudding sauce.

Meat Pie Covering

Use a biscuit dough made with 4 tablespoonfuls of fat instead of the 2.

Dumplings

Omit the fat in the recipe for Baking Powder Biscuits and use either milk or chicken broth for the liquid. Meat stock may be used instead of the chicken broth.

Biscuit Pies

Cover the bottom of a casserole with dried fruit, cooked and seasoned with spices. The fruit should be sweetened to taste. Cover with a layer of Baking Powder Biscuit dough and bake in

Even the best cooks a half-century ago treasured comparatively few recipes. They were clever at getting great mileage from those they had by inventing interesting variations. Biscuits came to country meals in many different dresses, such as hot breads, dumplings, meat and chicken pies and marvelous desserts.

a hot oven. Serve with a pudding sauce which may be made from the fruit juice, thickening it with cornstarch or flour.

Hot Cross Buns

2½ cupfuls flour	1 egg
4 teaspoonfuls baking powder	4 tablespoonfuls lard
½ teaspoonful salt	¾ cupful raisins
2 tablespoonfuls sugar	milk

Sift together 2 cupfuls of the flour, the baking powder, salt and sugar. Work in the lard with the tips of the fingers. Break the egg into a cup and beat it until light with a fork. Fill the cup with sweet milk and pour this on the flour mixture. Mix thoroughly, add the raisins which have been stirred into the ½ cupful of flour, turn on a floured board, roll ½ inch thick and cut in circles. Place in an oiled pan and bake. When almost baked, brush the tops with slightly beaten egg white.

When the buns are cool, make a frosting by beating powdered sugar into the white of 1 egg, adding sufficient sugar to make a frosting of the right consistency to spread. Either top these buns with the frosting or make a cross of it on top of every one. To make the cross, a piece of stiff paper may be rolled to form a cone and this is filled half-full with the frosting which is pressed out at the small end.

Scones

1 cupful flour	1 teaspoonful salt
3 cupfuls oatmeal	2 cupfuls milk
2 teaspoonfuls baking powder	2 tablespoonfuls butter
	1 tablespoonful sugar

Sift together the flour, baking powder and salt; add the oatmeal. Heat the milk to the boiling point and add the butter and sugar to it. Make a hollow in the sifted flour and add the milk gradually. Turn out on a floured board, roll into a thin sheet, cut with a biscuit cutter and bake on a hot griddle.

Cornbread

1 cupful cornmeal	1 cupful sour milk
1 cupful flour	1 tablespoonful butter
4 tablespoonfuls sugar	1 egg
½ teaspoonful salt	1 teaspoonful soda

These buns were as important at Easter time, at least in many families, as hard-cooked eggs dyed in brilliant colors. They were quicker to make than the traditional, yeast-leavened kind. Bake in hot oven (400° F.) about 15 minutes.

Made with yellow cornmeal, the hot bread was a rainy-day special. People considered it a cheerful food. Use ½ tsp. baking soda and 1½ tsp. baking powder for leavening. Sift with the flour. Substitute buttermilk for sour milk. Bake in a hot oven (425° F.) about 40 minutes if in a greased 8-inch-square pan. For a less sweet bread, use only 3 tblsp. sugar. Increase amount of fat for a richer, more tasty product. Substitute ¼ cup melted shortening for 1 tblsp. butter.

Sift the soda and flour together and mix with the dry ingredients. Beat egg and add it to the sour milk and the melted butter. Beat in the dry ingredients, pour into an oiled tin and bake in a hot oven about 25 minutes.

Bran Bread

2 cupfuls sour milk	1 teaspoonful soda
3 eggs	2 cupfuls Graham flour
2 cupfuls bran	1 teaspoonful salt
1 cupful raisins	½ cupful sugar

Add the sugar and salt to the milk, beat the eggs thoroughly and add them. Then stir in the other ingredients and bake 1 hour in a moderate oven. Chopped dates may be used instead of the raisins if one wishes.

Lucy's Walnut Bread

3 cupfuls Graham flour	2 teaspoonfuls baking powder
3 cupfuls white flour	1 cupful molasses
1 teaspoonful salt	1 teaspoonful soda
1 cupful walnut meats	3 cupfuls milk

Sift the dry ingredients together. Add the molasses in which the soda has been stirred. Then add the crushed and floured walnut meats and sufficient milk to make a drop batter. Pour in oiled bread pans and bake 45 minutes in a moderate oven. Serve with jelly and butter.

Nut Bread

3½ cupfuls white flour	1 cupful nuts, ground
3½ teaspoonfuls baking powder	1 egg
⅔ cupful sugar	1 cupful milk
	1 teaspoonful salt

Sift the dry ingredients together three times. Stir the mixture into the milk in which the beaten egg has been mixed. Add the floured nut meats and pour in an oiled bread pan. Let stand 20 minutes. Bake in a slow oven from 1 to 1½ hours.

Sour milk rarely is available today, but buttermilk is a splendid substitute. Bake in a greased loaf pan in moderate oven (350°F.) about 1 hour.

Cracking the nuts was a part of making this bread. They frequently were gathered in autumn on the farm and kept on hand for winter use. Use 1½ cups milk instead of 1 cup. Spread batter in a well-greased 9-by-5-by-3-inch loaf pan and bake in a moderate oven (350°F.) 60 to 70 minutes. Test with a wooden pick. Insert it into the center of the loaf. If it comes out clean, the loaf is done. Cool, wrap in waxed paper and store in refrigerator overnight, or longer, to insure neat slices when cut.

Substitute buttermilk for the difficult-to-find sour milk. To keep griddle cakes hot until serving time, countrywomen placed them in a single layer between folds of warm towels and put them in a very slow oven.

Bake griddle cakes that are as thin or thick as you like. Add a little more water or milk to make the batter thinner, a little more flour for thicker cakes.

CHAPTER 5

GRIDDLE CAKES AND WAFFLES

Sour Milk Griddle Cakes

1½ cupfuls flour	1 egg
¾ teaspoonful salt	1½ cupfuls sour milk
	¾ teaspoonful soda

Mix the flour, salt and soda together and add the sour milk and well beaten egg. Drop by spoonfuls on a hot griddle iron and cook on one side. When puffed, full of bubbles and cooked on the edges, turn and cook on the other side. Serve hot.

Sweet Milk Griddle Cakes

If one wishes to use sweet milk, follow the recipe for sour milk griddle cakes, substituting sweet milk and 1½ teaspoonfuls of baking powder for the sour milk and the soda.

Buckwheat Cakes

½ cake compressed yeast	1 teaspoonful melted butter
½ cupful lukewarm water	1 tablespoonful molasses
1 teaspoonful salt	8 cupfuls water
	buckwheat flour

Break the yeast in small pieces and soak in the ½ cupful of lukewarm water. Then put it in a pitcher and add 8 cupfuls of lukewarm water, the salt and sufficient buckwheat flour to make a smooth pour batter. Let stand overnight. In the morning dip out 2 cupfuls of batter and set aside. To the portion to be used add the molasses and melted butter. Mix together lightly and bake on the griddle.

If there is batter left after breakfast, pour it into the 2 cupfuls saved out and set away. The night before using add 2 cupfuls of lukewarm water, 1 teaspoonful of salt and sufficient buckwheat flour to make a pour batter. In the morning add 1

30

teaspoonful of melted butter and 1 tablespoonful of molasses. Stir in ¼ teaspoonful of soda, which has been dissolved first in a little cool water. In case one wishes to use the batter several mornings in succession, always save out some of the batter before adding the molasses and melted butter.

Buckwheat Cakes

1 cupful buckwheat flour	1 tablespoonful shortening
½ teaspoonful salt	3 teaspoonfuls baking powder
1 tablespoonful sugar	1 cupful cold water
	¼ cupful milk

Sift the dry ingredients together two times, add the other ingredients and mix. Bake at once on a hot griddle.

Rice Griddle Cakes

1 cupful boiled rice	1 egg
1 tablespoonful shortening	1 cupful flour
1 cupful milk	2 teaspoonfuls baking powder
	½ teaspoonful salt

Melt the shortening in the heated rice, add the milk and the beaten egg. Sift the dry ingredients together and add them to the other mixture. Mix thoroughly and bake at once on a hot griddle.

Crumb Griddle Cakes

3 cupfuls bread crumbs	1 cupful flour
3 cupfuls sweet milk	2 eggs
1 teaspoonful salt	4 teaspoonfuls baking powder
3 tablespoonfuls sugar	2 tablespoonfuls melted fat

Scald the milk and add the bread crumbs. Let stand 10 minutes and then beat to a paste. Add the salt, sugar, shortening and well beaten egg. Stir in the flour and baking powder which have been sifted together. Bake on a hot griddle until browned on both sides.

Corn Cakes

2 cupfuls flour	5 tablespoonfuls sugar
½ cupful cornmeal	1¾ cupfuls boiling water
1½ tablespoonfuls baking powder	1 cupful milk
1½ teaspoonfuls salt	1 egg
	2 tablespoonfuls melted butter

After cooking cornmeal with water, cool the mush before adding other ingredients. Sift together flour, baking powder and salt and stir in the sugar. Add with the egg, milk and melted butter, or shortening, to the cornmeal mixture.

Use 2 cups buttermilk for the liquid and 1 tsp. baking soda instead of 2 tsp. Waffles commonly were cooked in irons over coals in wood- and coal-burning stoves and served for breakfast or supper with sausage cakes. Add 6 tblsp. melted shortening instead of the butter for richer, more delicious waffles. Farm women liked to substitute fresh bacon fat for the shortening when they had it. When they were in a hurry, they did not separate the eggs. They beat the whole eggs well.

Make these substitutions: 2 cups sweet milk instead of 1 cup, 4 tsp. baking powder for the 3 tsp. and 6 tblsp. melted shortening for the melted butter.

Among the favorite suppers on a snowy evening was this menu: sweet potato waffles, grilled ham and fruit salad.

32 THE FARM COOK AND RULE BOOK

Add the meal to the boiling water and cook 5 minutes. Turn into a bowl and add the other ingredients. Bake on a griddle iron.

Waffles

2 cupfuls flour	2 tablespoonfuls melted butter
2 teaspoonfuls soda	2 cupfuls milk
½ teaspoonful salt	2 egg yolks
2 egg whites	

Mix and sift dry ingredients, add the milk gradually and stir in the beaten egg yolks. Add the melted butter and fold in the stiffly beaten egg whites. Cook on a hot, well oiled waffle iron.

Sweet Milk Waffles

1¾ cupfuls flour	1½ tablespoonfuls melted butter
3 teaspoonfuls baking powder	1 cupful sweet milk
¾ teaspoonful salt	2 egg yolks
2 egg whites	

Mix and sift the dry ingredients, add the milk gradually and stir in the beaten egg yolks. Add the melted butter and fold in the stiffly beaten egg whites. Cook on a hot, well oiled waffle iron.

Rice Waffles

1½ cupfuls flour	2 egg yolks
½ teaspoonful salt	2 egg whites
3 teaspoonfuls baking powder	2 tablespoonfuls butter
1 cupful boiled rice	1¼ cupfuls milk

Sift the dry ingredients together, add the melted shortening, the rice, beaten egg yolks and the milk. Mix thoroughly and fold in the stiffly beaten egg whites.

Sweet Potato Waffles

1 cupful mashed sweet potatoes	3 teaspoonfuls baking powder
1 cupful milk	½ cupful butter
1 egg	1 cupful flour
4 tablespoonfuls sugar	

Mix sweet potatoes, milk, melted butter, flour, sugar, beaten egg yolk and baking powder together. Fold in stiffly beaten egg white and cook.

Oven French Toast: When gas and electric ranges came to country kitchens, special French toast was made this way. Place dipped bread slices in a big, shallow pan, greased, and place in an extremely hot oven (500° F.). It takes about 8 minutes on each side for the toast to turn golden. Make the batter for 4 slices bread with 3/4 cup milk, 1/4 tsp. salt, 1 tblsp. sugar and 3 slightly beaten eggs.

Thick slices of homemade bread, browned deep over embers in a wood- and coal-burning stove and lathered with homemade butter, are only a beautiful memory.

CHAPTER 6

TOAST

Dry Toast

Cut bread that is at least a day old in ½ inch slices. The crust may be removed if desired. Put the slices in a wire toaster or hold on a fork and place over coals to dry and brown. Hold far enough from the coals that the bread will not burn. When dry and a golden brown on one side, turn and brown on the other side. Bread may be browned in the oven but this gives a harder toast.

Milk Toast

2 cupfuls milk	1 teaspoonful salt
2 tablespoonfuls flour	8 slices toast
2 tablespoonfuls butter	2 tablespoonfuls butter

Scald the milk and add the flour and butter which have been mixed together thoroughly. Add the salt and cook, stirring constantly, until the mixture thickens. Pour this hot sauce over the toast which has been buttered with 2 tablespoonfuls of butter.

French Toast

3 eggs	9 slices bread
1½ cupfuls milk	1 teaspoonful salt

Beat the eggs slightly and add the milk and salt. Dip the bread in this mixture and brown quickly on both sides in a frying pan containing a little fat.

Cinnamon Toast

Mix equal parts of powdered cinnamon and powdered sugar and sprinkle generously over buttered toast. Serve while hot.

33

Another method of serving, favored in country homes was to place the hot, buttered toast in a shallow soup plate or bowl. Hot milk was poured on just before serving. Or sometimes the toast was accompanied by a small pitcher of heated milk for adding just before the first bite was taken.

French toast was considered thrifty because it salvaged leftover dry bread, which makes the best toast. See French Toast recipes on the following page.

Country French Toast. To duplicate the French toast made with the rather firm homemade bread, use French bread. Cut 18 1-inch slices. Soak them on both sides in the batter. To make it, beat until smooth ½ cup flour, 2 tblsp. sugar, ¼ tsp. salt, 2 cups milk and 6 eggs. Melt 1 tblsp. butter in skillet over medium heat. Cook bread slices without crowding about 12 minutes on each side, or until golden brown.

Home-canned tomatoes from the fruit closet were featured in this supper toast. No need to add soda.

Tomato Toast

4 tablespoonfuls butter	1½ cupfuls strained tomato pulp
3 tablespoonfuls flour	¼ teaspoonful soda
¾ teaspoonful salt	½ cupful scalded cream
⅛ teaspoonful pepper	8 slices toast

Melt the butter in a saucepan and add the flour and salt. Gradually pour in the tomato which has been dissolved. Stir constantly and add the scalded cream. Pour the hot sauce over the toast and serve immediately.

Cake Baking in Country Kitchens

Countrywomen in the 1920 era built their culinary reputations to a large extent on the cakes they baked. This chapter features some of the superior layers and loaves popular in the days just before and after World War I. Superlative taste is what counted most; that they were simple cakes without fancy decorations made no difference.

Read the original recipes in the first Farm Cook and Rule Book and you will understand why baking a luscious cake was a triumph. Consider the variables. Pan sizes had not been standardized, so were not commonly listed in recipes. A woman had to experiment with the ingredients until they fitted the pans she had, which frequently differed from those of her neighbors down the road. Flours varied in hardness, or gluten content.

The ability to judge oven temperatures had to be acquired. Heat indicators built in oven doors of wood- and coal-burning stoves were not accurate. Even so, some of the best homemade cakes anyone ever tasted came from them. Portable oven thermometers rarely were available for use with kerosene- and gas-heated ovens. And no one had yet imagined heat regulators.

Any woman who outwitted all the variations and baked superb cakes deserved the local fame she won with them. She made the recipes her own and sometimes gave her name to the best cakes she baked. Notice Rachel's Dark Cake and Aunt Nellie's Cake in the old-time recipes.

Changes have continued. Sour cream is a classic example. It usually was thick cream skimmed from crocks of milk and allowed to sour naturally. The butter-fat content was larger than today's commercial sour cream. That is why one cannot be substituted for the other in cake recipes without adaptations.

Using the cake recipes in the first Farm Cook and Rule Book, due to the changes, is something like traveling

Country Plain Cake

¼ cup butter	2¼ cups sifted cake flour
¼ cup shortening	2½ tsp. baking powder
1½ cups sugar	¾ tsp. salt
1 tsp. vanilla	1 cup plus 2 tblsp. milk
2 eggs	

Cream together butter and shortening; gradually add sugar and cream until very light and fluffy. Add vanilla. Add eggs one at a time, beating after each addition.

Sift together flour, baking powder and salt. Fold into creamed mixture alternately with the milk.

Bake in 2 greased and paper-lined 9-inch layer-cake pans in moderate oven (375° F.) 20 to 25 minutes, or until wooden pick inserted in center comes out clean.

CHAPTER 7

CAKES

CAKES are divided into two classes, those which contain butter and those which do not contain butter.

To be successful in cake making the best ingredients, accurate measurements and the right oven temperatures must be used. Loaf cakes require an oven warm enough to turn a little flour light brown in 4 minutes, or a temperature of about 350 degrees Fahrenheit. Layer and cup cakes require a somewhat warmer oven, a temperature of 375 degrees Fahrenheit, while sponge cakes are best baked in a slower oven, or one with a temperature of approximately 300 degrees Fahrenheit. If a thermostat in the oven door is used to measure the temperature instead of an oven thermometer, subtract about 50 degrees from these temperatures. A small pan of water set in one corner of a kerosene or gas heated oven helps to insure even baking.

Baking Suggestions

The time of baking is divided into quarters. During the first quarter the cake should begin to rise, in the second it should continue to rise and begin to brown, in the third it should continue to brown, and in the fourth it should finish browning and shrink from the pan.

Cake pans are oiled lightly or are lined with oiled paper before the batter is poured into them. The pans should be about three-fourths full of the batter which is spread evenly toward the sides and corners. Cake is baked as near the center of the oven as is possible.

Mistakes to Avoid

When the cake breaks open on top, it is a sign that the oven was too hot when the batter was inserted or that too much flour

down a road marked by a sign: TRAVEL AT YOUR OWN RISK. You may turn out some delectable cakes, but you may not be pleased with all of them. Some of the recipes for the cakes were revised in the late 1930's. Several of them are included in this book. They retain that wonderful buttery taste so characteristic of popular country cakes just after World War I.

The fat contents of nuts and butter are compared. Because egg sizes vary, it takes 4 to 6 whole eggs, 8 to 10 whites and 14 egg yolks to measure 1 cup.

A cake referred to as plain was a basic cake. Sometimes this one was called Two-Egg Cake. See recipe for Country Plain Cake.

White Cake

⅓ cup butter

⅓ cup shortening

1¾ cups sugar

2 tsp. vanilla

3 cups sifted cake flour

3½ tsp. baking powder

¾ tsp. salt

1⅓ cups skim milk

4 egg whites, beaten

Cream together butter and shortening; gradually add sugar and cream until light and fluffy. Add vanilla.

Sift together flour, baking powder and salt. Add alternately to creamed mixture with the milk. Fold in egg whites. Pour into 2 greased and floured

was used. A soggy, heavy cake contains too little flour and too much sugar and fat. A cake which runs over the edges of the pan contains too much baking powder or it was baked in an oven that was not hot enough.

Since it is sometimes necessary to make substitutions in cake making, this table of equivalents may be helpful:

8 egg whites and 1 egg equal 4 eggs in a cake	1 cupful chocolate equals ⅓ cupful butter
1 cupful nut meats equals ⅓ cupful butter	¾ to ⅝ cupful bread flour equals 1 cupful pastry flour

Plain Cake

4 tablespoonfuls shortening	1½ cupfuls flour
1 cupful sugar	2½ teaspoonfuls baking powder
2 eggs	½ teaspoonful vanilla
½ cupful milk	¼ teaspoonful salt

Cream the shortening with a spoon and add the sugar. Beat until light and creamy. Then add the beaten egg yolks. Sift the flour and baking powder together and add them alternately with the milk. Add salt and vanilla, fold in the stiffly beaten egg whites and pour the batter in the tins for baking. This may be baked in layers or as a loaf.

Spice Cake

Add 1 teaspoonful of cinnamon and 1 teaspoonful of cloves to the plain cake batter.

Raisin Cake

Add ½ cupful of chopped and floured raisins to the batter for plain cake just before the egg whites are folded into the mixture.

Nut Cake

Add ½ cupful of chopped and floured nut meats to the plain cake batter just before folding in the egg whites. Since the plain cake is not very rich, the amount of fat does not need to be reduced when the nut meats are added.

Orange Cake

Add 2 tablespoonfuls of grated orange peel to the plain cake batter.

9-inch layer-cake pans, or in 1 13-by-9-by-2-inch pan.

Bake in moderate oven (350°F.) 30 to 35 minutes for layers, 35 to 45 minutes for oblong cake. Make wooden pick test for doneness.

Chocolate Cake

Add 2 ounces of melted chocolate to the plain cake batter just before the egg yolks are stirred into the sugar and butter.

White Cake

½ cupful butter	3 teaspoonfuls baking powder
1½ cupfuls sugar	¼ teaspoonful cream of tartar
½ cupful milk	6 egg whites
2½ cupfuls flour	½ teaspoonful flavoring

Cream the butter, add the sugar gradually and beat until light and creamy. Mix the dry ingredients together and add them alternately with the milk. Add the flavoring and fold in the stiffly beaten egg whites. Bake as a loaf.

White Layer Cake

½ cupful butter	4 teaspoonfuls baking powder
1⅓ cupfuls sugar	4 egg whites
1 cupful milk	¼ teaspoonful salt
3 cupfuls flour	1¼ teaspoonfuls vanilla

Cream the butter, add the sugar and beat until the mixture is light. Then add a tablespoonful or two of the dry ingredients which have been sifted together, then a little milk. Add these alternately until all are used, add the vanilla and then fold in the stiffly beaten egg whites. Bake in three medium-sized layer cake tins about 35 minutes.

Jelly Roll

4 eggs	1 tablespoonful cornstarch
1 cupful sugar	1 cupful flour
3 tablespoonfuls cold water	1 teaspoonful baking powder
	¼ teaspoonful flavoring

Separate the eggs and beat the yolks until they are a light lemon color. Add the sugar gradually and then stir in the cold water. Mix the flour, baking powder and cornstarch and add to the cake mixture. Stir in the flavoring and fold in the stiffly beaten egg whites. Pour in a pan lined with buttered paper, spreading the batter in about ¾ of an inch thick. Bake in a moderate oven. When baked, turn out on oiled paper sprinkled with powdered sugar and remove the paper on which it was cooked. Cut thin slices from the edges of the cake, spread with

See up-dated recipe. Sometimes slices of jelly-roll were served with topknots of vanilla ice cream.

Jelly Roll

3 eggs	1 tsp. baking powder
1 cup sugar	¼ tsp. salt
⅓ cup water	⅔ cup jelly
1 tsp. vanilla	Confectioners' sugar
1 cup sifted flour	

Beat eggs with rotary or electric beater until very thick and lemon-colored. Gradually beat in sugar. Beat in water and vanilla all at one time.

Sift together flour, baking powder and salt. Beat into egg mixture. Beat only until smooth. Pour into a 15½-by-10½-by-1-inch jelly-roll pan lined with greased paper, waxed or plain. Carefully spread batter into pan corners.

Bake in a moderate oven (375°F.) 12 to 15 minutes, or until a wooden pick inserted in center comes out clean. Loosen cake around edges and turn onto a towel sprinkled with confectioners' sugar. Gently peel off paper; trim edges if needed. Roll up cake and towel from narrow end. Place on rack to cool. When cool, unwind, remove towel, spread cake with jelly, beaten slightly with 1 tblsp. cold water so that it will spread more easily. Roll up and sprinkle with confectioners' sugar.

Note to Rachel's Dark Cake:

Rachel baked this cake in square layer-cake pans and frosted them with a fluffy white icing. The milk measurement in Part Two was ½ cup, not 1 cup.

Rachel's Chocolate Cake

½ cup hot water
3 squares unsweetened chocolate

Add hot water to cut-up chocolate and stir over low heat until chocolate is melted. Set aside to cool, first stirring until mixture thickens.

½ cup butter   ¼ tsp. baking soda
1⅓ cups sugar   2¼ tsp. baking powder
3 eggs   1 tsp. salt
2¼ cups sifted cake flour   1 cup buttermilk

Cream together butter and sugar, adding sugar gradually. Beat until light and fluffy. Beat in eggs and add the cooled chocolate mixture.
Sift together cake flour, baking soda, baking powder and salt. Add to chocolate mixture alternately with buttermilk. Pour into 2 greased and floured 9-inch round layer-cake pans. Bake in moderate oven (350°F.) 30 to 35 minutes. Test for doneness with wooden pick.

jam or jelly and roll tightly. The work must be done very rapidly or the cake will not roll neatly. Wrap the oiled paper about the cake so it will not unroll.

Gold Cake

3 eggs	¼ teaspoonful salt
1 cupful sugar	½ teaspoonful flavoring
4 tablespoonfuls cold water	1 cupful pastry flour or
1 teaspoonful baking powder	¾ to ⅝ cupful bread flour
4 tablespoonfuls melted butter	

Beat the eggs without separating until light and foamy. Stir in the sugar and beat thoroughly, then add the cold water and beat again. Sift together the pastry or bread flour, baking powder and salt. Add this to the cake mixture and beat again. When light pour in the melted butter and flavoring and bake in a moderate oven.

Feather Cake

Break 2 large eggs into a cup and then fill the cup with cream. Beat this mixture thoroughly and then beat in 1 cupful of granulated sugar and 1¼ cupfuls of flour sifted with 3 teaspoonfuls of baking powder. Flavor with ½ teaspoonful of flavoring extract. Bake in a slightly hotter oven than one uses for butter cakes.

Rachel's Dark Cake

½ cupful grated chocolate	1 cupful brown sugar
½ cupful milk	

Combine these ingredients and cook together until thick and smooth. Set away to cool.

Part Two

1 cupful brown sugar	1 cupful sweet milk
½ cupful butter	2 cupfuls flour
2 eggs	1 scant teaspoonful soda

Cream the butter, add the sugar and beat until light and creamy. Add the well beaten egg yolks. Sift the flour and soda together and add this mixture alternately with the milk. Then stir in the cooled chocolate mixture, fold in the stiffly beaten egg whites and bake as a loaf or in layers in a moderate oven.

Aunt Nellie's Cake

⅓ cupful drippings	1 teaspoonful salt
½ cupful sugar	1 teaspoonful cinnamon
½ cupful molasses	1 egg
½ cupful sour milk	½ teaspoonful cloves
1 teaspoonful soda	1 teaspoonful ginger
2 cupfuls flour	¾ cupful raisins

24 English walnuts

Add the sugar to the meat drippings and beat thoroughly with a spoon. Then add the well beaten egg yolk and the molasses in which the soda, first dissolved in a little water, has been stirred. Sift the flour and add the salt, spices, chopped raisins and nutmeats. Add this mixture alternately with the milk. Fold in the stiffly beaten egg white. Bake as a loaf.

Leftover chicken and pork fats, melted, strained through cheesecloth, frequently were salvaged in everyday spice cakes.

English Cake

1 cupful butter	1 teaspoonful cinnamon
2 cupfuls sugar	1 teaspoonful allspice
5 eggs	1 teaspoonful cloves
1 cupful black coffee	3½ cupfuls flour
1 teaspoonful soda	1 pound raisins

1 pound currants

Cream the butter with a spoon and stir in the sugar, beating thoroughly. Then add the well beaten egg yolks. Divide the flour into two parts and to one add the soda and to the other add the spices, raisins and currants. Add these flour mixtures alternately with the coffee infusion. Fold in the stiffly beaten egg whites and bake in two loaves.

Sour Milk Cake

½ cupful butter	½ cupful sour milk
2 cupfuls brown sugar	½ cupful cold water
2 squares chocolate	2½ cupfuls flour
2 eggs	1 teaspoonful soda

Cream the butter, add the sugar and beat until the mixture is creamy and light, then add the chocolate which has been melted over hot water. Stir in the beaten egg yolks. Sift the flour and soda together and add to the batter alternately with the

Some people called this chocolate cake devil's food.

milk and water. Bake in layers and use brown sugar filling between the layers and a chocolate icing on top.

Caramel cakes were extremely popular with many men. Some husbands insisted they married their wives because they baked superlative caramel cakes, which they often called burnt-sugar cakes. Some women considered it a temperamental cake and difficult to bake. See revised recipe.

Caramel Cake

¾ cupful sugar	1 tablespoonful caramelized sugar
¼ cupful butter	1½ cupfuls flour
1 egg	1½ teaspoonfuls baking powder
½ cupful water	½ teaspoonful vanilla

Cream the butter and add the granulated sugar. Beat until light and add the well beaten egg yolk. Caramelize the sugar by melting it in a frying pan without adding water and stirring constantly until the mass is a light golden brown. Dissolve this in the water. Sift the baking powder and flour together and add this mixture alternately with the water in which the caramelized sugar has been dissolved. Add the vanilla and fold in the stiffly beaten egg white. Bake in a loaf and ice with a burnt sugar icing.

Spice Cake

6 tablespoonfuls shortening	1 cupful raisins
1 cupful brown sugar	⅛ teaspoonful salt
⅓ cupful granulated sugar	3 teaspoonfuls baking powder
2 eggs	¾ teaspoonful cinnamon
½ cupful coffee infusion	¼ teaspoonful cloves
1¾ cupfuls flour	¼ teaspoonful nutmeg

Cream the shortening and beat until light. Add the sugar and beat thoroughly. Sift the dry ingredients together, add the raisins and then combine the egg yolks with the left-over coffee. Alternately add the flour and the coffee mixture. Fold in the stiffly beaten egg whites and bake in a loaf 45 minutes in a moderate oven.

An early version of applesauce cake. Was the applesauce sweetened? It is in the revised, smaller recipe.

Apple Cake

1 cupful sugar	1 tablespoonful cocoa
½ cupful apple sauce	1 teaspoonful cinnamon
½ cupful sour cream	½ teaspoonful cloves
1¼ teaspoonfuls soda	1 cupful raisins
2 cupfuls flour	

Mix the sugar, sour cream and the apple sauce together and add the soda to this mixture. Stir in the other ingredients, chopping and flouring the raisins.

Ruth's Boiled Cake

½ cupful sugar	½ cupful flour
4 tablespoonfuls cold water	1 teaspoonful baking powder
3 eggs	½ teaspoonful salt
	¼ teaspoonful vanilla

Boil the sugar and water together until the syrup thus made forms a thread when dropped from a spoon. Beat the egg whites until stiff and dry. Pour the hot syrup over them, beating constantly until cold. Then stir in the egg yolks, beaten until light and lemon colored. Sift the dry ingredients and add them gradually. Pour in oiled tins, or better still in tins lined with oiled paper, and bake in a moderate oven until firm. This requires about 20 or 25 minutes.

Hannah's Tea Cake

2 cupfuls butter	juice of 1 lemon
3 cupfuls brown sugar	4¼ cupfuls flour
5 eggs	1 teaspoonful soda
1 cupful milk	¼ teaspoonful salt
grated rind of 1 lemon	1 pound raisins
½ teaspoonful vanilla	1 teaspoonful nutmeg
	1 teaspoonful chopped citron

Cream the butter, add the sugar and beat until light. Then stir in the beaten egg yolks and the grated lemon rind. Sift the flour, salt and soda together and add this mixture alternately with the milk. Then add the nutmeg, vanilla, lemon juice, chopped raisins and the citron slightly floured and fold in the stiffly beaten egg whites. Bake in two loaves and ice with a white icing.

Angel Food

1 cupful egg whites	½ teaspoonful cream of tartar
1 cupful sugar	½ teaspoonful vanilla
1 cupful flour	speck of salt

Beat the egg whites to a froth, add the cream of tartar and continue beating until stiff. Sift the sugar and flour 5 times. Beat in the sugar gradually. Fold in the flour, salt and vanilla. Bake in a clean tin about 45 minutes in a slow oven.

Today's angel-food cakes, baked in heat-controlled ovens and made with cake flour, are baked in a moderate oven (375°F.) 30 to 35 minutes. Old-time cooks used a slow oven, but no one knows what the real temperature was.

Caramel Cake

1½ cups sugar	3 tsp. baking powder
½ cup butter	½ tsp. salt
1 tsp. vanilla	¾ cup cold water
2 eggs	3 tblsp. Caramel Syrup
2½ cups sifted cake flour	

Cream butter until light; gradually add sugar and cream until light and fluffy. Add vanilla and eggs, one at a time, beating well after each addition, at least for 1 minute.

Sift together cake flour, baking powder and salt. Add to creamed mixture, a small amount at a time, alternately with cold water. Beat until smooth after each addition. Add Caramel Syrup. Beat batter very well. Pour into 2 greased and paper-lined 9-inch layer-cake pans.

Bake in moderate oven (375°F.) about 20 minutes, or until cake tests done with a wooden pick. Cool in pans 10 minutes; turn out and complete cooling on cake rack. Frost with Fluffy Caramel Frosting (see recipe in chapter on fillings and icings).

Caramel Syrup. Melt ⅔ cup sugar in heavy skillet over low heat, stirring constantly. Remove from heat promptly when mixture is a dark brown to avoid scorching. Add ⅔ cup boiling water, a little at a time. Heat, stirring constantly, until mixture is smooth. Continue to boil until syrup measures ½ cup, which is the right amount for the cake and frosting.

Apple Loaf Cake

½ cup shortening	½ tsp. baking soda
1 cup sugar	3/4 tsp. ground cinnamon
2 eggs	¼ tsp. ground nutmeg
1¾ cups sifted flour	1 cup sweetened
1 tsp. salt	applesauce
1 tsp. baking powder	½ cup cut-up raisins

Cream shortening; gradually add sugar and cream until mixture is light and fluffy. Add eggs and beat well.

Sift together flour, salt, baking powder, baking soda and spices. Add to creamed mixture alternately with applesauce, beating well after addition. Stir in raisins. Pour into greased, paper-lined 9½-by-5-by-3-inch loaf pan.

Bake in moderate oven (350° F.) 55 to 60 minutes, or until cake tests done with wooden pick. Cool 10 minutes in pan set on rack; turn out. While still warm, sprinkle with sifted confectioners' sugar. Or add 1 tblsp. cold water to ½ cup sifted confectioners' sugar and spread on warm cake to form a glaze.

Sponge Cake

4 eggs	1 teaspoonful baking powder
1 cupful sugar	⅔ cupful boiling water
2 cupfuls flour	speck of salt
	grated rind of 1 lemon

Beat the egg whites until dry and fold in the well beaten egg yolks. Mix sugar, flour and baking powder and add to the first mixture alternately with the water and grated lemon rind. Bake in an oiled tin in a moderate oven until firm in the center, or about 30 minutes.

Cheap Sponge Cake

2 eggs	1 tablespoonful grated lemon rind
1 cupful sugar	1⅓ cupfuls flour
5 tablespoonfuls cold water	2 teaspoonfuls baking powder

Beat the egg yolks until they are a light lemon color, add the sugar and continue beating. Gradually add the water and lemon rind. Sift the dry ingredients together and add to the batter and fold in the stiffly beaten egg whites. Bake in an unbuttered tin in a moderate oven.

Gingerbread

1 cupful shortening	1 tablespoonful ginger
1 cupful brown sugar	3 eggs
1 cupful molasses	¾ teaspoonful salt
¾ teaspoonful cinnamon	2½ cupfuls flour
¼ teaspoonful cloves	1 teaspoonful soda
¼ teaspoonful nutmeg	1 cupful sour milk or buttermilk

Combine the shortening, sugar, molasses and spices. Place in a mixing bowl and set in a warm place near the range until the shortening is softened. Then beat the mixture with a spoon until it is light and creamy. Add the salt and eggs beaten until light. Stir in the flour and soda which have been sifted together alternately with the milk. Beat or whip the batter until light, then pour into oiled pans and bake 45 minutes in a moderate oven. When cool, ice with a thick white icing. This recipe makes two loaves and gives best results when a dark colored molasses and sugar are used.

Farm women dressed up gingerbread by cutting it in half crosswise and making a shortcake with it by combining sliced bananas and whipped cream for filling and topping. In the recipe for Speedy Gingerbread, a quick-loaf version (see recipe), a warm lemon- or orange-pudding sauce was a much-enjoyed accompaniment.

Coffee Gingerbread

Substitute 1 cupful of strong liquid coffee for the milk in the gingerbread recipes. Sprinkle a little powdered cinnamon and sugar over the batter just before placing it in the oven to bake.

Chocolate Gingerbread

Omit ½ cupful of flour in the gingerbread recipe and use ½ cupful of cocoa instead. Cover with a Mocha icing.

Fruit Gingerbread

Add 1 cupful of chopped nuts, raisins, currants, dates or cooked prunes to the gingerbread batter.

Cup Cakes

⅔ cupful shortening	4 teaspoonfuls baking powder
2 cupfuls sugar	¼ teaspoonful salt
4 eggs	¼ teaspoonful nutmeg
3 cupfuls flour	½ cupful milk
1¼ cupfuls raisins	

Cream the shortening and add the sugar slowly, beating the mixture until light and creamy. Add the well beaten eggs. Sift the dry ingredients together and add them and the milk alternately. Add the raisins dredged lightly in the flour. Pour into oiled muffin tins and bake in a moderate oven from 25 to 30 minutes.

Speedy Gingerbread

½ cup shortening	½ tsp. salt
½ cup sugar	¾ tsp. baking soda
1 egg	½ tsp. ground ginger
½ cup light molasses	½ tsp. ground cinnamon
1½ cups sifted flour	¼ tsp. ground nutmeg
	½ cup boiling water

Cream shortening and sugar until light; beat well until mixture is fluffy. Add egg and molasses and beat well.

Sift together flour, salt, baking soda and spices. Add to molasses mixture alternately with boiling water, beating after each addition. Pour into a greased 8-inch square pan.

Bake in moderate oven (350°F.) 35 to 40 minutes, or until gingerbread tests done with wooden pick. Serve warm with whipped cream.

To describe sugar cookies as plain was a way of saying they were basic and could be dressed in many pretty ways. Sprinkling cookie tops with colored sugar or tiny multicolored candies just before baking was quick and easy. Bake in moderate oven (375° F.) about 8 minutes, or until cookies are a light golden-brown.

When dough was cut with a small, round cutter having scalloped or fluted edges, and baked cookies were filled with a bright jelly such as currant, they won compliments at tea parties.

Bake in moderate oven (375° F.) until cookies are a light brown, about 8 minutes.

CHAPTER 8

COOKIES AND DOUGHNUTS

Plain Cookies

1 cupful shortening	2 eggs
2 cupfuls sugar	4 teaspoonfuls baking powder
½ cupful milk	4 cupfuls flour
	1 teaspoonful vanilla

CREAM the shortening, add the sugar and the eggs well beaten. Sift the baking powder with the flour and add to the mixture alternately with the milk. Chill. Add additional flour if needed in rolling the dough. Bake in a slightly oiled pan in a moderate oven.

Jelly Jumbles

Use the recipe for plain cookies. After cutting the dough, remove the centers from half of the circles with a thimble. Place a spoonful of jam or jelly on the whole cookies and cover with one having the whole in the center. Moisten the edges slightly and press together. Bake in a moderate oven.

Cooky Delights

½ cupful shortening	¼ teaspoonful salt
1 cupful sugar	1 tablespoonful milk
2 eggs	grated rind of 1 orange or
2 cupfuls flour	¼ teaspoonful nutmeg
2 teaspoonfuls baking powder	1 cupful raisins

Cream the shortening and add the sugar. Beat until light and creamy. Add the well beaten eggs. Sift the dry ingredients together and add to the sugar and shortening. Stir in the raisins, grated orange peel or nutmeg and the milk. If the mixture is not thick enough to roll, add more flour. Roll very thin, cut and bake in a hot oven from 10 to 15 minutes.

44

Hermits

1½ cupfuls sugar	1 teaspoonful cinnamon
1 cupful shortening	1 teaspoonful allspice
3 eggs	1 teaspoonful cloves
3 cupfuls flour	1 teaspoonful nutmeg
1 teaspoonful baking powder	½ teaspoonful soda
1 teaspoonful salt	1½ cupfuls raisins

Cream the shortening, add the sugar and beat until light. Add the well beaten eggs and sift in the dry ingredients. Add the raisins and drop the mixture by spoonfuls on a well greased tin and bake in a moderate oven from 20 to 25 minutes.

Bake rounded teaspoons of dough about 2 inches apart on a lightly greased baking sheet in a hot oven (400°F.) about 8 minutes. Test for doneness by touching lightly with finger. If almost no imprint remains, cookies are done.

Date Cookies

4 cupfuls flour	2 eggs
2 cupfuls sugar	¾ teaspoonful soda
1½ cupfuls sour cream	3 teaspoonfuls baking powder
1 teaspoonful vanilla	½ teaspoonful salt
	dates

Sift the dry ingredients together. Beat the eggs and add the sugar and cream to them. Combine the two mixtures. Drop in small patches on oiled tins, press whole stoned dates or four raisins on top of every cooky, sprinkle with brown sugar and bake.

They were made with heavy cream.

Festive Cookies

3 cupfuls sugar	1 teaspoonful nutmeg
1½ cupfuls shortening	2 teaspoonfuls cinnamon
5 egg yolks	1½ teaspoonfuls cloves
4 egg whites	½ pound raisins
1½ cupfuls molasses	½ pound currants
1½ cupfuls coffee	¼ pound citron
1 teaspoonful salt	6 teaspoonfuls baking powder
	6 cupfuls flour

Cream the shortening, add the sugar and beat thoroughly. Add the well beaten eggs. Sift the dry ingredients together and add them alternately with the molasses and coffee infusion. Then stir in the slightly floured raisins, currants and chopped citron. Bake in tiny muffin tins or in a large dripping pan, cutting with cutters after being baked. These cookies keep well for many weeks if stored in a tightly covered earthenware jar. They are especially delicious when covered with a white frosting. They are baked in a slow oven.

Dripping pans were of different sizes and were used for many purposes, such as holding 2 or more loaves of bread that were baked together, for roasting meats and for baking "spread cookies," known today as "bar cookies." The thickness of the dough in the pan affects the baking time, thicker layers taking more time than thinner ones. Bake in moderate oven (350° F.) 20 to 30 minutes, or until lightly browned. Cool in pan set on rack. Cut in bars with sharp knife. To play safe, test for doneness by touching with fingertip, as for Hermits.

Bake in moderate oven (375° F.) about 8 minutes, or until imprint made when touching cookie top lightly with fingertip disappears.

Snip raisins with kitchen scissors. No need to flour them. Bake in moderate oven, 375° F., until lightly browned.

Make this correction: use 6 tblsp. milk instead of 1 cup. Drop from tablespoon about 2 inches apart on greased baking sheet. Bake in hot oven (400°F.) 8 to 10 minutes. This recipe appeared before World War I in a churchwomen's cookbook in Dodge City, Kansas. The cookies were extremely popular in ranch homes for many years. Dried currants frequently took the raisin role.

Ginger Cookies

1 cupful fat	1 tablespoonful ginger
1 cupful molasses	3 tablespoonfuls sour milk
½ cupful sugar	1 teaspoonful soda
1 teaspoonful salt	4½ cupfuls flour

Cream the fat, add the sugar and molasses, then the salt, ginger and milk. Sift 2 cupfuls of the flour and soda together and mix into the molasses mixture. Then gradually add sufficient flour to make a mixture that can be rolled out. Roll very thin, cut in any desired shape and bake in a quick oven about 10 minutes. If one wishes, little men and women may be cut from this dough with cutters. Bits of nut meats, raisins, currants and white icing may be used to make features, buttons and clothes.

Mary's Gingersnaps

2 cupfuls molasses	1 tablespoonful ginger
1 cupful shortening	2 eggs
½ cupful sour milk	1½ teaspoonfuls soda
flour to make a soft dough	

Mix the molasses and shortening together and heat until the fat is melted. When cool add the beaten egg, 1 cupful of flour in which the ginger and soda have been sifted and the sour milk. Add enough flour to make a soft dough. Roll thin, sprinkle with sugar and cut.

Raisin Cookies

1 cupful shortening	1 teaspoonful soda
2 cupfuls sugar	½ cupful warm water
3 eggs	flour
½ pound chopped raisins	1 cupful nut meats

Cream the butter or other shortening, add the sugar gradually, beating thoroughly, and stir in the eggs without separating them. Stir in the soda which has been dissolved in the warm water. Add sufficient flour to make a soft dough. Stir in the floured and chopped raisins and nuts. Roll and bake.

Oatmeal Rocks

1 cupful sugar	1 cupful chopped raisins
½ cupful butter	1 cupful milk
½ cupful lard	1 cupful nuts
2 eggs	2 cupfuls flour
2 cupfuls oatmeal	1 teaspoonful soda

Cream the butter and lard with a spoon and add the sugar. Beat until light and creamy. Then stir in the well beaten eggs and add to the oatmeal. Sift the flour and soda together and add to it the chopped raisins and nut meats. Add this mixture alternately with the milk. Drop spoonfuls of the batter in oiled pans and bake in a moderate oven.

Vanilla Wafers

½ cupful butter   1 teaspoonful vanilla
1 cupful powdered sugar   ½ cupful milk
              1¾ cupfuls flour

Cream the butter, add the sugar and then drop the milk in slowly. If the mixture starts to separate, beat. Add the flour and the flavoring. Spread thinly in the bottom of a cake tin which has been oiled and crease in squares with a knife. Bake in a hot oven.

Bake in moderate oven (375° F.) about 8 minutes or until lightly browned around edges.

Potato Doughnuts

4 medium sized potatoes   flour
2 tablespoonfuls butter   2 cupfuls sugar
4 eggs   1 teaspoonful salt
              4 teaspoonfuls baking powder

Boil and mash the potatoes. Add butter, beaten eggs, sugar and salt. Mix the baking powder with 2 cupfuls of flour and add to the mixture. Add enough more flour to make a dough stiff enough to roll ½ inch thick. Cut and fry. Drain and roll in powdered sugar.

Crullers

6 eggs   6 tablespoonfuls sugar
6 tablespoonfuls melted shortening flour to make a stiff dough

Beat eggs until very light. Add sugar, shortening, and flour. Beat thoroughly and roll very thin. Cut in strips 3 inches long and 2 inches wide. Make three one-inch parallel gashes cross-wise at equal intervals. Take up by running the handle of a spoon in and out of the gashes. Fry in deep fat and sprinkle with powdered sugar.

Fry like doughnuts in fat heated to 370° F. Delicate and delicious!

Fry these chocolate doughnuts in fat heated to 365° F. for about 3 minutes.

Add 2 tsp. baking powder with 1 tsp. baking soda to 3½ cups sifted flour. Additional spices may be added. Substitute ¾ cup buttermilk for the 1 cup sour milk.

Fancy Doughnuts

1 cupful granulated sugar	4 teaspoonfuls baking powder
2 squares chocolate	3 cupfuls flour
1 egg	⅔ cupful nut meats
1 teaspoonful salt	1 teaspoonful vanilla
1 cupful milk	grated rind of ½ orange

Beat the egg and sugar together with a spoon and add the unsweetened chocolate which has been melted over hot water. Sift the dry ingredients together, saving out a little flour to mix with the chopped nut meats. Add the flour mixture alternately with the milk and then stir in the nuts and grated orange and lemon rind. Roll, cut and fry in hot fat.

Doughnuts

2 tablespoonfuls butter	1 teaspoonful salt
1 cupful sugar	½ teaspoonful cinnamon
1 egg	4 teaspoonfuls baking powder
flour to make a soft dough	1 cupful milk

Cream the butter, add the sugar and beat until light. Stir in the well beaten egg and the sweet milk. Sift the baking powder, salt and cinnamon with 1½ cupfuls of flour and stir this mixture in, adding sufficient flour to make a soft dough. Roll ½ inch thick and cut. Fry, drain and when partly cool, sprinkle with powdered sugar.

Sour Milk Doughnuts

2½ tablespoonfuls butter	1 teaspoonful soda
1 cupful sugar	1 teaspoonful salt
2 eggs	½ teaspoonful cinnamon
1 cupful sour milk	flour to make a soft dough

Cream the butter, add the sugar and beat until light. Stir in the well beaten egg and alternately add the sour milk and 1½ cupfuls of flour in which the soda, salt and cinnamon have been sifted. Add sufficient flour to make a soft dough. Roll ½ inch thick, cut and fry in hot fat. Drain and when somewhat cool, sprinkle with powdered sugar.

Overnight Cookies

3 cupfuls dark brown sugar	½ cupful lard
1 cupful granulated sugar	6 cupfuls flour
4 eggs	1 tablespoonful soda
¾ teaspoonful salt	1 tablespoonful cream of tartar
½ cupful butter	1 tablespoonful vanilla

When ice refrigerators arrived in farm kitchens in large numbers, overnight foods, including cookies, skyrocketed to popularity. These brown sugar cookies were among the first refrigerator cookies. Women, accustomed to shaping yeast dough in loaves, molded the cookie dough the same way. No one had thought of the now traditional cylindrical form.

Cream the sugars, butter and lard together until light. Add the beaten eggs and vanilla. Sift in the salt, flour, soda and cream of tartar. Mold in a loaf and let stand in a cool place, such as a refrigerator, overnight. Slice off in the morning and bake in a moderate oven. Do not let the loaf freeze during the night.

Delicious Butterscotchies

These delicious, crisp refrigerator cookies are an outgrowth of Overnight Cookies. Countrywomen insisted on using all or some butter for the shortening because it gets very hard when chilled. This makes it easier to slice the dough without crumbling.

1 cup butter	3 cups sifted flour
1 cup brown sugar, firmly packed	1 tsp. baking soda
	1 tsp. salt
2 eggs, beaten	½ cup finely chopped
1½ tsp. vanilla	walnuts or pecans

Cream butter until light. Gradually add brown sugar, creaming mixture until light and fluffy. Add eggs and vanilla; mix well.

Sift together flour, baking soda and salt. Add to creamed mixture, beating to blend. Stir in nuts. Shape dough in smooth rolls 1½ to 2½ inches in diameter. Wrap tightly in waxed paper, twisting ends to seal. Refrigerate overnight.

Cut in slices about ⅛ inch thick with a sharp knife. Place on ungreased baking sheet about 1 inch apart. Bake in hot oven (400°F.) 6 to 8 minutes or until light brown. Remove at once from baking sheet, spreading on racks to cool.

This is a big recipe. One roll of cookie dough may be sliced and baked, the other frozen. When baking the frozen roll, let thaw just enough to slice.

Breakfast at sunrise was not un-common 50 years ago. The meal was hearty. Bowls were filled with hot cereal, served with sugar and cream, frequently were followed by bacon and eggs. Cereals were cooked in the double boiler on wood- and coal-burning stoves with almost no watching. A universal practice was to cook them in the evening to reheat quickly at dawn. Quick-cooking cereals had not made their debut.

CHAPTER 9

CEREALS

MOST cereals are at their best when cooked slowly several hours in a double boiler. When this utensil is not available, a small saucepan set in a kettle containing water may be used. The fireless cooker is well adapted to the cookery of cereals, since the cooking can take place during the night so the food will be ready for breakfast in the morning. Cereals cooked the day before they are to be used should not be stirred when being reheated over hot water at breakfast time. If 2 tablespoonfuls of cold water are poured on top of the cooked cereal, no crust will form during the standing.

Directions for Cooking

Add ½ teaspoonful of salt to every cupful of boiling water used. Stir ½ cupful of whole or cracked cereal, such as cracked wheat or barley, macaroni, rice and hominy, into 2 cupfuls of boiling water and cook on the stove 10 minutes, stirring constantly. Then transfer to a double boiler and cook from 1 to 3 hours.

Use 1 cupful of flaked cereal, such as oatmeal or flaked wheat, in 2 cupfuls of boiling water and cook on the stove 10 minutes, stirring constantly. Then transfer to the double boiler and cook from ½ to 3 hours.

Three tablespoonfuls of granular cereal, of which cornmeal and cream of wheat, rye or barley are examples, are used in 1 cupful of boiling water. Cook on the stove 15 minutes, stirring constantly, and then cook from 1 to 4 hours in a double boiler.

Fruits Are Added

For the sake of variety fruits may be cooked with the cereal. Quartered dates, chopped figs, raisins, shredded prunes and quartered apples are some of the favorites.

50

Boiled Rice

1 cupful rice   1½ teaspoonfuls salt
1 quart water

Place the water in a saucepan, add the salt and bring to the boiling point. When the water is boiling rapidly, add the thoroughly washed rice slowly, stirring gently with a fork. When all the rice is added, let it boil until the kernels are tender. Then drain it through a sieve and pour cold water on the rice to separate the kernels. Place the cold rice in a colander or pan and set in the oven a few minutes to warm if it is to be served hot. One cupful of rice when cooked will measure almost 4 cupfuls.

Boiled Macaroni

Break the macaroni in one inch pieces and cook as boiled rice.

Browned Macaroni

Heat ¼ cupful of bacon fat in a frying pan and add 3 cupfuls of boiled macaroni. Brown until crisp and serve sprinkled with brown sugar.

Baked Macaroni

Place 3 cupfuls of boiled macaroni in an oiled baking dish and add ½ pimento chopped fine and a white sauce made by thickening 1 cupful of milk with 2 tablespoonfuls of flour. Sprinkle ½ cupful of grated cheese over the top and add 3 tablespoonfuls of melted butter. Bake in a slow oven until the cheese is brown.

Spanish Spaghetti

Fry 3 slices of bacon and to them add 2 cupfuls of spaghetti, boiled in the same way as macaroni, 2 finely chopped onions and 1 green pepper cut in pieces. After simmering for 10 minutes, add 2 cupfuls of canned tomatoes. Place alternate layers of this mixture and any cold chopped meat in an oiled baking dish. Add 1 cupful of milk and dot the top with 2 tablespoonfuls of butter. Bake 30 minutes in a moderate oven.

With a standard measuring cup, 1 cup regular white rice makes about 3 cups boiled rice.

Canned salmon was a staple item 50 years ago in Midwestern country cupboards. The fish was abundant, and cans of it were inexpensive.

Farm women knew men liked meat. They added it to macaroni and other casserole combinations, even in small amounts, to perform the magic of giving the dish appetite appeal.

Favored companion to ham and pork.

Macaroni with Salmon

1 cupful boiled macaroni	2 cupfuls milk
1 cupful canned salmon	3 tablespoonfuls flour
2 tablespoonfuls butter	1 teaspoonful salt
1 tablespoonful oil from salmon	dash of red pepper
¼ cupful buttered bread crumbs	

Arrange alternate layers of the macaroni and flaked salmon in a buttered baking dish. Prepare a sauce of the milk, flour and butter. Pour over the salmon and macaroni. Sprinkle bread crumbs on top and bake in a moderate oven 30 minutes or until the crumbs are browned delicately.

Italian Macaroni

1 cupful macaroni	1 cupful grated cheese
2 tablespoonfuls flour	½ teaspoonful salt
2 tablespoonfuls butter	¼ teaspoon paprika
1½ cupfuls scalded milk	¼ cupful cooked and chopped ham

Break the macaroni in 1 inch pieces and cook in 1 quart of boiling salted water. When tender, drain and reheat in a sauce made from the milk, butter and flour. Add the cheese to the hot sauce. When it is melted, add the salt, paprika and the ham. Turn on a platter and serve immediately. If one wishes, the ham may be used to sprinkle on top of the macaroni dish.

Macaroni with Pork Chops

2 cupfuls macaroni	1 teaspoonful salt
4 large pork chops	¼ teaspoonful pepper
4 cupfuls tomatoes	dash of paprika

Cook 1 inch pieces of macaroni in boiling salted water until tender. Drain. Cut the pork chops in small pieces, put them in a frying pan and cook until tender. Add the macaroni, seasonings and the canned tomatoes. Cook 10 minutes.

Hominy en Casserole

2 cupfuls cooked hominy	1½ teaspoonfuls salt
1¼ cupfuls milk	¼ teaspoonful pepper
2 eggs	2 tablespoonfuls butter

Drain the hominy and add to the milk. Beat the eggs until light, add them to the milk mixture, stir in the seasonings and bake in a greased baking dish until brown on top.

Mush Sticks

2 cupfuls boiling water	½ cupful cornmeal
1 teaspoonful salt	¾ cupful seeded raisins
½ cupful left-over meat	

Add the cornmeal gradually to the boiling salted water and stir continually for 5 minutes. Then place the mixture in a double boiler and cook 1¼ hours. Add the chopped seeded raisins and small bits of left-over meat. Pour into a shallow pan and cool. When firm, cut in long, narrow strips, dip in egg and bread crumbs and brown in fat. Serve with syrup for breakfast or supper.

Rice Patties

2 eggs	1 teaspoonful salt
1 cupful milk	2 tablespoonfuls butter
1 cupful boiled rice	1 cupful flour

Beat the egg yolks and add the milk, rice, salt, melted butter and flour. Fold in the stiffly beaten egg whites and form in round cakes. Brown in hot fat.

Prized as a thrifty use of leftover boiled rice and a good substitute for potatoes.

Spanish Rice

2 thin slices bacon	2 cupfuls tomatoes
1 onion	½ teaspoonful chili pepper
1 teaspoonful salt	2 cupfuls boiled rice
	1 egg

Cut bacon in small pieces with the onion and fry until hot and slightly browned. Add the boiled rice and stir constantly until it is a little brown. Add the canned tomatoes, chili pepper and salt. When piping hot, place in a serving dish and garnish with slices of hard cooked egg.

Rice with Cheese

3 cupfuls boiled rice	1¼ cupfuls cheese
3 egg whites	1½ tablespoonfuls butter
bread crumbs	1 cupful milk
	¼ teaspoonful salt

Place the rice in a mixing bowl and beat with a spoon until light. The rice should be warm. Add the stiffly beaten egg whites and beat these together. Grease a baking dish and sprinkle a thin layer of bread crumbs over the bottom. Then place

A supper specialty that often stretched rather skimpy leftover fried chicken or slices of cold beef pot roast. It sometimes escorted boiled ham.

one-third of the rice in the dish.   Sprinkle with one-third of the grated cheese, dot with butter and sprinkle with a few bread crumbs.   Repeat until three such layers are made.   Then add the milk and salt and bake in a moderate oven about 30 minutes.

Rice, Country Style

3 cupfuls cooked rice	3 eggs
1 cupful bacon	¼ teaspoonful pepper
½ teaspoonful salt	

Cut the bacon in small pieces before measuring, then fry it until crisp.   Then pour off about half of the fat and place the bacon on a small dish and set in a warm place.   Beat the eggs thoroughly and combine them with the rice; add the salt and pepper.   Turn in the skillet with the bacon fat and scramble. Place on a hot platter and garnish with the bacon.

CHAPTER 10

CANDIES AND CONFECTIONS

THE secret of successful candy making is to keep the syrup from crystallizing. Several precautions may be heeded to accomplish this. First of all, boil the sugar and liquid together in a thick kettle or saucepan.

Stir until the sugar is dissolved and then cook without moving or shaking the kettle containing the boiling syrup. Wipe off the crystals of sugar that form on the sides of the kettle with a cloth moistened in water and tied over the tines of a fork. If one wishes, a few drops of any acid, such as vinegar or lemon juice, may be added to prevent crystallization. Cream of tartar may also be used for this purpose. If the candy contains grains, add water to soften it and reboil.

Testing Candy

If one has a candy thermometer, it is easy to determine when the candy is cooked. The soft ball stage is reached when the thermometer registers from 236 to 240 degrees F.; the hard ball at 254 degrees F.; the soft crack at 260 degrees F.; and the hard crack at 290 degrees F.

Without a thermometer the tests are made by dropping a small portion of the boiling syrup from the spoon into a cupful of cold water. If the mixture makes up into a soft ball, it is the soft ball stage; if it forms a rather hard ball, it is the hard ball stage; if the mixture becomes crisp and too hard to form a hard ball when crushed between the fingers, it is the soft crack stage; and if it cracks or breaks when crushed between the fingers, the hard crack stage is reached.

To Caramelize Sugar

When caramelized sugar is called for in a recipe, it may be prepared by placing granulated sugar in a frying pan and melt-

55

Corn syrup has largely replaced the crystallization preventatives once used.

Standard Temperature Chart

Soft ball — 232 to 240°
Firm ball — 242 to 248°
Hard ball — 250 to 268°
Soft crack — 270 to 290°
Hard crack — 300 to 310°

Practically all countrywomen 50 years ago were skilled in caramelizing sugar in their heavy iron skillets. To use low heat and stir constantly were the cardinal rules in producing one of the best-liked food flavors.

This candy is what grandmothers used to call white fudge. Using today's ingredients, combine 3 cups sugar, ¾ cup milk, 3 tblsp. light corn syrup and ½ tsp. salt. Heat and stir until sugar dissolves; cook without stirring to soft ball stage, 236°. Add 3 tblsp. butter without stirring. Cool until lukewarm, add 1 tsp. vanilla and beat until candy loses its gloss and starts to thicken. Stir in ¾ cup flaked cocoanut and spread in a buttered 8-inch square pan. Cool. Cut as desired. For Christmas, substitute ½ cup finely chopped candied cherries for cocoanut if desired.

ing it on the stove without the addition of water. The sugar must be stirred constantly while being melted. When it becomes a light brown, or a golden brown, mass, it is caramelized.

Caramelized syrup is made by boiling water and sugar together beyond the hard crack stage or until the syrup becomes a golden brown. The main precaution to heed in this process is to stir the syrup and to remove it from the stove as soon as it is caramelized, in this way avoiding all traces of scorch.

Peppermint Circles

½ cupful sugar	3 tablespoonfuls water
	5 drops oil of peppermint

Stir the ingredients together and place on the stove. When the sugar begins to melt, stir for several minutes. Drop small spoonfuls of the syrup on oiled paper.

Cocoanut Candy

1½ cupfuls sugar	3 tablespoonfuls butter
½ cupful milk	¾ cupful shredded cocoanut

Boil the sugar and milk together until they form a soft ball when dropped in cold water. Add the butter and cocoanut. Boil 3 minutes and pour into an oiled pan. Mark in squares. Soak the cocoanut in a little milk before using.

Maple Squares

2½ cupfuls maple sugar	1 teaspoonful vanilla
¾ cupful water	¾ cupful nut meats
¾ pound marshmallows	½ cupful preserved fruit

Boil the sugar and water to the soft ball stage. Remove from the stove and add the marshmallows, nuts, preserved or candied fruit and the vanilla. Beat until the mixture begins to harden. Pour into oiled pans and mark in squares.

Caramel Squares

2 cupfuls sugar	1 cupful corn syrup
	3 cupfuls thin cream

Put the sugar and syrup in a saucepan and add 1 cupful of the cream. Bring to the boiling point and cook to the soft ball stage. Stir constantly to prevent burning, but do not beat. When the soft ball stage is reached, add a second cupful of cream and cook again until a soft ball is formed when a few drops are tried in cold water. Then add the third cupful of cream. Cook until a firm ball is made when a little of the syrup is dropped in cold water. Pour the hot syrup in oiled pans and mark off in squares. One cupful of nut meats or shredded cocoanut may be added to the caramel syrup just before it is poured into the pans. If this candy is packed, wrap every piece in oiled paper.

Peanut Brittle

2 cupfuls sugar   1 cupful shelled peanuts

Melt the sugar in a frying pan, stirring constantly until the mixture is a golden brown syrup. Remove from the stove immediately, stir in the chopped peanuts and pour on a well oiled platter. When cold, break in pieces with the handle of a knife.

Layer Candy

2 cupfuls sugar	1 teaspoonful vanilla
1 cupful milk	½ cupful nut meats
2 tablespoonfuls butter	fruit preserves
2 squares chocolate	speck of salt

Boil the sugar and milk together until a rather firm ball is formed when a small portion of the syrup is dropped in cold water. Add the chocolate which has been melted over hot water, the nut meats, salt and vanilla. Remove from the fire and beat until creamy. Then pour in an oiled pan. Spread generously with raspberry, strawberry and other fruit preserves.

Part Two

1 cupful sugar	1 egg white
1 cupful water	¼ teaspoonful cream of tartar

Boil the sugar, water and cream of tartar together until the hard ball stage is reached. Then pour the hot syrup slowly on the stiffly beaten egg white, beating constantly. Beat until the mixture is light and foamy and then pour it on the candy covered with the fruit preserves. When cold, cut in squares.

Combine sugar, milk and chocolate; add 1 tsp. light corn syrup. Heat and stir until sugar dissolves. Cook without stirring to soft ball stage, 334°. Add butter without stirring and cool until lukewarm. Add vanilla and beat until mixture starts to lose its gloss and becomes very thick. Quickly fold in nuts and pour into buttered pan.

This is one version of old-fashioned chocolate fudge. Combine 2 squares unsweetened chocolate, 2 cups sugar, ¾ cup milk, a dash of salt and 1 tsp. light corn syrup. Cook like Layer Candy. Black walnuts, hickory nuts and pecans are favorites in this candy.

Use a candy thermometer when making taffy, if available. Combine 3 cups sugar, 2 cups light corn syrup minus 2 tblsp. and 1 cup water. Cook and stir over low heat until sugar is dissolved. Then cook over medium-high heat, stirring only if necessary, to the hard ball stage, 256°. Add 2 tblsp. butter and cook to 262°. Pour into lightly buttered platter or shallow pan. When cool enough to handle, pull with fingertips, working 1 tsp. vanilla into candy. If candy sticks, dip fingers in cornstarch.

Chocolate Squares

2 cupfuls sugar	1 cupful milk
1 square chocolate	2 tablespoonfuls butter

Boil the sugar and milk to the soft ball stage. Do not stir during the cooking, that is, not after the sugar is dissolved. Just before taking the mixture from the stove, add the chocolate and butter which have been melted over hot water. Cool; then beat until thick. Pour into a buttered pan and mark in squares. If one wishes, ¾ cupful of nut meats may be added.

Taffy

2 cupfuls corn syrup	2 tablespoonfuls butter
1 cupful sugar	1 tablespoonful vinegar

Stir the ingredients together and cook until the soft or hard crack stage is reached. Chewing taffy is cooked to the soft crack stage and hard taffy to the hard crack. Pour on a buttered platter. When cool, pull with the tips of the fingers. Cut in pieces with scissors.

Sugar Taffy

2 cupfuls sugar	½ cupful vinegar
	2 tablespoonfuls butter

Combine the ingredients and boil until the soft or hard crack stage is reached. Stir while cooking until the sugar is dissolved. Turn on a buttered platter to cool. When cold enough to handle, pull until porous and white. Cut in pieces with scissors.

Butter Scotch

1 cupful sugar	1 tablespoonful vinegar
4 tablespoonfuls molasses	2 tablespoonfuls boiling water
	½ cupful butter

Stir the ingredients together and cook, without stirring, to the hard crack stage. Turn into a buttered tin. When partly cool, mark in squares, or break into pieces with the handle of a knife when the candy is cold.

Divinity Delicious

1½ cupfuls brown sugar	1 egg white
½ cupful corn syrup	1 teaspoonful vanilla
¾ cupful boiling water	1 cupful nut meats

Recipe is obsolete. Compare it with a 1976 recipe. Stir together 2⅔ cups sugar, ⅔ cup light corn syrup and ½ cup water over low heat. When sugar is dissolved, cook without stirring to hard ball stage, 260°

Beat 2 egg whites in electric mixer's bowl until stiff peaks form. Continue beating while pouring thin stream of hot syrup into egg whites. Add 1 tsp. vanilla. Beat until mixture holds its shape and turns slightly dull.

Cook syrup, sugar and water to 240 degrees Fahrenheit or until the syrup forms a rather firm soft ball when dropped in cold water. Pour a part of this on the stiffly beaten egg white, beating constantly. Return the rest of the syrup to the stove and cook to 260 degrees F. or to the soft crack stage. Pour this on the egg white mixture slowly, beating all the time. Add the vanilla and nuts. When the mixture begins to thicken so it cannot be beaten, pour it into a pan lined with oiled paper. When nearly cold, remove from the pan and cut in squares.

Fairyland Fondant

2½ pounds sugar	¼ teaspoonful cream of tartar
1½ cupfuls water	flavoring

Cook the sugar and water together slowly, stirring constantly until the sugar is dissolved. Then bring quickly to the boiling point, add cream of tartar and cease stirring. Boil until the syrup forms a rather firm soft ball when dropped in cold water. Then wipe the sides of the pan with a fork, having the tines wrapped with a moistened cloth. Pour the candy quickly on a moistened platter; the platter should be rinsed in cold water and not dried. Do not let the syrup drain from the pan but pour quickly. Cool until the mixture is lukewarm. Then stir with a knife until it is creamy and white. Form into a large ball with the hands, place in an earthen jar or crock and cover with a dampened cloth. It may be left overnight or molded right away.

When ready to mold the candy, rub some powdered sugar on the hands so the work may be done quickly. Work any desired flavoring, such as vanilla, lemon, orange, clove, peppermint and wintergreen into the fondant, color with a vegetable coloring if white candy is not desired, and mold in small pieces. Nut meats, candied fruits, dates or raisins may be used as centers.

Mints

Melt some of the fondant over hot water, flavor with a few drops of oil of peppermint, wintergreen, cinnamon, clove or orange and color delicately if desired. Drop from a spoon on to oiled paper. These mints may be dipped in chocolate when cold.

If mixer balks in handling candy, beat with a spoon. Fold in ⅔ cup broken nuts. Drop from a buttered teaspoon onto waxed paper.

An old-time rule still holds, even if the recipe does not. It is: choose a bright day with low humidity to make Divinity. In damp, rainy weather the candy has a habit of not becoming firm. If you want to make Divinity on a rainy day, use 1 tblsp. less water.

Bonbons

Prepare the centers for bonbons by adding flavoring, chopped nuts, candied fruit or any coloring desired to fondant. Shape this into balls and let stand overnight. Nuts, candied cherries or other fruits may be used as the centers if one wishes.

To make the chocolate for dipping, cut a ½ pound cake of dipping or coating chocolate in small pieces and place in the upper part of a double boiler. Do not let the water below it boil. To the chocolate add 1 level tablespoonful of butter, olive oil or any good salad oil. When the chocolate is melted, pour a part of it in a shallow dish. If you have a candy thermometer, insert it in the chocolate and let the mass cool to 80 degrees F., manipulating the mixture all the time with the fingers. This distributes the butter or oil throughout the chocolate, making it smooth and glossy. When the chocolate begins to harden a little on the sides of the dish, it is time to dip the candies, and this work should be done quickly.

Roll the center in the chocolate, pick it up with the thumb and first finger and rub off the surplus chocolate with the other hand. Place on a pan covered with oiled paper, bringing the fingers up over the top to form any desired design on the bonbon. When the chocolate becomes too cool for dipping, it is no longer smooth and it will not slip from the fingers easily. Add to it some of the chocolate in the double boiler over hot, but not boiling, water and proceed as before.

Honey Kisses

2 tablespoonfuls honey	1 cupful brown sugar
1 cupful white sugar	½ cupful cream
2 tablespoonfuls hot water	¾ teaspoonful vanilla
	nut meats

Stir the honey, brown and white sugar, hot water and cream together until they are melted. Boil without stirring until a little of the mixture dropped in cold water forms a hard ball. Add the vanilla and pour into an oiled pan. While warm cut into squares and press a nut meat in every piece.

Fruit Balls

1 cupful raisins	1½ cupfuls dates
2 tablespoonfuls lemon juice	1 cupful nut meats

Mothers encouraged their children to eat healthy confections made with dried fruit. They liked to pack a few Fruit Balls in school lunchboxes for a pleasing surprise.

Put the stoned dates, seedless raisins and nut meats through a food grinder and mix in the lemon juice. Shape into balls the size of marbles and dip in chocolate.

Bonbon Delights

1 pound raisins	3 figs
½ cupful cocoanut	1 pound nuts
2 tablespoonfuls grated orange peel	

Put the raisins, cocoanut, figs and nuts through a food chopper. Add the orange peel and thoroughly mix the ingredients. Shape the paste into balls the size of marbles and dip in chocolate.

Marshmallows

2 cupfuls sugar	1 teaspoonful vanilla
½ cupful hot water	2 tablespoonfuls gelatin
½ cupful cold water	

Soak the gelatin in the cold water. Cook sugar and hot water nearly to the soft ball stage. Add gelatin, pour into a large bowl and beat until stiff. Add vanilla, beat thoroughly and pour into a tin. Let stand until stiff. Cut in strips, pull out of tin, cut in squares and roll in equal parts of cornstarch and powdered sugar.

Pralines

1⅛ cupfuls powdered sugar	1 cupful maple syrup
½ cupful cream	2 cupfuls chopped nut meats

Boil the powdered sugar, cream and maple syrup together until the soft ball stage is reached. Remove from the stove and beat until creamy. Add the nuts and drop from a spoon on buttered paper.

Popcorn Balls

1 cupful sugar	½ cupful cold water
½ cupful white corn syrup	2 tablespoonfuls butter

Cook the sugar, syrup, water and butter to the soft ball stage, or until a small portion of the syrup dropped in cold water forms a firm soft ball. Pour this over popped corn. Mix well and when slightly cool press into balls. Use enough corn to make about 18 balls from this amount of syrup.

Use 5 quarts popped corn; keep it warm and crisp in a slow oven (300 to 325° F.) while cooking syrup. Combine 2 cups sugar, 1½ cups water, ½ tsp. salt, ½ cup light corn syrup and 1 tsp. vinegar. Cook to hard crack stage, 250°. Add 1 tsp. vanilla. Slowly pour over popped corn, stirring to mix. Butter hands lightly and shape mixture into 15 balls.

Cool this basic syrup and store in refrigerator. Use to sweeten lemonade and other cold drinks.

Fruit syrups to serve with pancakes and waffles had their beginning on farms when almost every acreage had fruit trees and berry patches. Bottles of them now are offered in supermarkets and food specialty stores — and usually at fancy prices!

SYRUPS

Sugar Syrup

1 cupful sugar   ½ cupful hot water

Boil these ingredients together 5 minutes. Serve hot, or if the syrup is to be kept, bottle.

Fruit Syrup

Add the juice and pulp of any fresh fruit to the sugar syrup. Orange and lemon syrups are winter favorites. Canned pineapples may be used in this way. Strawberry and raspberry syrups are delicious in the berry season.

Jam Syrup

To the sugar syrup recipe add 4 tablespoonfuls of strawberry, raspberry, blackberry, grape, plum or any other fruit jam. Orange marmalade may be used.

Winter Fruit Syrup

Add 1 cupful of the juice from canned apricots, peaches, strawberries or other canned fruit to ½ cupful of sugar. Boil until the syrup thickens slightly. Add a few bits of the canned fruit and serve warm on pancakes, fritters, biscuits or waffles.

CANDIED FRUITS

Candied Apples

6 small apples   2¾ cupfuls sugar
                                  1¼ cupfuls water

Pare and core the apples and cut in fourths. Make a syrup by boiling the sugar with the water 3 minutes. When the syrup is boiling, add the apples and simmer, but do not boil, 4 minutes. Remove from the stove and let stand overnight in the syrup. The next morning simmer the apples until tender, drain and roll in shredded cocoanut.

Taffy Apples

Remove the cores from red apples and fill the cavities with chopped nuts, raisins or dates. Fasten every apple to a small stick or skewer to be used in holding them while dipping and eating the fruit. Make a syrup by boiling 1 cupful of white sugar, 1 cupful of brown sugar, ½ cupful of water and ½ cupful of vinegar together. Cook until the mixture cracks when a small portion is dropped in cold water and pushed together with the fingers. Dip the apples in this, making certain that they are coated thoroughly.

Candied Cherries

Stone the cherries, saving any juice that is extracted. Place 2 cupfuls of sugar and 2 cupfuls of water in a kettle and stir until the sugar is dissolved. Then add a pinch of cream of tartar and boil until a thick syrup is made. Skim thoroughly, add the stoned cherries and cook gently until the fruit is tender. Drain the cherries and place on platters to dry. When thoroughly dry, pack in boxes, lining them with oiled paper, placing this paper between every layer of fruit and sprinkling liberally with sugar. Put cover on box, wrap with paper and store in a dry place.

Candied Pears

Peel, core and cut the pears into halves. Make a thick syrup by boiling 2 cupfuls of sugar and 1 cupful of water together. Drop the pears in this and let them cook slowly until they are tender, but not broken. Remove from the stove and let stand in a cool place for 2 days. Then drain and sprinkle sugar over the pears. Let them dry slowly in the sun or in a slow oven, leaving the oven door open. Pack in glass jars, sprinkling generously with sugar, and cover.

Candied Pineapple

Peel the fruit and cut in thick slices. Remove the cores and cut the slices in halves. To every pound of pineapple use 1 cupful of water. Cook slowly until the fruit is clear. Then drain and to the liquid add 2 cupfuls of sugar for every pound of fruit.

If apples are not cored, they are easier to eat. For an up-to-date, from-scratch recipe (not made with caramel candy), wash and dry 5 or 6 medium-small apples. Remove stems and blossoms. Combine 2 cups sugar, ⅔ cup light corn syrup, 1 cup water and a dash of salt. Heat and stir until sugar dissolves. Cook without stirring to 300° on candy thermometer, reducing heat after thermometer reaches 280°. Remove from heat, add a few drops of cinnamon extract and tint a bright red with food color. Set pan of syrup in a larger pan of boiling water to keep it hot. Insert wooden skewers in blossom ends of apples. Dip them, one at a time, in hot syrup. Twirl to cover apples with syrup. Cool on waxed paper.

Boil the syrup down until about one-third of it is gone; then add the fruit and cook gently until it is transparent. Remove the pineapple again and spread on platters. Set in the sun to dry. Cook the syrup down again and pour over the pineapple. Let dry thoroughly and pack away in glass jars, placing sugar and rounds of oiled paper between every layer.

Candied Orange Peel

Cut the orange peel in long one-fourth inch wide strips, using the kitchen scissors for this purpose. Place in a saucepan, add a little cold water and bring to the boiling point. Drain off the liquid and add cold water and repeat the process of boiling and draining three times in all.

After draining off the liquid the third time, measure the orange peel and to every cupful add 1 cupful of sugar and sufficient hot water to cover. Cook until the white of the skin is translucent. Then remove from the syrup, roll in granulated sugar, place on plates to dry and when thoroughly dry, pack in boxes between pieces of oiled paper. This candied peel cut in bits makes delicious flavoring for many cakes, gingerbreads, cookies and puddings.

Candied Citron

Peel small citron melons and slice or cut into small pieces. Let soak in weak salt water overnight. In the morning drain and cover with fresh water; add a tiny pinch of alum and simmer until the melon is clear. Drain and cool. When cold add 2 cupfuls of sugar to every 2 cupfuls of melon and sufficient water to moisten the sugar thoroughly. Return to the fire and simmer 2 hours. Place the citron on platters and let dry in the sunshine. When thoroughly dry, pack in boxes between layers of sugar. A few pieces of ginger root may be added with the sugar if one desires.

Citron melons once were available in food stores and were candied in home kitchens. They are sold now in candied form.

Home canning has been simplified and made so much safer since 1923 that the original chapter in the first _Farm Cook and Rule Book_ is replaced with a new one. Research has shown that anyone following some of the old-time directions might encounter spoilage and, of greater importance, serious poisoning.

Open-kettle canning is not recommended. It provides too many opportunities for bacteria to enter the food and cause spoilage. The two methods of canning today are to process the filled jars in a boiling-water bath or under 10 pounds pressure in a pressure canner.

The water-bath canner is recommended for fruits and the high-acid vegetables, rhubarb and tomatoes. The pressure canner is recommended for the remaining vegetables, meats and poultry. There are steps to take that are the same for both types.

Use standard canning jars. Inspect the rim by running fingers around the sealing edge. If there are cracks or chips, discard jars. Wash jars in sudsy water, rinse thoroughly in hot water and place in a pan of hot water to keep warm until filled.

Use pot holders to lift hot jar for filling. Turn it upside down on a folded towel to drain briefly. Then fill with food, using a ladle. Add liquid. Always leave headspace.

With flexible spatula or knife work out air bubbles in filled jars, using care not to break food. Wipe off rim of jar to remove bits of food or syrup, which might affect the seal. Prepare and adjust jar lids as the manufacturer directs. Follow the directions for the food being canned.

When processing time ends, remove jars from canner and set on folded towels a few inches apart so they do not touch. They should be free of drafts. In about 12 hours, inspect seals. The self-sealing lids dip a little, which may be felt with the fingers. Or tap the lid lightly with a metal spoon. If the seal is good, there will be a clear, ringing sound. Jars with screw-on tops and wire clamps will not leak when inverted. If seals are not perfect, either add new lids and reprocess, or refrigerate and use within a couple of days.

Kinds of Packs

Foods are canned either by the raw pack or hot pack method. In one the food is not heated before added to canning jars, in the other it is partially cooked. Some foods may be canned either way, for others one pack is preferred over the other. The directions for the different foods indicate which pack gives the best product unless there is no difference.

Canning Fruits and High-Acid Vegetables

Use the water-bath canner with fruits, rhubarb and tomatoes.

Syrups for Fruits

Thin — 2 cups sugar to 4 cups water
Medium — 3 cups sugar to 4 cups water
Heavy — 4¾ cups sugar to 4 cups water

Altitude Adjustments

Processing times are for altitudes of 1,000 feet or less. When processing food for 20 minutes or less, increase processing time 1 minute for every 1,000-foot increase in altitude, 2 minutes for foods processed more than 20 minutes.

To Prevent Fruits from Darkening

Some fruits, such as peaches, pears and apples, darken quickly when pared. Drop them into a solution made by adding 2 tblsp. each salt and vinegar to 1 gallon cold water. Do not let fruit stand in this solution more than 15 minutes. If the time does exceed 15 minutes, rinse in cold water.

Operation of Canner

About 10 minutes before filling jars, fill water-bath canner about half full of hot water and heat. Water should be hot, but not boiling, when jars are put into it. As each jar is filled, place on rack in canner, leaving enough space between jars for water to circulate. When all the jars are in the canner, add boiling water to cover them by 1 to 2 inches. Do not pour boiling water directly on jars. Cover and heat to the boiling point; reduce heat and keep the water gently boiling throughout processing. Start counting processing time when the water boils.

Canning Fruits

Apples. Wash, pare, core and quarter or slice. Use hot pack only. Boil apples in thin syrup or water 5 minutes. Pack in hot jars, to within ½ inch of jar top. Cover with hot thin syrup or water, leaving ½-inch headspace. Process pint jars 15 minutes, quart jars 20 minutes.
Applesauce. Make sweetened or unsweetened applesauce. Heat to simmering, stirring to prevent scorching. Use hot pack only. Pack

applesauce to within ½ inch of jar top. Process pint jars 10 minutes, quart jars 10 minutes.

Apricots. Can firm but ripe fruit, unpeeled or peeled, whole or cut in halves and pitted. To peel, dip into boiling hot water for ½ minute, then into cold water. Raw pack tends to keep shape better. Pack apricot halves overlapping, whole ones close together. Add boiling medium syrup, leaving 1½-inch headspace. Process pint jars 25 minutes, quart jars 30 minutes. For hot pack, prepare apricots as for raw pack. Bring to a boil in medium syrup and cook about 3 minutes. Pack fruit in hot jars and cover with hot medium syrup, leaving ½-inch headspace. Process pint jars 20 minutes, quart jars 25 minutes.

Berries, Soft (except strawberries). Among the soft berries are raspberries, dewberries, loganberries and blackberries. Wash gently, lifting from water with hands. Remove stems and caps if necessary. Use raw pack only. Pack berries into hot jars, shaking down several times, using care not to crush. Cover with boiling medium syrup, leaving 1- to 1½-inch headspace. Process pint jars 10 minutes, quart jars 15 minutes.

Berries, Firm. Blueberries, huckleberries, currants and elderberries are in this group. Wash and prepare berries as for soft berries. Add ½ cup sugar to each quart of fruit in saucepan; cover and shake to prevent scorching while heating to a boil.

Blueberries are best blanched before canning. Place in a square of cheesecloth, gather up the corners and dip in boiling water for 30 seconds, or until juice spots show on cheesecloth. Remove and cool. Use the raw pack. Add ½ cup sugar to each quart of fruit and pack in hot jars, leaving ½-inch headspace. Process pint jars 10 minutes, quart jars 15 minutes.

Use hot pack for other firm berries. After heating with sugar to a boil, pack berries and juices to within ½ inch of top of jar. Process pint jars 10 minutes, quart jars 15 minutes.

Cherries, Tart or Sweet. Stem, wash and remove pits if desired. If not pitted, prick skins to prevent splitting. Pie cherries are best pitted and may be canned in water or syrup. Use raw pack or hot pack. For hot pack, pack cherries in jars, shaking down several times to get a firm pack. Cover with boiling thin syrup for sweet cherries, heavy syrup for tart cherries. Leave 1- to 1½-inch headspace. Process pint jars 20 minutes, quart jars 25 minutes.

Prepare cherries for hot pack as for raw pack. Add ½ cup sugar to each quart of fruit. Add a little water to help prevent sticking to pan; cover and heat to simmering. Ladle hot into jars, leaving ½-inch headspace. Process pint jars 10 minutes, quart jars 15 minutes.

Gooseberries. Wash, drain and with scissors snip off blossom ends and stems. Taste will be better if berries are pierced with a fork. Use hot pack only. Work with 1 quart berries at a time. Add 3 cups boiling heavy or medium syrup, let stand 30 seconds and drain in colander. When several quarts are ready, pack in hot jars, shaking down for a close pack. Cover with boiling syrup in which berries were heated, leaving ½-inch headspace. Process pint jars 15 minutes, quart jars 20 minutes.

Peaches. Select firm, ripe peaches. Dip in boiling water for ½ minute, then into cold water. Slip off skins. To prevent darkening, drop into salt-vinegar solution (2 tblsp. each vinegar and salt to 1 gallon water), draining before packing or heating. Use raw or hot pack.

For raw pack, place peach halves cut side down and overlapping in hot jars. Cover with boiling medium syrup, leaving 1- to 1½-inch headspace. Process pint jars 25 minutes, quart jars 30 minutes.

For hot pack, prepare as for raw pack, but heat peaches in medium syrup. Pack hot fruit in hot jars to within ½ inch of jar top. Pour in boiling syrup in which fruit was heated, leaving ½-inch headspace. If peaches are very ripe and juicy, syrup may be omitted. Then heat them with ½ cup sugar added to each quart of fruit. Heat gently. Pack in jars, leaving ½-inch headspace. Process pint jars 20 minutes, quart jars 25 minutes.

Pears. Use firm, ripe pears. Pare, cut in halves or quarters and core. Work rapidly to prevent darkening, or drop in salt-vinegar solution. Pears canned by hot pack have higher quality than those packed raw. Boil pears 3 to 5 minutes in thin or medium syrup. Pack fruit hot cupside or coreside down in hot jars to within ½ inch of jar top. Cover with boiling syrup, leaving ½-inch headspace. Process pint jars 25 minutes, quart jars 30 minutes.

Plums. Select firm, ripe fruit. Plums mush easily in canning; pricking skins with needle will not prevent splitting but keeps them from bursting. For the raw pack, pack gently but close together in hot jars. Add boiling syrup to cover, heavy syrup for tart plums, medium for sweeter varieties. Leave 1- to 1½-inch headspace. Process pint jars 20 minutes, quart jars 25 minutes.

For hot pack, prepare plums as for raw pack. Heat in boiling medium syrup. If plums are juicy, omit syrup, add ½ cup sugar to each quart of fruit and heat. Pack fruit and juices to within ½ inch of jar top. Ladle the fruit heated in syrup into jars within ½ inch of jar top. Cover with the boiling syrup, leaving ½-inch headspace. Process pint jars 20 minutes, quart jars 25 minutes.

Rhubarb. Use tender, young stalks of rhubarb. Wash and cut in ½-inch pieces. Use raw or hot pack. For raw pack, pack tightly in hot jars and pour boiling heavy syrup to within 1 or 1½ inches of jar top. Rotate jar between hands to remove air bubbles. Process pint jars 10 minutes, quart jars 10 minutes.

For hot pack, prepare rhubarb as for the raw pack. Add ½ cup sugar to each quart of rhubarb. Let stand a few minutes to draw out juices. When juice appears, heat to simmering; simmer 2 or 3 minutes. Fill jars with care to prevent mushing, leaving ½-inch headspace. Instead of heating rhubarb with sugar on top of range, it may be placed in the oven until it is hot and juicy. There will be less danger of mushing. Process pint jars 10 minutes, quart jars 10 minutes.

Tomatoes. Use firm, ripe tomatoes of about the same size. Dip in boiling water for ½ minute, then plunge at once into cold water. Slip off skins and cut out cores and stem ends. Small tomatoes may be packed whole, as may those of medium size, but cut large tomatoes in quarters. Use either raw pack or hot pack.

For raw pack, pack tomatoes in hot jars, pressing gently to fill spaces. Leave ½-inch headspace. To each pint jar add ½ tsp. salt and ½ tsp. lemon juice, 1 tsp. salt and 1 tsp. lemon juice to each quart jar. Process pint jars 35 minutes, quart jars 45 minutes.

For the hot pack, bring tomatoes to boiling, stirring constantly but gently. Use an 8-quart kettle. Pack hot tomatoes into hot jars, leaving ½-inch headspace. Add ½ tsp. salt and ½ tsp. lemon juice to pint jars, 1 tsp. salt and 1 tsp. lemon juice to quart jars. Process pint jars 10 minutes,

quart jars 10 minutes.

Note: Do not can tomatoes without processing in boiling-water bath. Many of the varieties grown today have less acid than old-time tomatoes. Since the home canner does not know how much acid the tomatoes she is using contain, it is recommended that they be processed in boiling water, and that lemon juice, which does not affect flavor, be added.

Canning Low-Acid Vegetables

Use a pressure canner. Do not attempt to can low-acid vegetables in a boiling-water bath. It is not recommended as safe. Process at 10 lbs. pressure for the time specified in directions that follow. The processing time is for altitudes up to 2,000 feet.

Before the canning season arrives, read instructions for using canner. If it has a spring-dial gauge, have it checked. Ask your county extension office where it can be checked. If it is more than 5 pounds off, replace the gauge. Or ask home service department of utility company — that is, gas or electric company.

Follow directions in instruction booklet that came with your canner.

Always put the packed jar in the canner while filling the next one.

Count the processing time from the minute 10 pounds pressure is reached. Regulate the heat to keep the pressure constant during processing. Fluctuations draw liquid from the jars. And if pressure goes below 10 pounds, the processing time cannot be counted until it attains the correct pressure.

Altitude Adjustments for Pressure Canner

The pounds of pressure given in directions that follow are for up to 2,000 feet above sea level. Make the following adjustment for spring-dial gauge: add 1 pound pressure for every 1,000 feet. On a weight gauge use 15 pounds pressure instead of 10 pounds in altitudes above 2,000 feet. Do not use raw pack in altitudes above 6,000 feet.

After processing ends, turn off heat and set canner out of drafts on a wooden board or a wire rack to cool to normal. The gauge will register zero and the safety plug will be in normal position. Never open canner until you are certain the pressure is down.

Add ½ tsp. salt to pint jars and 1 tsp. salt to quart jars of vegetables when ready to adjust the lid and put the jar in the canner. If less or more salt is desirable, directions will so state.

Asparagus. Use young, tender stalks. Wash. Trim bracts (scales) and tough ends. Cut in 1-inch pieces or in lengths 3/4 inch shorter than jar in which they will be canned.

For raw pack, pack 1-inch pieces tightly, the longer lengths in bundles in hot

pint or quart jar to within ½ inch of top. Cover with boiling water, leaving ½-inch headspace. Add salt. Process at 10 pounds pressure 25 minutes for pint jars, 30 minutes for quart jars.

Precook asparagus in boiling water to wilt it; cook 3 minutes when using the hot pack. Plunge asparagus at once into cold water. Pack at once and very loosely to within ½ inch of jar top. Cover with boiling hot water or hot liquid in which asparagus was wilted, leaving ½-inch headspace. Add salt. Process at 10 pounds pressure 25 minutes for pints, 30 minutes for quarts.

Beans, Snap. Wash and trim tender beans; remove strings if necessary. Cut in 1-inch lengths or leave whole.

For raw pack, pack lightly within ½ inch of jar top; if whole, stand beans on end. Fill with boiling water, leaving ½-inch headspace. Add salt. Process at 10 pounds pressure 20 minutes for pint jars, 25 minutes for quart jars.

For hot pack, heat prepared beans 5 minutes in boiling water. Pack loosely and at once to within ½ inch of jar top. Cover with boiling water or the liquid in which beans were heated, leaving ½-inch headspace. Add salt. Process at 10 pounds pressure 20 minutes for pint jars, 25 minutes for quart jars.

Beets. Remove tops except for 2 inches of stem; do not remove roots. Use beets of uniform size if possible. Wash beets and cover with water. Bring to a boil and cook

25 to 30 minutes. Drain, dip in cold water and slip off skins. Cut off stems and roots. Tiny beets (diameter under 2 inches) may be left whole; slice the larger beets.

Use only hot pack. Pack hot beets in jars to within ½ inch of top. Cover with hot water to which vinegar has been added, 1 tblsp. for pints, 2 tblsp. for quarts. The vinegar protects the color. Leave ½-inch headspace. Process at 10 pounds pressure 30 minutes for pint jars, 35 minutes for quart jars.

Carrots. Can only young, tender carrots. Wash, scrape or pare and slice or dice. Tiny carrots may be left whole.

For raw pack, pack tightly to within 1 inch of jar top. Cover with boiling water, leaving ½-inch headspace. Add salt. Process at 10 pounds pressure 25 minutes for pint jars, 30 minutes for quart jars.

For hot pack, prepare carrots as for raw pack. Cover with boiling water and bring to a boil. Pack carrots to within ½ inch of jar top. Cover with boiling water, leaving ½-inch headspace. Add salt. Process at 10 pounds pressure 25 minutes for pint jars, 30 minutes for quart jars.

Corn, Cream-Style. Harvest corn when it is at its best for table use. Use it as soon as possible after gathering, working with a small quantity at a time. Cut off ends of ears; remove husks and silk. Cut out any blemishes. Cut kernels from cob about ⅔ of their depth. Scrape cob to remove any remaining corn, using care not to add any of the cob. Can only in pint jars. For raw pack, fill jars with corn to within 1 inch of top, using care not to pack or shake it down. Add salt. Fill with boiling water and process at 10 pounds pressure 95 minutes for pints.

For hot pack, add 1 pint boiling water to each quart of corn. Heat to boiling. Pack corn in jars to within 1 inch of top. Add salt. Process at 10 pounds pressure 85 minutes for pints.

Corn, Whole-Kernel. Prepare as for hot-pack cream-style corn, only do not scrape cobs. Use only whole kernels. Add 1 pint boiling water to each quart of corn and heat to boiling. Fill jars with hot corn to within 1 inch of jar top. Cover with hot cooking liquid, leaving 1-inch headspace. Add salt. Process at 10 pounds pressure 55 minutes for pint jars, 85 minutes for quart jars.

Peas, Green. Harvest peas when at their best for table use. Can them immediately after picking for the best flavor. For the raw pack, wash and shell peas; do not press down. Fill jars to within 1 inch of top. Add boiling water to cover, leaving 1-inch headspace. Add salt. Process at 10 pounds pressure 40 minutes for pint jars, 40 minutes for quart jars.

For hot pack, cover prepared peas with boiling water. Bring to a boil and pack peas hot in jar to within 1 inch of top. Cover with liquid in which peas boiled or with boiling water, leaving 1-inch headspace. Add salt. Process at 10 pounds pressure 40 minutes for pint jars, 40 minutes for quart jars.

Strained Pumpkin (or Winter Squash). Wash, remove seeds and fibrous material from flesh. Cut in 1-inch cubes or in strips, cover with water and bring to a boil. Cook until tender, about 25 minutes. Scrape flesh from rind and put through a colander or food mill. Simmer just to heat through, stirring to prevent sticking. Pack hot to within ½ inch of jar top. Add no liquid and no salt. Process at 10 pounds pressure 65 minutes for pint jars, 80 minutes for quart jars.

Summer Squash. Wash, trim and cut off any blemishes from small, tender squash, but do not pare it. Cut in ½-inch slices, in quarters or halves. To pack raw, pack tightly to within 1 inch of jar top. Cover with boiling water, leaving ½-inch head-space. Add salt. Process at 10 pounds pressure 25 minutes for pint jars, 30 minutes for quart jars.

For the hot pack, add boiling water to prepared squash and heat to boiling. Pack hot squash loosely, to within ½ inch of jar top. Add hot cooking water to within ½ inch of jar top. Add salt. Process at 10 pounds pressure 30 minutes for pint jars, 40 minutes for quart jars.

Canning Meat, Poultry and Game

Freezers hold most of the meat, poultry and game stored in farm homes. While canning and curing these foods interest fewer people than they did 50 years ago, occasionally there are requests asking for help with the old skills of preserving these protein foods.

Canning rates as an old country art, but the steps in practicing it are changed. Only the pressure canner is recommended for processing the proteins, meat, poultry and game, as well as the low-acid vegetables. The time required to process these foods may seem long, but it is correct. It takes the number of minutes specified in the directions that follow to kill bacteria that otherwise might cause spoilage and possibly endanger health.

Here are the recommended methods for canning meat.

Beef, Pork, Lamb and Veal. Select fresh, clean meat that was well-bled in slaughtering. Chill at once until all the animal heat has gone. If the meat can be held at 40° F., it will handle more easily. If frozen, the meat will not be of top quality when canned. In case it is frozen, do not thaw it. Cut in pieces with a saw or a sturdy, sharp knife. Place meat in boiling water long enough to soften it for packing in jars.

Wipe the meat with a damp cloth; washing draws out the juices. Cut in slices that can be packed easily in canning jars. Cut across the grain when possible. Trim off most of the fat and remove the larger bones. For the larger pieces, select the more tender cuts commonly used for roasts and steaks.

Cut less tender cuts in smaller pieces for stews. Add ½ tsp. salt to pint jars, 1 tsp. to quart jars.

For the hot pack, place cut meat in a large, shallow pan. Pour in a little water to prevent sticking. Cover with a lid or aluminum foil and cook in a moderate oven (350°F.) until the pink color is almost gone from the center of the pieces of meat. Stir occasionally to insure even cooking.

Pack hot meat in jar to which salt has been added. Spoon in 2 tblsp. broth or juices, first skimming off fat, to pint jars, ¼ cup broth to quart jars. The broth should not cover the meat, because the juices cook out during processing. If the fat in them reaches the jar lid, it may affect the seal. Leave 1-inch headspace. Wipe off sealing edge with a damp cloth. Adjust lids.

Process at 10 pounds pressure 75 minutes for pint jars, 90 minutes for quart jars.

For raw pack, pack raw, lean meat pieces loosely in jars to which salt has been added. Leave 1-inch headspace. Add no liquid. Wipe off sealing edge and adjust lids. Process at 10 pounds pressure 75 minutes for pint jars, 90 minutes for quart jars.
Big Game, such as Venison and Elk. Follow directions for canning beef, pork, lamb and veal.

Canning Ground Meat

Grind small pieces of meat from less tender cuts, trimming off large chunks of fat. Keep very cold.

Add 1 tsp. salt to each pound of ground meat and mix thoroughly. Shape in rather thin patties that can be packed in jars without breaking.

Place patties in a large pan and cook in moderate oven (350°F.) until medium done, or until pink color is almost gone from patties.

Pack patties in clean, hot jars. Leave 1-inch headspace. Skim off fat from juices in pan in which meat was heated. Cover with juices, leaving 1-inch headspace. Use spatula or knife to work out air bubbles. Wipe off sealing edge. Adjust lids.

Process at 10 pounds pressure 75 minutes for pint jars, 90 minutes for quart jars.

Canning Pork Sausage

Follow directions for canning ground beef, but omit sage when making sausage. It is a good idea to use less of other seasonings, which sometimes change flavor during processing. The sausage may be seasoned when heating the patties for serving.

Canning Chicken, Other Poultry and Small Game Chicken. Can only birds that

are plump and healthy. Be sure they are bled well or meat may have a reddish color. Remove feathers and chill birds under running cold water or place them in a pan of cold water. When thoroughly chilled, wash and dry. Dress as for the table, but separate in three groups: meaty pieces, bony pieces and giblets. Can giblets separately.

Cook bony pieces in water to cover to make broth. Simmer until tender. Remove meat from bones. The small pieces may be canned for sandwich-making and creaming. Skim fat from broth.

Meaty Pieces with Bone. Saw off drumsticks to shorten them so they will fit in jars. Remove bone from breasts. Leave bones in other pieces, such as second joints. Trim off fat. Heat broth, pour over chicken and heat until almost all pink color disappears from center of pieces. Stir occasionally to heat evenly.

Put 1 tsp. salt in each quart jar. Pack second joints and drumsticks in jars with skin side next to glass. Fit breasts in center. Tuck in smaller pieces where needed. Leave 1-inch headspace.

Cover with hot broth, using ½ to 3/4 cup in each quart jar. Leave 1-inch headspace. Wipe off sealing edge. Adjust lids.

Process at 10 pounds pressure 65 minutes for pints, 75 minutes for quart jars.

Chicken without Bone. Follow directions for canning meaty pieces with bone, except remove the bones, but not the skin, before or after cooking to make broth.

Process at once at 10 pounds pressure 75 minutes for pint jars, 90 minutes for quart jars.

Turkey and Other Poultry. Follow directions for canning chicken.

Canning Giblets. Freeze livers if possible, or can them separately. Place gizzards and hearts in kettle, cover with chicken broth made by cooking bony pieces and simmer until medium done, stirring occasionally. Add ½ tsp. salt to each pint jar. Pack hot giblets in jar; add 2 or 3 tblsp. hot broth or water. Work out air bubbles with spatula or knife. Leave 1-inch headspace. Adjust lids.

Process at 10 pounds pressure 75 minutes for pint jars.

Game Birds. Cut birds in pieces suitable for canning. Follow directions for canning chicken as closely as possible.

Rabbits. Skin rabbits, remove entrails and cut out waxy glands under front legs where they join the body. Wash carcass in salty water. Cut in pieces and can like chicken.

Reader's Notes

The women who invented and prized the pickle and relish recipes in this chapter used fresh fruits and vegetables from their own or their neighbors' gardens and orchards. Sharing abundant foods was the rule. The recipes follow the methods employed a half-century ago.

Pickled fruits and vegetables today are packed hot in standard canning jars with metal lids that have screw-on rings and are processed in boiling-water bath canners to insure against spoilage.

CHAPTER 12

PICKLES, CATCHUPS AND RELISHES

MOST meals are improved by the use of pickles which add zest and variety. On the farm where there are gardens and orchards, various kinds of pickles can be made during the summer and fall.

In making pickles the first precaution to heed is that of using only sound, never over-ripe, vegetables and fruits. Unless badly soiled, these should be cleansed by being wiped with a damp cloth and then with a dry one, for even a little water may prevent the pickle from keeping.

If possible, use pure cider vinegar. Some commercial vinegars, other than that made from cider, frequently contain chemicals that soften the pickles, making them flabby. Cooking too long in vinegar also softens pickles. The purpose of heating is to cause the vinegar to "strike in" or if there are mixed vegetables, cooking is an excellent way to blend the flavors.

Precautions to Heed

Adding a little grated horseradish or nasturtium leaves helps to keep the pickles from molding, while the addition of grape leaves is supposed to make the pickles green. A little powdered alum may be added to make pickles crisp, but this material must be used in very small quantities, if at all, since it is an astringent and large amounts impart an undesirable flavor.

In making or storing pickles no metal utensils should be used. An enameled kettle gives best results in cooking, and for storing glass fruit jars or stoneware, not earthenware, jars are best.

As a rule, best results are obtained by sealing the pickles in sterilized glass jars although they may be left in the brine. If this is done, they must be examined frequently to make certain that none of them are soft. Too strong a brine causes them to become soft. When spices are used, they are tied in thin muslin or cheesecloth.

Cucumber Pickles

4 quarts cucumbers   4 quarts vinegar
                4 red peppers

Wash and wipe until dry, small unripe cucumbers. Put into a stone jar and cover with a brine made by adding 1 cupful of salt to every quart of water used. Have the brine cool when added to the cucumbers. Let stand 24 hours. Heat to near the boiling point, drain and wipe the cucumbers dry. Cover them with fresh, cold water, the colder the better. Bring to the boiling point. Drain and cook the cucumbers, a few at a time, in the cider vinegar boiled with the peppers. Can in sterilized jars, pouring the hot vinegar over the pickles. Seal. Sweet pickles may be made by adding sugar and spices to the vinegar.

Process in boiling-water bath canner 15 minutes.

Dill Pickles

Use cucumbers about 8 inches long. Wash and wipe until dry and arrange in layers in a stone jar, placing between every layer a small red pepper cut in pieces, a large bunch of dill seed on the stalk and a few clean grape leaves. Repeat the process until the cucumbers have been used. Then add 4 cupfuls of salt to 3 gallons of water, boil and skim, adding sufficient water to make 3 gallons of the brine after the boiling. When cool, pour over the cucumbers. Spread more dill, grape leaves and a clean cloth over the top. Cover with a plate weighted down with a heavy block and let stand 3 weeks before using any of the pickles. Wash the cloth over the top of the jar two times every week.

Fermented pickles do not require processing in boiling-water bath. The cucumbers frequently were taken from the brine as needed, soaked in water to desalt and a pickle solution was added.

Dill Pickles

50 medium-sized cucumbers   6 quarts water
1 large bunch dill   1½ quarts vinegar
½ cupful mustard seed   1½ cupfuls salt
½ cupful grated horseradish   brine

Wash the cucumbers and place in a brine overnight. Make a brine by using ½ cupful of salt to every gallon of water. Drain the cucumbers in the morning and arrange them in layers in sterile glass fruit jars. Between every layer place some of

Process pints and quarts in boiling-water bath canner 15 minutes.

the dill, horseradish and mustard seed. Heat the vinegar, water and salt together. When boiling hot, pour the liquid over the cucumbers and seal.

Beet Pickles

Wash the beets carefully, but do not cut off the roots, and leave at least 3 inches of the tops on to prevent "bleeding" during the cooking. Boil the beets until almost tender, plunge in cold water, remove skins and cut or slice as desired.

For sour pickles boil the beets in vinegar until thoroughly cooked. Then pour in sterilized cans, add 1 teaspoonful of salt to every quart and pour in the boiling vinegar. Seal.

Sweet beet pickles are made by using a syrup instead of the vinegar and salt. To make the syrup boil 4 cupfuls of sugar with 2 cupfuls of vinegar and 2 tablespoonfuls of whole cloves and 1 tablespoonful of stick cinnamon. Tie the spices in a piece of thin muslin. Bring the syrup to the boiling point and boil the beets in it 5 minutes. Pour in sterilized jars and seal.

Sweet Sliced Cucumber

1 quart large cucumbers	18 whole cloves
1 onion	1 tablespoonful mustard seed
1 green pepper	¼ teaspoonful celery seed
1 cupful brown sugar	salt
1 teaspoonful turmeric	vinegar to cover

Peel and slice the cucumbers. Remove the seeds from the pepper and cut in small, thin slices. Slice the onion and sprinkle with a little salt, and let stand overnight. In the morning, drain, add the other ingredients, using white mustard seed, and boil until tender. Can in sterilized jars and seal.

Mustard Pickles

Use equal quantities of cucumbers, green tomatoes, cauliflower and small onions. Cover with boiling brine made from 1 cupful of salt to every quart of water. Let stand 24 hours. Drain and cover with fresh boiling water. Let stand 30 minutes. Drain and cover with mustard sauce made by cooking 1 cupful of brown sugar, ½ pound of mustard and ¼ pound of flour, which have been mixed together, with 1 quart of vinegar. Seal the pickles while hot in sterile jars.

Countrywomen depended on pickled beets to add color and flavor to winter meals. Process pint and quart jars in boiling-water bath canner 30 minutes.

Process in boiling-water bath canner 10 minutes.

Mustard pickles were great favorites when served with roast pork, pork chops or baked beans. Heat pickles thoroughly before packing in hot pint or quart jars. Process in boiling-water bath canner 10 minutes.

Delicious Relish

2 small cabbages	4 tablespoonfuls flour
5 onions	1½ cupfuls sugar
10 ears corn	3 hot peppers
4 tablespoonfuls salt	4 cupfuls vinegar
3 tablespoonfuls mustard	

Steam the corn until tender, cut from the cob and add to the chopped cabbage, onions and peppers. Mix the dry ingredients together and add to the vinegar. Pour this over the vegetables and simmer 40 minutes. Pour into large bottles or jars which are sterile and seal while hot.

Simmer this corn-cabbage relish only 20 minutes, pack in hot pint jars and process in boiling-water bath canner 15 minutes.

Pepper and Onion Relish

24 red peppers	3 tablespoonfuls salt
18 large white onions	2 cupfuls sugar
6 cupfuls cider vinegar	

Remove the seeds from the peppers, skin the onions and put both vegetables through the food grinder. Cover with boiling water and let stand 5 minutes. Drain and add the vinegar, sugar and salt. Boil 25 minutes and can or bottle while hot.

Simmer 15 minutes and pack in hot pint or half-pint jars. Process in boiling-water bath canner about 5 minutes.

Tomato Relish

2 pecks ripe tomatoes	6½ cupfuls vinegar
½ peck white onions	½ cupful salt
2 teaspoonfuls cayenne pepper	

Skin onions, wash the tomatoes and cut both vegetables in small pieces. Cook together until soft, strain and cook again until the mixture is as thick as catchup. Add vinegar, salt and cayenne pepper and cook again until the mixture is as thick as catchup. Seal in sterile jars or bottles.

Process in boiling-water bath canner 10 minutes.

Tomato Catchup

1 peck ripe tomatoes	1 teaspoonful ground mace
¼ cupful salt	1 tablespoonful cinnamon
1 cupful sugar	2 teaspoonfuls ground cloves
1 teaspoonful cayenne	1 tablespoonful mustard
1 quart cider vinegar	

Stew the tomatoes until tender. Then rub them through a sieve, add the spices and vinegar and cook until of the right consistency. Bottle in sterile bottles and seal.

Process like Tomato Relish.

Chili Sauce was a traditional companion to pan-fried country ham and to baked beans. Process in boiling-water bath canner 15 minutes.

Apples were plentiful and often countrywomen went to great efforts to salvage their crops of the fruit. That was when Apple Chutney enjoyed its greatest popularity. Process in boiling-water bath canner 10 minutes.

Lemon and raspberry catchups were considered exotic relishes. They were made less often than many kinds.

Chili Sauce

1½ dozen tomatoes	1 teaspoonful cinnamon
3 small onions	½ teaspoonful chili pepper
3 green peppers	1 teaspoonful powdered cloves
2 teaspoonfuls salt	2 cupfuls vinegar
1 cupful sugar	1 teaspoonful ginger

Use ripe tomatoes, remove the skins, peel the onions and discard the pepper seeds. Put the vegetables in a kettle, after chopping them in small pieces. Cook slowly until they are tender. Add the sugar, salt, spices and vinegar and cook 10 minutes. Bottle and seal.

Apple Chutney

1 dozen sour apples	2 cupfuls vinegar
3 small onions	½ cupful lemon juice
3 green peppers	2 cupfuls sugar
1 small red pepper	½ cupful cranberry jelly
1 cupful raisins	1 tablespoonful ginger
1 tablespoonful salt	

Chop the apples, onion and peppers in fine pieces and add the vinegar and jelly. Simmer gently 1½ hours, stirring frequently. Add the other ingredients, using brown ginger, and cook 1 hour. Pour in sterilized jars and seal.

Lemon Catchup

7 lemons	2 teaspoonfuls salt
3 tablespoonfuls grated horseradish	5 blades mace
1½ tablespoonfuls celery seeds	8 cloves
1½ tablespoonfuls mustard seeds	6 grains red pepper

Grate the rinds from the lemons and add the strained juice of the fruit, the spices and salt. Boil gently 45 minutes. Pour into glasses and seal. This will be ready for use in about 2 months.

Raspberry Catchup

1 gallon ripe raspberries	1 teaspoonful cinnamon
1 quart cider vinegar	1 small piece ginger root
½ teaspoonful mustard seeds	2 cupfuls sugar

Cook the berries slowly in the vinegar for 1 hour, then strain and add the spices and mustard seed. Boil slowly 20 minutes, strain and measure. To every quart, add 2 cupfuls of sugar. Simmer gently until the mixture is thick, then bottle and seal.

Walnut Catchup

Use walnuts which are soft enough that they may be pierced with a needle. Mash them to a pulp and allow them to lie in salt water 2 weeks, using ½ cupful of salt to 20 walnuts and sufficient water to cover them. Drain off this liquid and pour on a pint of boiling vinegar and let stand for 5 minutes; then drain. To every quart of this liquor add 3 tablespoonfuls of pepper, 1 tablespoonful of ginger, 2 tablespoonfuls of cloves and 3 tablespoonfuls of nutmeg. Boil 1 hour and when cool, bottle and seal.

Once an enjoyed, commonplace relish in country kitchens, Walnut Catchup now is a stranger.

Apple Catchup

2 quarts tart apple sauce	2 teaspoonfuls powdered cloves
4 small onions	1¾ teaspoonfuls pepper
2 quarts vinegar	2 teaspoonfuls salt
2 cupfuls sugar	4 teaspoonfuls cinnamon
2 teaspoonfuls mustard	1 teaspoonful mace

Put the apple sauce through a sieve, add the chopped onions, vinegar, salt, sugar and spices. Simmer until thick. Bottle and seal while hot.

Cucumber Catchup

10 cucumbers	1 teaspoonful ginger
8 onions	½ teaspoonful pepper
5 cupfuls sugar	1 teaspoonful powdered mace
2 tablespoonfuls mustard seed	½ teaspoonful turmeric
1 teaspoonful cinnamon	1 teaspoonful celery seeds
vinegar	salt

The catchup that has more than held its own during the last half-century is Tomato Catchup. Process all catchups in boiling-water bath canner for 10 minutes.

Slice the unpeeled cucumbers, sprinkle with salt and let stand 2 hours. Drain, add the sliced medium-sized onions, the spices, sugar and sufficient vinegar to cover. Put into a saucepan and boil until tender. If this is not salt enough, add 1 teaspoonful of salt. Seal while hot in sterile jars or bottles.

Elderberry Catchup

4 cupfuls ripe elderberries	24 whole cloves
6 cupfuls boiling vinegar	40 white peppercorns
¾ teaspoonful salt	2 blades mace
small piece of ginger root	4 shallots

Remove the elderberries from the stems, measure and add the boiling vinegar. Let stand overnight in a cool place. Next

Elderberries once were free for gathering on countless farms. While pies made with them were regarded their greatest gift to good eating, the catchup also had some enthusiastic champions.

Grape catchups had their heyday when most farms had miniature vineyards, usually a few vines. The standard variety of grapes grown in the Midwest was the blue-purple Concord, developed in New England from several kinds of American wild grapes.

Spicy, clove-studded, golden peach pickles were as essential in country fried chicken dinners as mashed potatoes and cream gravy. Simmer peaches in the syrup just until tender instead of soft and process in boiling-water bath canner 20 minutes.

Old-time pickle makers made a point of using very firm pears. Simmer them until barely tender and process in boiling-water bath canner 15 minutes.

day strain the liquor through a muslin bag without pressure and boil it five minutes with the salt, spices and chopped shallots. Bottle and seal while hot.

Grape Catchup

3 quarts ripe grapes	1½ tablespoonfuls cinnamon
vinegar to cover	1½ tablespoonfuls cloves
1½ cupfuls sugar	1½ tablespoonfuls allspice

Cook grapes in vinegar until they are soft. Rub through a sieve, add sugar and spices to the pulp and cook slowly, stirring occasionally to avoid burning, until of the consistency of catchup.

PICKLED FRUITS

Sweet Peach Pickles

16 peaches	1 cupful vinegar
1 pound brown sugar	16 whole cloves
	2 large sticks cinnamon

Dip the peaches in hot water and remove immediately, rubbing them with a towel to remove the skins. Boil the sugar, vinegar and cinnamon, broken in small pieces, 5 minutes. Pierce every peach with a clove. Put them in the syrup and simmer until soft. The slower and longer the cooking, the better the color and flavor. Place in sterilized jars and seal.

Sweet Pickled Pears

Follow directions for sweet pickled peaches, using pears instead of the peaches.

Spiced Apples

8 apples	½ cupful vinegar
¾ cupful brown sugar	1 large stick cinnamon
	whole cloves

Boil the sugar, vinegar and cinnamon, broken in bits, 5 minutes. Wash, pare and core the apples and cut in eighths. Pierce every piece with a clove. Simmer gently until tender in the syrup. Can in sterile jars.

Process in boiling-water bath canner 15 minutes.

Cantaloupe Pickles

Select firm under-ripe melons, cut in small sections and discard the seeds. Soak in a brine made by dissolving ¼ cupful of salt in a quart of water. After the melon has stood in this 3 or 4 hours, drain and add the well-drained sections to a syrup made by boiling 4 cupfuls of sugar, 1 cupful of vinegar, 1 quart of water, 1 tablespoonful of cloves and 1 tablespoonful of allspice together. Boil the melon rapidly in this 10 minutes. Remove from the stove and let stand overnight. In the morning drain the syrup from the melon and boil it until the back of a spoon dipped in it is coated. Then add the cantaloupe and cook slowly 1 hour.

A favored melon for eating and pickle making in Kansas and neighboring states was the Rocky Ford cantaloupe, developed in the Arkansas River valley of eastern Colorado. The flesh of the melon, even when dead-ripe, was firmer than that of most muskmelons. Process cantaloupe pickles in boiling-water bath canner 10 minutes.

Of all the pleasing aromas of country kitchens, none surpassed those from steaming kettles at pickle-making time. In the thoughts of older people they bring memories of happy company, holiday and other special-occasion meals when home-canned, spicy vegetable and fruit relishes and pickles played important roles in menus.

In warm climates, where cool, dry storage quarters are at a premium or are impossible, much spoilage of preserves, jams, conserves, fruit butters and marmalades may be prevented by pouring the hot mixture into half-pint canning jars with self-sealing lids and processing them in a boiling-water bath canner 5 to 10 minutes.

CHAPTER 13

FRUIT PRESERVES, JAMS AND BUTTERS

PRESERVES are fruits canned in a thick syrup. Usually these are cooked by the open kettle method. They are stored in glasses covered with a layer of paraffin which keeps the air from entering. Properly preserved fruits are saturated with sugar so they have a transparent appearance. Uncooked fruits should never be dropped into a thick syrup as this causes them to shrivel.

Strawberry Preserves

Pick over, hull, wash and drain berries. Weigh and make a syrup by using ¾ their weight in sugar mixed with water. Use 1 cupful of water to every 2 cupfuls of sugar. Boil the syrup 5 minutes. Add the berries and bring to the boiling point. Lift out the fruit and place in the sterilized glasses. Boil the syrup 10 minutes longer and pour over the berries. When cool, pour melted paraffin over the top, cover and set away in a cool dark place.

Raspberry Preserves

Follow the directions for making strawberry preserves, substituting raspberries for the strawberries.

Blackberries

Substitute blackberries for the strawberries and make like strawberry preserves.

Plum Conserve

5 pounds fruit	2 pounds raisins
5 pounds sugar	½ cupful nut meats
	3 oranges

Grind the fruit and chopped nuts through the food chopper. Cook until as thick as desired and seal in sterile fruit jars or in glasses like the strawberry preserves.

Jams

Use sound fruit or berries. Wash carefully and stem or pare as is necessary. Weigh or measure the fruit. Cut large fruit in pieces and crush berries and place in a saucepan with just enough water to prevent sticking. Stir to keep from burning and cook until the mixture begins to thicken. Then add ¾ as much sugar as fruit. Simmer until the desired consistency is reached, pour into hot sterilized jars, cool, seal with paraffin, cover and store in a cool, dark place.

Fruit Butters

Fruit butters are made like jams, only the cooked fruit or berries are rubbed through a colander before the sugar is added. As a rule, fruit butters are not so thick as jams. After the sugar is added, the butter may be set in the oven to finish cooking so it will not have to be stirred so much.

Watermelon Conserve

6 cupfuls watermelon rind	4½ lemons
5 cupfuls apples	6 cupfuls sugar
4 oranges	5 cupfuls water

Chop or cut the rind into small cubes, discarding the green portion. Peel the apples, remove the cores and chop. Chop oranges, peeling and all, removing the seeds. Use the juice of the lemons. Mix all the ingredients and boil slowly from 2 to 3 hours. Can and seal in sterile jars.

Splendo Marmalade

2 pounds quinces	2 pounds peaches
2 pounds pears	3 lemons
½ pound sour apples	sugar

Peel the quinces, pears, apples and peaches, removing the cores and pits. Cut or chop in fine bits. Slice the lemons in thin wafer-like slices, discarding the seeds. Weigh the combination

Putting up fruit spreads in summer to enjoy in the months ahead sometimes led to adventure. After a day's outing searching for, discovering and gathering wild plums, a mother and her young helpers anticipated two busy days of activity. On the first, the plums yielded jelly; next day the leftover fruit pulp, mixed with sugar and spices in a big pan, simmered softly in the oven. It came out a lovely plum butter to spread throughout the winter on homemade bread warm from the oven.

of fruits and add ¾ as much sugar as fruit. Let stand several hours in a cool place. Then boil gently until the marmalade is very thick, stirring frequently so the mixture will not stick to the pan or burn. If one wishes, 1 pound of finely ground nut meats may be added just before the marmalade is taken from the stove. Seal while hot in sterilized jars.

Prune Marmalade

1 pound prunes	1¼ cupfuls sugar
1 cupful vinegar	½ teaspoonful cinnamon
½ teaspoonful cloves	

Soak the prunes overnight in cold water and cook the next morning in the same water in which they soaked. After cooking slowly 45 minutes, drain, saving the liquor, and cut the prunes in small pieces. Discard the pits. Place the prunes and the liquor in a saucepan with the vinegar, sugar and spices and cook slowly 45 minutes, or until the marmalade is thick.

Dried Peach Butter

1 pound peaches	1 cupful sugar
	2 cupfuls water

Wash the peaches carefully and soak overnight in cold water. Cook slowly in the same water the next morning until the fruit is very tender. Rub through a sieve, add the sugar and simmer gently until the butter is of the desired consistency.

Winter Jam

2 oranges	1 grapefruit
2 lemons	sugar

Wash the fruit and cut in small pieces, discarding the seeds but saving all the juice. Use only the pulp of the grapefruit. Measure the fruit and juice and pour three times its quantity of water over it. Let stand overnight. Then cook 30 minutes, measure again and add an equal amount of sugar. Mix together thoroughly and let stand overnight again. In the morning simmer until the marmalade is thick. Use an enameled saucepan for cooking this marmalade, or if desired, a stone crock may be used.

Making this three-citrus marmalade during February was as traditional in many country kitchens as baking cherry pie for a treat on Washington's birthday. Oranges, grapefruit and lemons most years were plentiful at that season, when their cost was usually lower than at any other time.

Quince Honey

5 large quinces	2 cupfuls water
	5 cupfuls sugar

Pare and grate or grind the quinces. To 2 cupfuls of water add 5 cupfuls of sugar. Stir over the fire until the sugar is dissolved. Add the quinces and cook 20 minutes. Turn into sterile glasses and seal.

Pear Honey

1 peck pears	1 quart grated pineapple
	sugar

Pare and core the ripe pears and put through the food grinder. Measure and add ¾ as much sugar as fruit and cook without adding water until the mixture is the color of rich preserves. Add the pineapple, cook 3 minutes and can in sterile jars.

Cider Fruit Butters

10 pounds fruit	Cinnamon or other spices as desired
5 pounds sugar	
Cider enough to barely cover	

Apples, peaches, pears, plums, grapes and other fruits may be used. When using the larger fruits, peel and remove the seeds, add sugar, cider and spices. Cook together until of a thick consistency, stirring frequently to prevent burning. It is easier to cook fruit butters in the oven since fewer stirrings are required. When using small fruits as plums and grapes, cook with the cider until soft and then rub through a sieve to remove the skins and seeds. Add sugar, return to the stove and cook like other fruit butters. Seal in sterile jars.

Pumpkin Butter

4 cupfuls pumpkin pulp	½ teaspoonful ground ginger
2 cupfuls sugar	⅛ teaspoonful ground cloves
¾ teaspoonful cinnamon	⅛ teaspoonful ground nutmeg
	2 lemons

Steam the pumpkin until tender, drain and put through a sieve. To every 4 cupfuls of the pulp add the spices and the juice of the lemons. Cook slowly in the oven until thick. Pour into glasses, cool and seal.

Apple butter won more praise than other kinds flavored with cider. Farmers claimed it was the perfect topping for hot buttered biscuits.

This old-fashioned country special of years when the fruit crop was not abundant rarely is made now. When it is, canned strained pumpkin (see canning chapter) is the basis for it. The butter is made in small amounts, or enough to use without canning. Keeping it in the refrigerator eliminates possible storage problems.

An unwritten rule among old-time experts in making clear, sparkling jellies that quivered but held their shape was to select slightly underripe fruit for it. They did not know the reason it helped was that such fruits contain more acid and pectin.

Bottled and packaged pectin had not arrived in many Midwestern farm kitchens a half-century ago.

CHAPTER 14

JELLY MAKING

THE success of jelly making depends largely on three factors —the amount of acid in the fruit, the amount of pectin present and the quantity of sugar used. If the fruit tastes sweet, it needs acid, which may be supplied by the addition of lemon juice or some other tart fruit juice. An excellent way to test fruit juice for the acid it contains is to compare its taste with that of a tart apple. If the apple is more tart, sour fruit juice is needed for the jelly. Another test is made by mixing together 1 teaspoonful of lemon juice, 3 tablespoonfuls of cold water and ½ teaspoonful of sugar. If the fruit juice is not so tart as this mixture, it is best to add lemon juice or some other tart fruit juice when cooking the fruit for the jelly.

Testing for Pectin

Pectin may be supplied by the addition of apple juice or the white portion of lemon and orange peelings. Since this substance is found more abundantly in under-ripe fruits than ripe ones, very ripe fruits should not be used for jellying purposes.

To test for pectin, place 1 tablespoonful of wood alcohol in a cup and add to it 1 tablespoonful of fruit juice. Let stand at least 30 minutes. If pectin is present, a gelatinous mass will appear in the liquid. If this can be taken up in a spoon without breaking apart and if the mass is quite firm, there is an abundance of pectin present. When the mass is rather loose and breaks apart when shaken or lifted in a spoon or if there is little of it, the juice contains less pectin. When the pectin forms in small globules but not in a jelly-like mass, the juice needs to be cooked more and the test repeated. Pectin may be prepared from oranges or apples and kept on hand during the jelly making season or it may be purchased at most grocery stores.

Sugar Proportions Important

The amount of sugar required varies with the amount of pectin. If the pectin test shows an abundance of pectin is present, 1 cupful of sugar is used to every cupful of fruit juice, but if the test shows a loose and less firm pectin, ¾ cupful of sugar is used to every cupful of fruit juice.

Adding too much sugar produces a soft jelly, while not enough produces a tough, stringy product. Experiments have shown that the sugar should be added gradually after the juice begins to boil. It does not need to be heated in the oven first if stirred into the juice carefully.

Watch for Jellying Point

Care must be exercised in watching for the jellying point, for jelly cooked too long is stringy and tough and frequently it is dark in color. Uncooked jelly is syrupy and soft and it has a tendency to sour. By dipping some of the jelly in a spoon, allowing it to cool a few minutes and pouring it gently from the edge of the spoon, one can determine when the jellying stage is reached. If the juice runs off like syrup, it is not cooked enough, but if it breaks in flakes or sheets off, the jellying stage is reached. A safe way of determining when the jelly is cooked enough is to use a thermometer. When the temperature of the boiling mass is 221 to 223 degrees Fahrenheit or 106 degrees Centigrade, the jellying point has been reached.

The hot jelly is skimmed, poured into sterilized glasses which have been boiled in water 12 minutes and set in a warm place, such as a sunny window, to cool. When firm, it is sealed with paraffin, labeled and stored in a cool, dark place. In sealing, pour the hot paraffin on top of the jelly and run a small pointed knife around the edge of the glass while the paraffin is still hot. Sterilize the glass covers in boiling water before putting them over the jelly. Wrapping glasses in paper helps to keep out light and prevent fading.

Straining the Juice

After the fruit is cooked to a pulp, strain the juice through dampened flannel without squeezing. This juice makes the

When using a candy or jelly thermometer to test for the jellying point, first place it in boiling water to determine the exact temperature at which the water boils. Altitudes affect the temperature. Add 8° to the temperature at which water boils. Water boils at 212°F. at sea level. In making jelly there, the jellying point is 220°F.

best jelly. Then return the pulp to the stove, add cold water to cover and boil 20 minutes. Strain through the flannel again without squeezing. Make jelly as with the first extraction of juice, making the pectin test first to determine how much sugar to add. Cloudy jelly usually is the result of cooking the juice too long with the fruit or not using sufficient care in straining it.

Best results are obtained in making 8 glasses or less at a time. The kettle used should have a capacity four times as great as the volume of juice to be cooked. Cooking too much juice at one time frequently results in a slower cookery, thus a destruction of pectin and a loss of color.

Apple Jelly

Wipe, quarter and core apples. Cover with cold water and heat slowly until the apples are a pulp. Drain through dampened flannel and do not squeeze. Boil the juice about 10 minutes, add ¾ as much sugar as juice and boil 10 minutes. Skim, fill glasses, and when cool, seal with paraffin. After straining the juice from the apple pulp, return it to the stove, cover with cold water and boil 20 minutes. Strain this juice through flannel and make the pectin test to determine how much sugar will be needed. Make jelly with it just like the first extraction of juice.

Crab Apple Jelly

Make as apple jelly, using crab apples instead of the apples.

Small Fruit Jelly

Pick over, wash and drain the fruit or berries, such as grapes, raspberries, currants, blackberries and cranberries, and cook with enough water to cover until the juice is extracted from the fruit. Drain through flannel cloth, but do not squeeze. Measure the juice and use ¾ as much sugar as juice. Cook the juice 10 minutes, add the sugar and cook 10 more minutes. Skim, pour in sterilized glasses and seal with paraffin when cool.

Quince Jelly

Wash the quinces, cut in quarters, cover with cold water and cook until soft. Strain, measure and add ½ cupful of lemon juice to every 4 cupfuls of quince juice. Test for pectin and finish the same as for apple jelly.

Strawberry Jelly

4 cupfuls strawberry juice	4 tablespoonfuls strained lemon
4 cupfuls sugar	juice

Bring the strawberry juice to the boiling point and add the lemon juice and sugar. Boil until the jellying stage is reached.

Apple Pectin

1 pound apple pulp	3 tablespoonfuls lemon juice
	5 cupfuls cold water

Wash the apples thoroughly, remove the stem ends and cut the apples in quarters without removing the skin or cores. Add the lemon juice and water and simmer until the apples are soft. Place in a jelly bag and let drip, squeezing out the juice gently. Then strain through a flannel without squeezing. Test with wood alcohol for pectin.

Orange Pectin

1 cupful white portion of orange peel	3 tablespoonfuls lemon juice
	6 cupfuls cold water

Cut the white portion from the orange peel and put through the food chopper and measure. Add the lemon juice and 3 cupfuls of the cold water and let stand in an enameled or earthenware dish about 5 hours. Boil 12 minutes and cool. Add the rest of the cold water and bring to the boiling point, cool and let stand 12 hours or overnight. Boil 10 minutes and strain through two layers of cheesecloth, squeezing the bag to obtain all the juice. Then strain through a flannel bag without squeezing. Test with alcohol to see how much pectin is present.

Strawberry Jelly

2 cupfuls orange or apple pectin	2 cupfuls strawberry juice
2 cupfuls sugar	

Combine the pectin and strawberry juice and bring to the boiling point. Skim and add the sugar gradually and cook until the jellying stage is reached.

Orange Jelly

2 cupfuls orange pectin	2 cupfuls orange juice

2 cupfuls sugar

Combine the pectin and orange juice and bring to the boiling point. Skim and add the sugar gradually and cook until the jellying stage is reached.

Cherry Jelly

2 cupfuls apple pectin	2 cupfuls cherry juice

2 cupfuls sugar

Combine pectin and cherry juice and bring to the boiling point. Skim and add the sugar gradually and cook until the jellying stage is reached.

Rhubarb Jelly

1 cupful apple pectin	2 cupfuls rhubarb juice

2½ cupfuls sugar

Use tender rhubarb stalks. Wash but do not peel. Cut into one inch pieces and add just enough water to prevent sticking or burning and simmer until soft. Strain through a jelly bag. Combine the juice with the pectin and bring to the boiling point. Skim and add the sugar gradually and cook until the jellying stage is reached.

Mint Jelly

½ cupful chopped mint leaves	2 cupfuls apple pectin
⅓ cupful boiling water	2 cupfuls sugar

green vegetable coloring

Pour boiling water over the mint and allow the mixture to steep 1 hour, keeping the bowl covered. Strain and press to extract the juice. Bring pectin to the boiling point and skim, add the mint juice and sugar. When the jellying stage is reached, stir in a little green vegetable coloring mixed with a little syrup to give a green tint, stir well and pour in sterilized jars.

Cranberry Jelly

4 cupfuls cranberries   2 cupfuls sugar
water to cover

Wash and pick over the cranberries. Place in a saucepan and add barely enough water to cover. Cook 20 minutes. Rub through a colander or sieve and add the sugar to the pulp. Cook 5 minutes and pour in molds or jelly glasses.

If possible, make pudding with firm-textured bread similar to many homemade loaves. Bake in moderate oven (350°F.) about 1 hour, or until knife inserted in center of pudding comes out clean.

Melt chocolate in milk before adding bread. Strain.

CHAPTER 15

PUDDINGS AND DESSERTS

THE dessert is the last part of the meal and therefore is of great importance. If good, it crowns the meal with success and sends everyone from the table in a happy state of mind. There is almost no end to the different kinds of desserts, the recipes in this book being examples of types which can be prepared with ease in the farm home.

Bread Pudding

1½ cupfuls bread	3 cupfuls milk
2 tablespoonfuls butter	1 egg
¾ cupful sugar	1½ teaspoonfuls vanilla
½ teaspoonful salt	speck of nutmeg

Break the bread in small pieces and add it to the scalded milk. Let stand a few minutes until the bread is soft, then stir in the butter, flavoring, beaten egg, salt and sugar. Pour in an oiled baking dish and bake in a moderate oven about 40 minutes, taking care that the pudding mixture does not boil. Best results are obtained by setting the pudding dish in a pan containing a little water. Serve hot or cold with cream or a pudding sauce.

Chocolate Bread Pudding

1½ cupfuls bread	1 egg
3 cupfuls milk	½ teaspoonful salt
1½ squares chocolate	1 teaspoonful vanilla
¾ cupful sugar	speck of cinnamon

Break the bread in small pieces and pour the scalded milk over it. When the bread is soft, add the other ingredients, first melting the chocolate over hot water. Bake in a moderate oven about 40 minutes and serve with cream or a pudding sauce.

Peach Shortcake

1½ cupfuls flour	½ cupful fat
½ cupful cornstarch	½ teaspoonful salt
4 teaspoonfuls baking powder	¾ cupful milk

Sift dry ingredients. Work in the fat and add sufficient milk to make a soft dough. Cut dough into two parts and fit one of the halves into a tin. Butter the top and lay the other half on it. Bake and serve with peach sauce between the layers and on top.

Peach Sauce

½ cupful butter	1 cupful powdered sugar
⅔ cupful sliced canned peaches	1 egg white

Cream the butter, add the sugar and beat until light. Whip in the fruit and the stiffly beaten egg white.

Fruit Puffs

½ cupful butter	2 cupfuls hot water
5 eggs	1½ cupfuls flour
2 ounces chocolate	½ cupful preserved fruit
½ cupful milk	1 teaspoonful vanilla
½ cupful sugar	¼ teaspoonful salt
	1 egg

Melt the butter in the hot water and bring to the boiling point. Then stir in the flour gradually and boil until it leaves the sides of the pan. Stir constantly during the cooking. Usually 1 minute is long enough to cook the flour mixture. Turn into a bowl to cool. Beat the five eggs in, one at a time, beating the batter 1 minute for every egg. When all five are added, beat the mixture 5 minutes. Set in a cold place, on ice if possible, for at least 1 hour. Then drop by spoonfuls in paper lined pan. Use oiled paper or grease plain wrapping paper. Bake in a hot oven 15 minutes. These should puff up and have cavities in the center.

Make a filling for these by grating the 2 squares of chocolate and melting it over hot water. When melted add the sugar, 1 tablespoonful of butter, 1 well beaten egg and the salt. Cook in a double boiler until the mixture thickens. Then add the fruit preserves and vanilla. Pear, strawberry and peach preserves make delicious fillings.

Apple Betty

3 cupfuls bread crumbs	¾ teaspoonful cinnamon
3 cupfuls apples	¼ teaspoonful cloves
¾ cupful sugar	4 tablespoonfuls butter

These are cream puffs with chocolate filling. Bake in hot oven (400°F.) about an hour, or until puffs are puffed and golden. Cool away from drafts. Cut off tops, fill as desired and replace tops. Countrywomen liked to fill them with whipped cream with bananas or strawberries folded in and with chocolate sauce or crushed and sweetened berries spooned over.

Grease a baking dish and sprinkle a layer of the pared and chopped apples in the bottom. Sprinkle with a little of the sugar and spices which have been mixed together, dot with some of the butter and cover with a layer of fine bread crumbs. Repeat this process until all the ingredients are used, making certain that the top layer is of bread crumbs. Cover and bake 40 minutes in a hot oven, then remove the cover and brown the top quickly. Serve when quite warm with cream or a pudding sauce.

Fig Pudding

3 tablespoonfuls cornstarch	⅓ pound figs
½ cupful sugar	½ cupful boiling water
½ teaspoonful salt	2 tablespoonfuls sugar
3 cupfuls milk	1 tablespoonful lemon juice
2 egg yolks	2 egg whites
2 tablespoonfuls powdered sugar	

Use dried figs.

Mix the cornstarch with the salt and ½ cupful of sugar and place in the upper part of a double boiler. Add the scalded milk, a little at a time, while stirring constantly. Cook in the double boiler 25 minutes, then add the beaten egg yolks and cook 5 minutes longer. Put the figs through a food grinder, add the boiling water and 2 tablespoonfuls of sugar to them and cook gently until the figs are soft and the water has boiled down. Then stir in the lemon juice and combine the two mixtures. Fold in the beaten white of 1 egg and place the pudding mixture in an oiled baking dish. Beat the other egg white until stiff and add the powdered sugar. Cover with this meringue. Brown in a slow oven.

Fruit Tapioca

4 tablespoonfuls pearl tapioca	¼ teaspoonful salt
2 cupfuls milk	1 egg
½ cupful sugar	2 cupfuls sliced bananas
1 tablespoonful lemon juice	

Pudding is best chilled. Fold in or top with bananas at serving time.

Wash the tapioca and let stand overnight in cold water. Drain in the morning and add the scalded milk. Cook in a double boiler until the tapioca is clear or transparent. Then add the sugar, salt and the beaten egg yolk. Cook until the mixture thickens. Remove from the stove and fold in the stiffly beaten egg white. Slice the bananas and sprinkle the lemon juice on them. Stir the fruit into the tapioca pudding and serve with cream.

Date Pudding

1 egg	1 cupful breadcrumbs
1 cupful sugar	1 teaspoonful baking powder
1 cupful dates	1 tablespoonful butter
1 cupful nuts	1 teaspoonful vanilla
	½ teaspoonful salt

Beat the egg well and add the sugar to it. Then mix the bread crumbs, baking powder, chopped dates and nuts and combine the two mixtures. Add the milk, vanilla and melted butter. Mix thoroughly and turn into a well oiled baking dish. Set in a pan of cold water and place in a moderate oven. Bake 45 minutes and serve with whipped cream or lemon pudding sauce.

Blueberry Pudding

Line a pudding dish with stale bread buttered lightly, sprinkle with a few grains of salt and fill the dish almost full of blueberries mixed with a little sugar. Cover the berries with slices of bread buttered on both sides and sprinkled with salt. Cover the baking dish, set in a pan of cold water and bake 1 hour in a moderate oven. Remove the cover just long enough to brown the top of the pudding. Serve hot with a pudding sauce or sugar and cream.

Steamed Pudding

¼ cupful shortening	2 cupfuls flour
½ cupful raisins	½ teaspoonful soda
½ cupful molasses	¼ teaspoonful cloves
½ cupful milk	½ teaspoonful mace
	¾ teaspoonful salt

Cream the shortening, beat in the chopped raisins and molasses and add the milk alternately with the dry ingredients which have been mixed together. Place in an oiled can and steam 3 hours. Serve warm with a pudding sauce.

Cream Pie

2 tablespoonfuls butter	2 cupfuls flour
2 tablespoonfuls lard	3 teaspoonfuls baking powder
1 egg yolk	¾ teaspoonful salt
1 cupful sugar	1 egg white
1 cupful milk	½ teaspoonful vanilla

Cream the shortening; beat the egg yolk until very light and whip ½ cupful of sugar into this. Cream the other ½ cupful

Correction: add ½ cup milk to the list of ingredients. Sometimes called November pudding, the dessert was enjoyed during the Thanksgiving season. Black walnuts or hickory nuts were added to it in families who gathered these nuts on the farm.

A Midwestern version of Boston cream pie.

of sugar with the shortening and beat until light. Combine the two mixtures. Add the milk alternately with the dry ingredients which have been sifted together and fold in the stiffly beaten egg white. Bake in two layers, put together with a cake filling and sprinkle powdered sugar on top.

Dutch Apple Cake

2 cupfuls flour	1 egg
6 tablespoonfuls butter	½ teaspoonful salt
1 cupful milk	4 tart apples
4 teaspoonfuls baking powder	2 tablespoonfuls sugar
½ teaspoonful cinnamon	

Sift the salt, baking powder and flour together and work in the shortening. Add the egg yolk to the mixture and fold in the stiffly beaten egg white. Spread the mixture ½ inch thick in a shallow baking tin. Wipe, pare, quarter and core the apples. Cut every quarter into two pieces lengthwise. Then place them in parallel rows on top of the mixture with the sharp edge down. Sprinkle the apples with the sugar and cinnamon which have been mixed together. Bake in a hot oven 30 minutes, or until the apples are soft. Serve with a pudding sauce or with whipped cream.

Indian Pudding

½ cupful milk, scalded	¼ cupful molasses
2 tablespoonfuls cornmeal	¼ teaspoonful salt
½ cupful cold water	½ teaspoonful cinnamon
¼ cupful sugar	¼ teaspoonful ginger
1 egg	¼ cupful milk

Stir the cornmeal into the cold water and add the scalded milk. Cook 20 minutes. Then add the other ingredients except the ¼ cupful of milk. Pour into a greased baking dish and bake in a moderate oven 35 minutes. Pour the cold milk on top and bake 2 hours longer without stirring.

Pineapple Cream

1 cupful canned pineapple	¼ pound marshmallows
1 cupful cream	1 tablespoonful lemon juice
¼ cupful powdered sugar	1 tablespoonful pineapple juice

Drain the grated pineapple. Whip the cream until stiff and fold in the powdered sugar, the cut marshmallows and the fruit

Bake in a slow oven (325°F.) 2 hours. Serve warm with topknots of vanilla ice cream, or pass a pitcher of cream to pour over the pudding.

juices. Then fold in the pineapple and serve in dishes lined with sponge or angel food cake.

Berry Dumplings

2 cupfuls flour	2 tablespoonfuls butter
½ teaspoonful salt	milk to moisten
4 teaspoonfuls baking powder	berries

Work the butter into the dry ingredients which have been sifted together. Add sufficient milk to moisten. Roll out ¼ inch thick and cut in circles with a diameter of 4 or 5 inches. Place 1 large strawberry or 3 small ones or several raspberries or blackberries in the center of every circle and cover with the dough, pressing the edges together firmly. Brush with milk, sprinkle with sugar and bake in a hot oven 20 minutes. Serve with a pudding sauce or Berry Butter.

King Apple Dumplings

1½ cupfuls flour	½ teaspoonful salt
1 cupful sugar	2 teaspoonfuls baking powder
¾ teaspoonful cinnamon	4 tablespoonfuls shortening
½ teaspoonful nutmeg	½ cupful cold water
	2¼ cupfuls apples

Mix the flour, salt and baking powder together thoroughly and work in the shortening, using either butter, lard or a mixture of these fats. Add the water and roll ½ inch thick. Sprinkle the dough with chopped or sliced apples, the sugar and spice. Roll like a jelly roll, cut off 2-inch pieces and place in a pudding dish cut side down. Pour a part of the apple syrup on them and bake 25 minutes in a hot oven.

Apple Syrup

1 cupful brown sugar	1 teaspoonful vanilla
3 tablespoonfuls butter	2 tablespoonfuls flour
1 cupful water	¼ teaspoonful salt

Mix the sugar and flour, add the water, salt and any pieces of apples that were not used in the dumplings. Cook until the mixture thickens. Add the butter. Use a part of this when baking the dumplings and the rest as a sauce when serving the dessert.

Rich and luscious. Chill several hours or overnight before serving. Bread crumbs may be substituted for cake crumbs.

Make with dried figs.

Prune Pudding

3 cupfuls cake crumbs	1½ cupfuls cooked prune pulp
1½ cupfuls whipped cream	½ teaspoonful lemon extract

Combine the prune pulp and cake crumbs and beat until they form a light paste. Then fold in the stiffly whipped cream and the lemon extract. Set in a cold place several hours before serving. Serve with or without whipped cream.

Fruit Fritters

1 cupful flour	2 eggs
½ teaspoonful salt	2 teaspoonfuls butter
⅔ cupful milk	fruit

Mix together the dry ingredients, beat in the milk gradually, and then stir in the egg yolks, beaten until they are a light lemon color. Add the melted butter and stiffly beaten egg whites. Then dip the fruit in this batter, drain it for a moment and drop it in deep fat. Fry until a golden brown on one side, then turn and brown on the other side. When cooked, drain and dust with powdered sugar. Serve with a hot pudding sauce. Among the fruits which may be used are bananas, apples, peaches, and oranges. In every case pare or peel the fruit, slice the cored apples in rings, divide the bananas into halves lengthwise and then into quarters, quarter the peaches and separate the orange into sections or cut in circles.

Steamed Fig Dessert

1½ cupfuls molasses	¾ teaspoonful nutmeg
1½ cupfuls suet, chopped	1½ teaspoonfuls soda
3 cupfuls chopped figs	1½ cupfuls sour milk
1½ teaspoonfuls cinnamon	3 eggs
	3¾ cupfuls flour

Mix together molasses, suet, figs and spices. Add soda which has been dissolved in the milk. Add well beaten eggs and gradually stir in the flour. Beat thoroughly and pour into an oiled mold. Steam 2 hours. Serve with a sweet pudding sauce.

Apple Pudding

3 cupfuls flour	3 tablespoonfuls butter
6 teaspoonfuls baking powder	1¼ cupfuls milk
¾ teaspoonful salt	6 apples cut in eighths

Mix the dry ingredients, work in the butter and add the milk. Toss on a floured board and roll out as for biscuits. Sprinkle with 1 tablespoonful of sugar. Place apples on the dough and sprinkle them with a dash of sugar and cinnamon. Roll dough around the apples and place in a greased dish or mold. Cover tightly and steam 1 hour and 20 minutes. Serve with a pudding sauce.

Shortcake

1 egg	3 tablespoonfuls butter
½ cupful sugar	2 teaspoonfuls baking powder
½ cupful milk	1 cupful flour

Cream the butter, stir in the sugar and beat until light. Then stir in the well beaten egg yolk and add the milk alternately with the flour to which the baking powder has been added. Fold in the egg white which is beaten stiff and bake in two layers. Spread crushed and sweetened berries between the layers and over the top of the cake. Serve with cream.

Chocolate Dessert

½ cupful sweet chocolate	½ cupful milk
2 egg yolks	2 egg whites
	4 cupfuls cooky crumbs

Melt the chocolate over hot water and when cooled slightly, stir in the beaten egg yolks, the milk and stiffly beaten egg whites. Break cookies in small pieces or use crumbs of cookies or cake. Pour the chocolate mixture over them and set in a cool place for a few hours. Serve with whipped cream.

Lucy's Pudding

½ cupful sugar	½ cupful flour
2 tablespoonfuls butter	1 teaspoonful baking powder
1 egg	2 squares chocolate or
½ cupful milk	2 tablespoonfuls cocoa

Cream the butter and sugar together and add the well beaten egg yolk. Stir in the cocoa or the chocolate which has been melted over hot water. Alternately add the milk with dry ingredients which have been sifted together and fold in the stiffly beaten egg white. Pour in an oiled pan and bake in a moderate oven about 30 minutes. Cut in squares and serve hot or cold with a pudding sauce.

Revise recipe by combining 2 cups sifted flour, 2 tblsp. sugar, 3 tsp. baking powder and 1 tsp. salt in mixing bowl. Work in ⅓ cup butter until mixture looks like cornmeal. Stir in 1 cup milk just enough to blend. Pat soft dough with fingers into a greased round 8-inch layer-cake pan. Bake in hot oven (425° F.) about 20 minutes, or until golden brown. Split while warm and fill and top with 1 quart ripe strawberries, crushed and sweetened with sugar. Serve warm with cream. For added richness spread cut side of shortcake with butter before adding berries.

Plum Pudding

½ cupful suet	½ cupful sour milk
½ cupful molasses	¾ teaspoonful soda
¼ teaspoonful salt	1 cupful flour
½ teaspoonful cinnamon	4 tablespoonfuls raisins
¼ teaspoonful cloves	4 tablespoonfuls cloves

Chop the suet fine, wash and dry raisins and currants and mix with the flour and suet, first cutting the raisins in small pieces. Mix the milk and molasses and to this mixture add all the other ingredients. Pour into an oiled mold and steam 3 hours. Serve hot with a pudding sauce.

When refrigerators came to farm kitchens, Icebox Plum Pudding sometimes replaced the traditional steamed plum pudding. Here is a recipe that was circulating from one home to another in rural neighborhoods during 1925.

Icebox Plum Pudding

1 envelope unflavored gelatin	½ cup each chopped raisins, dried figs and dates
¼ cup cold water	1½ cups orange juice
½ tsp. ground cinnamon	½ square unsweetened chocolate, melted
¼ tsp. ground nutmeg	
¼ tsp. ground cloves	½ cup chopped nuts
⅛ tsp. salt	2 tblsp. lemon juice
½ cup sugar	

Add gelatin to water. Mix together spices, salt, sugar and dried fruits. Add orange juice and heat, but do not let come to boil. Stir in gelatin and chocolate. Continue to stir over low heat to dissolve gelatin and mix thoroughly. Remove from heat; stir in nuts and lemon juice. Pour into a mold rinsed with cold water. Chill several hours or overnight. Serve topped with whipped cream. Sliced dates were a favored garnish.

CHAPTER 16

CUSTARDS

A CUSTARD is a mixture of sweetened and flavored milk and eggs which is either baked or cooked over water. In combining the ingredients care should be taken not to add too much sugar to the egg or little yellow threads will appear through the liquid when the milk is added. The eggs should not be beaten too light because overbeating causes a porous custard. To prevent lumps, pour the milk over the eggs and stir constantly.

Cooking a custard too long causes it to curdle. A curdled custard may be made smooth by beating with a Dover egg beater. As soon as the steamed custard coats the bowl of the spoon and when a knife inserted in a baked custard comes out clean, it should be removed from the heat to prevent overcooking. By stirring occasionally during the cooling, a steamed custard will not be coated.

Substitutions in Custard Making

Two egg yolks will thicken as much as one egg and they produce a smoother custard.

Two egg whites used instead of 1 egg give a white custard.

Three-fourths tablespoonful of cornstarch may be substituted for one egg.

One tablespoonful of flour may be used in place of 1 egg.

Very thick custards are made by decreasing the amount of milk, and thin ones by adding more milk.

Steamed Custard

2 cupfuls milk	6 tablespoonfuls sugar
3 eggs	¼ teaspoonful salt
	½ teaspoonful vanilla

Scald the milk and pour it over the egg which has been beaten with the sugar and salt. Place the mixture in a double boiler

103

Rotary beaters were once called Dover beaters.

Good Idea: Pour custards through a fine strainer into baking cups or dish.

Blend slightly beaten eggs, sugar and salt in top of double boiler. Gradually stir in 2½ cups milk instead of 2 cups. Add water to lower part of double boiler, but do not let it touch the bottom of the upper container that holds the custard mixture. Cook over medium heat, stirring con-

stantly. Do not let water boil. Cook until custard coats a metal spoon. Remove top of double boiler, stir in 1 tsp. vanilla and set in a pan of cold water to hasten cooling. If custard curdles, beat with rotary beater. Chill at least 2 to 3 hours before use.

or in a saucepan over hot water and stir constantly until the custard will coat a metal spoon. Set in a pan of cold water and when cool, add the vanilla.

Steamed Caramel Custard

3 cupfuls milk	¼ teaspoonful vanilla
3 eggs	2 tablespoonfuls sugar
¼ teaspoonful salt	6 tablespoonfuls caramelized sugar

Dissolve the caramelized sugar in the milk, scald and pour it over the egg which has been beaten with the salt and sugar. Cook over water until the mixture coats the back of a spoon. Remove from the stove at once and set in a pan of cold water to cool. When cold, add the vanilla.

Steamed Chocolate Custard

1½ squares chocolate	¼ teaspoonful salt
3 cupfuls milk	3 tablespoonfuls water
3 eggs	½ cupful sugar
½ teaspoonful vanilla	

Combine the grated chocolate with the water and add 3 table-spoonfuls of sugar. Cook until the mixture is smooth and glossy. Then add the heated milk. Mix thoroughly and then pour it over the eggs beaten with the rest of the sugar. Add the salt and cook over water until the back of a spoon is coated with the mixture. Take from the stove, set in a pan of cold water and when cool, add the vanilla.

Baked Custard

3 cupfuls milk	6 tablespoonfuls sugar
6 eggs	¼ teaspoonful salt
½ teaspoonful vanilla	

Beat the egg white with the sugar and salt. Add the cold milk and flavoring, pour into molds or a pudding dish, set in pans of cold water and bake until a silver knife comes out clean when inserted.

Baked Caramel Custard

3 cupfuls milk	2 tablespoonfuls sugar
6 eggs	¼ teaspoonful salt
6 tablespoonfuls caramelized sugar	¼ teaspoonful vanilla

Use 2 to 2½ cups milk. Cook like Steamed Custard.

Add chocolate to milk and heat in double boiler, stirring, until chocolate melts. Then follow directions for Steamed Custard.

To make 6 servings, use 4 eggs, ¼ cup sugar, ¼ tsp. salt and 2 to 2½ cups milk or milk and cream. Flavor with 1 tsp. vanilla. Strain custard mixture into 6 buttered custard cups, set in pan and pour in hot water to reach within ¾ inch from top of cups. Bake in slow oven (300° F.) 1¼ hours, or until knife inserted in center comes out clean.

Dissolve the caramelized sugar in the hot milk. Cool. Beat the egg with the granulated sugar and the salt, pour on the cooled milk and add the vanilla. Bake in molds or in a pudding dish set in pans of cold water.

Baked Chocolate Custard

1½ squares chocolate	3 tablespoonfuls water
3 cupfuls milk	¾ cupful sugar
6 eggs	⅛ teaspoonful salt
¼ teaspoonful vanilla	

Boil the grated chocolate with the water and 3 tablespoonfuls of sugar until the mixture is smooth and glossy. Add the chocolate to the milk. When mixed, cool and add to the egg beaten with the sugar and salt. Add the vanilla and pour into individual molds or one large one. Set in a pan of cold water and bake.

Raisin Custard

2 cupfuls milk	3 tablespoonfuls flour
½ cupful sugar	2 eggs
¾ teaspoonful salt	½ cupful raisins
½ teaspoonful vanilla	

Heat 1½ cupfuls milk; mix sugar, salt and flour with the ½ cupful of cold milk. Combine the two mixtures, stirring the flour and milk combination into the hot milk. Cook over water until the mixture thickens. Remove from the fire, add the beaten eggs, raisins and vanilla. Pour into an oiled baking dish and bake from 30 to 35 minutes in a slow oven. Serve with cream.

Many country families now fill the freezer tub ¼ full of crushed ice and then add alternate layers of salt and ice, 6 parts ice to 1 part rock salt.

Children were the champion crank turners and taste testers when the dasher was removed. They also helped crush the ice by placing it in a heavy feed bag and pounding it with a hammer.

Combine sugar, salt and slightly beaten egg yolks in double-boiler top; slowly add milk. Cook as for Steamed Custard, stirring constantly. Cool, strain and add the vanilla and cream. Ice cream is very rich.

CHAPTER 17

FROZEN DESSERTS

The first requirement in making good ice cream is the use of materials of a high quality. Smooth, rich cream or milk mixtures produce velvety ice creams, while thin, watery ones make a coarse-grained product. As the freezing is taking place the ice cream expands. Therefore the freezer should never be filled more than three-fourths full. If it is, a coarse ice cream will be the result.

One part of salt to 3 parts of crushed ice are used in freezing ice creams and equal parts of ice and salt are used in making fruit ices. Since some of the flavor is destroyed in freezing, the ice cream mixture is always flavored too highly and is made a little too sweet for taste when being poured into the freezer.

After the cream is frozen, the salt water is drained off, the dasher is removed and the ice cream is packed down with a spoon. The cover is then adjusted and a cork placed in the opening in it. One part of salt to 4 parts of ice is used in repacking the freezer.

Neapolitan Ice Cream

2 cupfuls milk	6 egg yolks
1 cupful cream	1 cupful sugar
⅛ teaspoonful salt	1 tablespoonful vanilla

Scald the milk, pour slowly on the egg yolks which have been beaten with the sugar and stir constantly so the eggs will not cook, but blend with the hot milk. Place in a double boiler and cook until the mixture coats the back of a silver spoon. Strain through a sieve into a bowl, chill, add the vanilla and cream and freeze.

Philadelphia Ice Cream

4 cupfuls cream	1 tablespoonful vanilla
1 cupful sugar	⅛ teaspoonful salt

Mix all the ingredients and freeze.

106

Chocolate Ice Cream

4 cupfuls cream	⅛ teaspoonful salt
1 cupful sugar	1 tablespoonful vanilla
4 tablespoonfuls cocoa	½ cupful boiling water

Dissolve the cocoa in the boiling water and boil until the mixture is smooth and glossy, stirring constantly. Add it to the cream, sugar and flavoring. Freeze.

Stir sugar and salt into melted cocoa. Cool, add vanilla and heavy cream.

Caramel Ice Cream

2 cupfuls milk	½ cupful sugar
2 eggs or 4 egg yolks	½ cupful caramelized sugar
	2 cupfuls thin cream

Scald the milk, dissolve the caramelized sugar in it, pour this over the egg which has been beaten with the granulated sugar. Cook over water until the mixture coats the back of a spoon. Strain, chill and freeze. To caramelize the sugar, stir it in a pan directly over the fire without adding water, and stir until it melts and becomes a light brown color.

Tastes great. Combine sugars and slightly beaten eggs in double-boiler top. Slowly stir in milk and cook like Steamed Custard. Strain, cool and add thin or heavy cream.

Peach Ice Cream

1 quart peach pulp	½ lemon
2 cupfuls sugar	1½ teaspoonfuls vanilla
1 cupful water	5 egg whites

Put pared ripe peaches through a sieve until 1 quart of pulp is secured. Make a syrup by boiling the sugar with the water a few minutes. When cool, add it and the juice of the lemon and the vanilla to the peaches. Mix and then add the slightly beaten egg whites. Freeze. The vanilla may be omitted if one wishes.

Pineapple Ice Cream

6 cupfuls thin cream	½ cupful sugar
	1 cupful grated pineapple

Add pineapple to the cream and let stand 30 minutes. Strain, add sugar and freeze.

The grated pineapple is now called crushed pineapple.

Strawberry Ice Cream

2 cupfuls milk	2 cupfuls sugar syrup
2 cupfuls cream	4 cupfuls berries

Crush the berries and combine with the syrup made by boiling 1 cupful of sugar with 1½ cupfuls of water. Cool the syrup before adding it to the berries. After the strawberries have stood in the syrup 30 minutes, rub them through a fine sieve, add the cream and freeze until the mixture is very cold, then stir in the milk and continue the freezing.

Honey Cream

¾ cupful strained honey	1½ cupfuls whipped cream
4 eggs	½ teaspoonful vanilla
	¼ teaspoonful salt

Separate the eggs and beat the yolks slightly, stirring in the honey gradually. Heat in the double boiler, stirring constantly, until the mixture thickens. Cool, add the stiffly beaten whites and the whipped cream, salt and vanilla. Pack in ice and salt and let stand 4 or 5 hours.

Raspberry Sherbet

4 cupfuls water	1 teaspoonful gelatin
2 cupfuls sugar	1 tablespoonful cold water
	2 cupfuls raspberry juice

Boil the sugar and water 10 minutes. Add the gelatin which has been softened in the cold water. When cool, add the raspberry juice and freeze.

Frozen Orange Jelly

2 cupfuls orange juice	2 tablespoonfuls lemon juice
4 cupfuls water	1 tablespoonful gelatin
2 cupfuls sugar	2 egg whites

Soak the gelatin in 1 cupful of the cold water and boil the rest of the water with the sugar 10 minutes. Remove from the fire, add the gelatin and strain. Cool and then stir in the fruit juices. Freeze until thick, but not hard, then stir in the stiffly beaten egg whites. Continue the freezing, remove the dasher and pack for an hour before serving.

Grape Freeze

2 cupfuls thick cream	½ cupful water
1 cupful sweet milk	1 cupful grape jelly
4 tablespoonfuls sugar	1 tablespoonful gelatin

Soak the gelatin in the milk and heat over water until it is dissolved. Then add the sugar and water which have been boiled

---

This is an old-fashioned orange sherbet, country style. Combine sugar and gelatin in double-boiler top; stir to mix. Slowly add water and heat, stirring until gelatin dissolves. Cool to lukewarm, stir in fruit juices and freeze until mixture thickens. Fold in beaten egg whites and continue freezing.

Combine sugar and gelatin in double-boiler top; stir to mix. Slowly add water and milk and cook, stirring, until gelatin dissolves. Remove from heat and cool until lukewarm. Fold grape jelly into heavy cream, whipped, and fold into gelatin mixture.

together to a fairly thick syrup. Cool. Whip the cream until stiff and fold the jelly into it. Beat it into the milk and gelatin mixture. Pour into a mold and pack in ice and salt for 3 or 4 hours.

Apricot Ice

1 quart canned apricots	2 cupfuls sugar
	1 quart water

Put the apricots through a sieve. Add the sugar and water and stir until the sugar is dissolved. Freeze.

Orange Ice

3 cupfuls orange juice	2 cupfuls water
4 tablespoonfuls lemon juice	2 cupfuls syrup

Make the syrup by boiling 1 cupful of sugar with 1½ cupfuls of water 5 minutes. Cool, mix with other ingredients and freeze.

Cherry Ice

4 cupfuls cherry juice	1 quart water
4 cupfuls sugar	2 egg whites
	2 lemons

Boil sugar and water together 5 minutes. Cool, add the fruit juices. When partly frozen, add the beaten egg whites.

Pineapple Ice

2 cupfuls shredded pineapple	1½ cupfuls cold water
	2 tablespoonfuls lemon juice

Mix water and pineapple, sweeten to taste, and let stand 30 minutes. Strain, add lemon juice and freeze.

Old-time ices consisted of fruit pulp or juice, sweetened to taste and frozen. Women taste tested as they prepared the mixture to freeze. Almost always they added a little more sugar or lemon juice and sometimes both flavor helpers.

Tart red cherries were the fruit in this dessert. Practically every farm had at least a couple of cherry trees, which were covered with mosquito netting when the fruit was ripe to protect it from eager birds.

Use canned crushed pineapple. This and other fruit ices frequently were served as a part of the main course of holiday dinners as an accompaniment to roast chicken or turkey. They answered for dessert in hot weather and often were served with sponge or angel cake.

The molded dessert recipes in this chapter call for unflavored gelatin. A new technique with it has developed since this book first appeared. Instead of soaking gelatin in cold water to soften it, the granules may be combined with sugar and dissolved in liquid over heat. One envelope holds 1 tblsp. gelatin.

Combine gelatin and sugar in double-boiler top. Add 1¾ cups water, stirring. Heat, continuing to stir, until gelatin is dissolved. Cool until lukewarm, add lemon juice. Pour into mold rinsed in cold water and chill.

CHAPTER 18

GELATIN DISHES

Gelatin is always soaked in cold water or other liquid before being added to foods. It swells and then must be dissolved in a hot liquid or by being heated over hot water. Stirring helps to hasten the dissolving.

Attractive results may be obtained by molding gelatin desserts in various shapes. The molds used for this purpose are first dipped in cold water, and without drying them the gelatin mixture is poured in and allowed to stand in a cold and level place until firm. In unmolding a knife blade is run around the edge of the mold, then the mold is dipped quickly in hot water. An inverted serving dish is placed on top and both are turned over. Then the mold is lifted off carefully.

Amounts to Use

Allow ½ cupful of liquid for every person to be served.

Use 2 tablespoonfuls of granulated gelatin to 4 cupfuls of water.

Less liquid is used in the gelatin dish during the warm weather when fruit is added to it, that is, 3 cupfuls of liquid to 2 tablespoonfuls of granulated gelatin. The use of more gelatin than this hastens the setting of the dish but produces a tough mixture which frequently has a disagreeable taste.

Lemon Jelly

1½ tablespoonfuls gelatin	1¼ cupfuls boiling water
½ cupful cold water	1 cupful lemon juice
2 cupfuls sugar	

Swell the gelatin in the cold water and dissolve the sugar in the lemon juice and hot water. Combine the two mixtures. Strain into wet molds and chill.

Orange Jelly

2 tablespoonfuls gelatin	¼ cupful sugar
½ cupful cold milk	¼ teaspoonful salt
2½ cupfuls scalded milk	1 cupful orange juice
¼ cupful lemon juice	

Swell gelatin in the cold water and dissolve sugar in the lemon juice. Combine the two mixtures. Strain into wet molds and chill.

Make like Lemon Jelly, dissolving sugar-gelatin mixture in 3 cups milk.

Vanilla Jelly

2 tablespoonfuls gelatin	¼ cupful sugar
½ cupful cold milk	¼ teaspoonful salt
2½ cupfuls scalded milk	¾ teaspoonful vanilla

Swell gelatin in cold milk and dissolve in the scalded milk. Add sugar, salt and vanilla. Strain into wet molds and chill.

Make like Lemon Jelly, dissolving gelatin combined with sugar and salt in 3 cups milk. Serve molded dessert with crushed berries or other fruit, topped with whipped cream.

Lemon Sponge

1½ tablespoonfuls granulated gelatin	1¼ cupfuls boiling water
¼ cupful cold water	½ cupful lemon juice
3 egg whites	¾ cupful sugar

Swell the gelatin in the cold water and dissolve the sugar in the lemon juice and hot water. Combine the two mixtures. Strain. Cool until it begins to thicken. Beat thoroughly, add the stiffly beaten egg whites and beat until the mixture will hold its shape. Pile in a dish or mold and serve with cream or a boiled custard.

Make like Lemon Jelly. When cooled and thickened to the consistency of unbeaten egg white, beat thoroughly with rotary beater. Fold in stiffly beaten egg whites. Beat until mixture will hold its shape. Pile in molds and chill. Serve with Steamed Custard.

Orange Sponge

1 tablespoonful gelatin	½ cupful orange juice
¼ cupful cold water	¼ cupful lemon juice
1 cupful boiling water	½ cupful sugar
3 egg whites	

Swell the gelatin in the cold water and dissolve the sugar in the fruit juices and the hot water. Combine the two mixtures and strain. Cool until it begins to thicken. Beat thoroughly, add stiffly beaten egg whites and beat until the mixture will hold its shape. Pile in dish or mold and serve cold with cream or with a boiled custard.

Make like Lemon Jelly, dissolving sugar-gelatin mixture in 1¼ cups water. When cooled and thickened to the consistency of unbeaten egg whites, beat and fold in stiffly beaten egg whites.

Dissolve gelatin-sugar mixture in water in double-boiler top. Heat, stirring constantly until gelatin dissolves. Cool slightly and add fruit or fruit juice. Cool until mixture begins to thicken. Beat thoroughly and fold in whipped cream. Continue beating until mixture will hold its shape.

Strawberry Bavarian

1½ cupfuls whipping cream	1 tablespoonful gelatin
¾ cupful sugar	¼ cupful cold water
1½ cupfuls crushed berries	¼ cupful boiling water

Swell the gelatin in the cold water and dissolve the sugar in the hot water. Combine the two mixtures and add the crushed berries. Cool until the mixture begins to thicken. Beat thoroughly and stir in the stiffly whipped cream, continuing the whipping until the bavarian will hold its shape. Pile in a dish or mold and serve cold. Decorate with a few whole berries.

Orange Bavarian

1½ cupfuls cream	1 tablespoonful gelatin
¾ cupful sugar	¼ cupful cold water
1½ cupfuls orange juice and pulp	¼ cupful boiling water

Swell the gelatin in the cold water and dissolve the sugar in the hot water. Combine the two mixtures and add the orange juice and pulp. Cool until the mixture begins to thicken. Beat thoroughly and add the stiffly whipped cream, beating until the bavarian will hold its shape. Pile in a dish or mold and serve cold. Garnish with orange sections.

Banana Bavarian

1½ cupfuls cream	4 tablespoonfuls orange juice
1½ cupfuls banana pulp	4 eggs
1 tablespoonful lemon juice	2 teaspoonfuls gelatin
¼ cupful cold water	

Soak the gelatin in the cold water. Put the banana pulp through a sieve and heat over water. Add the sugar and the softened gelatin, cool until lukewarm and add the fruit juices. When this has thickened a little, fold in the whipped cream, pour into slightly oiled molds and let stand until cold and firm. Serve garnished with sliced banana.

Pineapple Whip

1 cupful grated pineapple	½ cupful sugar
4 tablespoonfuls lemon juice	4 eggs
½ cupful orange juice	2 teaspoonfuls gelatin
2 tablespoonfuls cold water	

Combine the fruit juices with the sugar and egg yolks and heat in the double boiler until the egg is cooked. Remove from the fire and stir in the gelatin which has been soaking in the cold water. When cool enough to begin to thicken, beat in the stiffly beaten egg whites. Pour into a cold serving dish and set in a cold place until ready to be served with whipped cream.

Peach Bavarian

2 tablespoonfuls gelatin	6 ripe peaches
1 cupful water	½ cupful powdered sugar
	2 cupfuls cream

Soak the gelatin in the cold water and dissolve it over boiling water. Add to it the pulp of the peaches which have been pushed through a sieve. When the mixture begins to thicken, fold in the stiffly whipped cream. Serve cold.

Grape Bavarian

2 cupfuls grape juice	½ cupful cold water
2 tablespoonfuls gelatin	1 cupful sugar
	1½ cupfuls cream

Soak the gelatin in the cold water and dissolve it over hot water. Stir in the sugar and grape juice and when the mixture begins to thicken, fold in the whipped cream.

Note: Since the first edition of *The Farm Cook and Rule Book* was published, desserts made with flavored gelatin have climbed to great popularity in farm homes. Their bright colors, interesting flavors and ease of preparation have contributed to their success.

Note to Soft Cooked Eggs:

Take eggs from refrigerator, place in a bowl and cover with warm, not hot, water. It keeps shells from cracking when heated. In a saucepan, heat enough water to cover eggs, and bring to a full rolling boil. Remove eggs warmed in water. Carefully drop them into hot water. Remove from heat. Let stand, covered, 6 to 8 minutes, the time depending on the stage of doneness desired. Cool at once for a few seconds to prevent further cooking before serving.

Follow directions for soft-cooked eggs, but when eggs are dropped in boiling water, reduce heat, cover and simmer, not boil, 20 minutes.

Good Idea: Break each egg into a greased 5- or 6-inch baking dish or a custard cup. Add 1 tblsp. milk or light cream, sprinkle with salt and pepper and top with 1 tblsp. shredded cheese. Bake in a slow oven (325°F.) 15 to 18 minutes, or until egg whites are set.

CHAPTER 19

EGGS AND CHEESE

THE whites of eggs and cheese are composed largely of protein, a substance which becomes hard and tough when intense heat is applied to it. For this reason these foods are cooked at as low a temperature as is possible and for as short a time as will make them palatable.

Soft Cooked Eggs

Pour boiling water over eggs, using ¾ cupful of water to every egg. Draw to a cool part of the range and let stand from 8 to 10 minutes.

Hard Cooked Eggs

Prepare as soft cooked eggs only let stand from 30 to 40 minutes.

Baked Eggs

Cut 6 large, thin slices of bacon in one-inch squares and place them in a dripping pan. Set the pan in a hot oven. In 5 minutes turn the bacon squares and cook on the other side. Then remove the pan from the oven and break 6 eggs, taking care not to break the yolks, on top of the bacon, sprinkle lightly with salt and pepper and cook until the eggs are set. Serve immediately.

Eggs with Cheese

Take 1 cupful of stale cheese, cut in thin slices and arrange ¾ cupful of it in the bottom of a greased baking dish. Break 6 eggs, taking care not to break the yolks, on top of the cheese, sprinkle with salt and pepper and dot with 3 tablespoonfuls of butter and the rest of the cheese. Bake in a moderate oven 15 minutes and serve hot from the baking dish.

114

Coddled Eggs

6 eggs	3 tablespoonfuls butter
2¼ cupfuls milk	½ teaspoonful salt
	⅛ teaspoonful pepper

Scald the milk in a saucepan and add the slightly beaten eggs. Cook over hot water, stirring constantly until of a soft, creamy consistency. Add the seasonings and serve with buttered toast.

A version of scrambled eggs.

Plain Omelet

5 eggs	⅛ teaspoonful pepper
4 tablespoonfuls water	1½ teaspoonfuls salt
	1 tablespoonful butter

Beat the egg yolks until light and lemon colored. Add the salt, pepper and water. Heat a large frying pan and melt the butter in it. Fold the stiffly beaten egg whites into the yolk mixture and pour it into the frying pan. Cook gently, lifting the omelet around the edges with a knife. When it is set, brown on the bottom and then place in an oven so it will dry on top. Fold over and turn on a hot platter.

This is a puffy omelet. Beat egg whites until stiff peaks form. Combine egg yolks, beaten with water, salt and pepper. Fold in egg whites. Heat skillet just hot enough to sizzle a drop of water. Add 1 tblsp. butter and pour in egg mixture. Reduce heat and slowly cook until bottom is slightly browned. Place in a slow oven (325° F.) and bake until knife inserted in center of omelet comes out clean, 12 to 15 minutes. Fold and serve.

Fancy Omelets

Before folding the omelet various foods may be spread on top. Among them are these: 4 tablespoonfuls chopped ham or other cooked meat, slightly thickened canned tomatoes, creamed chicken or dried beef, creamed peas, creamed asparagus or creamed onions. Cheese sauce may be used in the fold or the plain omelet may be served on a bed of creamed vegetables.

Potato Omelet

1½ cupfuls boiled potatoes	4 eggs
½ teaspoonful onion juice	4 tablespoonfuls water
2 tablespoonfuls butter	¼ teaspoonful salt
½ teaspoonful salt	¼ teaspoonful pepper

Cut the cold boiled potatoes in small cubes, add the onion juice and turn into a frying pan in which the butter has been melted. Cook the potatoes, stirring constantly, until they are hot and slightly browned. Beat the eggs until light, add water, salt and pepper and pour over the potatoes. Let stand a few minutes; then move the pan to distribute the uncooked egg. When all the egg is cooked, roll and turn on a hot dish.

A variation of scrambled eggs enjoyed for supper, especially when accompanied by sliced, juicy tomatoes from the garden. A bowl of creamy cottage cheese, hot whole wheat muffins and homemade jelly or jam rounded out a typical main course.

Bake in slow oven, 325°F.

Bread and Jelly Omelet

4 eggs	1 tablespoonful butter
½ cupful milk	½ cupful bread crumbs
1 teaspoonful salt	⅛ teaspoonful pepper
	jelly

Soak the bread crumbs in the milk until the milk is absorbed. Add the beaten egg yolks, salt and pepper and fold in the stiffly beaten egg whites. Cook as a plain omelet. Spread with jelly before folding and sprinkle with sugar.

Rice Omelet

1 cupful boiled rice	3 eggs
1 cupful milk	1 teaspoonful salt
1 tablespoonful butter	⅛ teaspoonful pepper

Beat the eggs until light and add to them the warm rice, heated milk, melted butter and the seasonings. Pour in an oiled baking dish and bake in a hot oven, folding over once.

Shirred Eggs

Break eggs into oiled individual molds or ramekins, sprinkle lightly with salt and pepper and generously with coarse bread crumbs. Place a few dots of butter or a thin slice of bacon on top of every egg. Set the ramekins in a pan of warm water, place in the oven and bake until the eggs are set and the crumbs are delicately browned.

Tomato Eggs

Follow the directions for making shirred eggs, only place 3 teaspoonfuls of tomato sauce in every ramekin before breaking the egg into it.

Scalloped Eggs

6 hard cooked eggs	1 teaspoonful salt
2 cupfuls milk	¼ teaspoonful pepper
2 tablespoonfuls flour	½ cupful bread crumbs
2 tablespoonfuls butter	1 tablespoonful melted butter

Make a sauce by thickening the heated milk with the flour, which is mixed thoroughly with the 2 tablespoonfuls of butter. Add the salt and pepper. Cut the hard cooked eggs in thin slices and arrange a layer of them in the bottom of an oiled baking dish. Pour a little of the sauce on top and continue this process until all the egg and sauce are used. Cover the top with bread crumbs which have been mixed with 1 tablespoonful of melted butter. Brown in a hot oven.

Eggs with Peas

5 eggs
⅓ cupful milk
½ teaspoonful salt

¼ teaspoonful black pepper
1 cupful cooked peas
2 tablespoonfuls butter

Beat the eggs with a spoon until a full spoonful can be lifted. Add the milk, salt and pepper. Melt the butter in a frying pan and turn in the egg mixture. Stir constantly and cook until the egg begins to thicken. Then add the peas and continue to cook and scrape until creamy throughout. Turn on a hot plate and serve at once.

Rarebit

2 cupfuls grated cheese
½ cupful milk
1 teaspoonful mustard

1 teaspoonful salt
2 eggs
4 tablespoonfuls butter
speck of cayenne

Put the cheese and milk in a double boiler or in a saucepan over hot water. Mix the mustard, salt and cayenne, add the eggs and beat thoroughly. When the cheese is melted, stir in the egg mixture and the butter. Cook until thick, stirring frequently. Pour over toasted bread or crackers and serve at once.

Country-Style Rarebit. Use 4 cups cut-up Cheddar or process American cheese. Melt over hot, not boiling, water. Gradually stir in ¾ cup cream; add ½ tsp. each dry mustard and Worcestershire sauce. Season with salt. Serve at once on crackers.

Macaroni and Cheese

2 cupfuls cooked macaroni
2 cupfuls milk
2 tablespoonfuls flour
2 tablespoonfuls butter

1 teaspoonful salt
¼ teaspoonful pepper
1 cupful grated cheese
½ cupful buttered bread crumbs

Thicken the hot milk with the flour which is mixed thoroughly with the butter and add the salt and pepper. Arrange the macaroni, thickened milk and grated cheese in layers in a buttered baking dish and sprinkle crumbs over the top. Bake in a moderate oven until browned.

Cover and bake 30 minutes in a moderate oven (350°F.). Uncover and bake 20 minutes longer.

Cheese Fondu

1 cupful scalded milk
1 cupful bread crumbs
¼ pound mild cheese

1 tablespoonful butter
½ teaspoonful salt
3 egg yolks
3 egg whites

Revised recipe. Cut 10 slices of bread in cubes. Beat 6 eggs, add 3 cups milk, 1 tsp. salt and ½ tsp. dry mustard. Stir in bread cubes, 2 cups shredded sharp process American cheese and 2 tblsp. finely chopped onion. Turn into an ungreased baking dish, 10 by 7½ by 1½ inches. Bake uncovered in a slow oven (325°F.) until center is set, about 1 hour. Remove crusts from bread slices if you wish.

Mix the milk, bread crumbs, the cheese cut in small pieces, melted butter and salt together. Beat the egg yolks until light and lemon colored and add them to the mixture. Fold in the stiffly beaten egg whites. Pour into a buttered baking dish and bake 20 minutes in a moderate oven.

Cheese Balls

3 cupfuls grated cheese
2 tablespoonfuls flour
¾ teaspoonful salt

4 egg whites
⅛ teaspoonful pepper
cracker crumbs

Mix cheese, flour and seasonings. Add the stiffly beaten whites, shape in balls and roll in the cracker crumbs. Fry until brown in deep fat.

Cheese Soufflé

1 cupful milk
3 tablespoonfuls flour
3 tablespoonfuls butter

1 teaspoonful salt
¼ teaspoonful pepper
3 eggs

1 cupful grated cheese

Thicken the hot milk with the flour which is mixed thoroughly with the butter. Add the seasonings and the grated cheese. When the cheese is melted, add the egg yolks and fold in the stiffly beaten egg whites. Turn in a greased baking dish, set in a pan of cold water and bake in a moderate oven until browned.

Cottage Cheese

3 quarts sour milk
2 tablespoonfuls butter

salt
pepper

Pour the milk in a crock and let stand in a warm place (about 98 degrees Fahrenheit). When the curd is separated from the whey, strain through a cloth and shake until dry. Stir in butter, salt and pepper and cool before serving.

Homemade cottage cheese does not taste like commercial cottage cheese. It is so rare now that most people have to acquire a liking for it. Adding lactic acid starter is necessary when using pasteurized milk.

CHAPTER 20

FILLINGS AND ICINGS

FILLINGS and icings not only make the cake more attractive but they also increase its palatability. Fancy cakes may be made by decorating the icing with candied cherries, designs cut from candied orange peel, the use of small candied cherries and by forcing icings colored with vegetable colorings through pastry tubes.

Icing the Cake

Unless the cake is symmetrical, trim it to obtain the desired shape. Then place a filling or icing between the layers and last of all ice the top and sides. Let the cake stand in a warm room until the icing is dry. In dipping small cup cakes or cookies in icing, they may be placed on a knitting needle while being coated.

Boiled Icing

1 cupful sugar	1 egg white
½ cupful water	½ teaspoonful vanilla

Put the sugar and water in a saucepan and stir until the sugar is dissolved. Then bring to the boiling point, washing off the sugary sides of the saucepan with a piece of soft cloth moistened in cold water and tied over the tines of a silver fork. Beat the egg white until stiff and dry and add slowly a tablespoonful of the boiling syrup, beating constantly. Then add 4 more tablespoonfuls of the hot syrup and beat constantly. Allow the rest of the syrup to cook until it forms a long thread when dropped from a spoon. In making this test remove the pan of syrup from the stove, insert the spoon in the syrup, taking care not to stir it, and lift up the spoon so the syrup can drop off. If it spins a thread 10 inches long, it has cooked sufficiently, but if not, it is returned to the fire and tested frequently. The

Frostings were known as icings to many cake bakers.

When corn syrup became a staple in country cupboards, the chances of success with cake frostings increased greatly. This recipe uses it. Combine 2 cups sugar, 1 tblsp. light corn syrup, 3/4 cup water and a dash of salt in saucepan. Cook over low heat, stirring until sugar dissolves. Cover for 2 or 3 minutes to dissolve any sugar crystals that form. Remove cover and bring to a rapid boil over medium heat without stirring. Cook to the soft-ball stage, 236° on candy thermometer. While syrup is cooking, beat 2 egg whites until stiff peaks form. Pour hot syrup very slowly on egg whites, beating constantly. Add 1 tsp. vanilla and continue beating until frosting is of spreading consistency. Add ½ cup finely chopped nuts if desired.

This is a White Fudge Frosting.
Cook it like Chocolate Fudge Frosting,
using the same ingredients, omitting
chocolate.

This is the real McCoy, with corn
syrup added to insure a velvety
frosting. Combine 2 squares unsweetened chocolate, 3 cups sugar, 3 tblsp.
light corn syrup, a dash of salt and
1 cup milk in a large saucepan. Cook
on low heat, stirring until chocolate
melts. Cook without stirring to the
soft ball stage, 234° on candy thermometer. Remove from heat; add ¼ cup
butter without stirring or beating.
Let stand until lukewarm, add 1 tsp.
vanilla and beat until of spreading
consistency.

right consistency is reached usually when the thermometer registers 240 degrees Fahrenheit. When the syrup is ready, it is added in a fine stream to the egg white which is beaten constantly. The flavoring is added. The icing is beaten until almost stiff enough to hold its shape.

When Icing Is Too Soft

If the cooled boiled frosting is too thin to spread on the cake, the dish containing it may be set over hot water. Fold the icing over and over with the spoon until it becomes stiff enough to hold its shape or begins to get sugary on the sides of the dish. Then remove from the fire and fold over and over until cool. Spread on the cake quickly with the back of a spoon.

Fudge Frosting

2 tablespoonfuls butter	½ cupful milk
1½ cupfuls sugar	½ teaspoonful vanilla

Melt the butter in a saucepan; when melted, add sugar and milk. Stir to prevent the sugar sticking to the bottom, heat to the boiling point and boil without stirring until a firm soft ball is formed when a little of the syrup is dropped in cold water or until the mixture reaches 238 degrees Fahrenheit. Remove from the fire, cool, add flavoring and beat until of the right consistency to spread.

Chocolate Fudge Frosting

To Fudge Frosting add from 2 to 3 squares of chocolate as soon as the boiling point is reached.

Cream Fudge Frosting

Use ¾ cupful of cream instead of the milk in making Fudge or Chocolate Fudge Frosting.

Brown Sugar Fudge Frosting

Use brown sugar instead of the white in making Fudge Frosting.

Maple Fudge Frosting

Use 4 tablespoonfuls of butter, 1 cupful of sugar, ½ cupful of maple sugar and ½ cupful of milk. Make like Fudge Frosting. If any Fudge Frosting becomes too hard before being spread on a cake, it may be stirred over hot water until soft and then spread on the cake with a spoon.

Cream Frosting

2 tablespoonfuls butter	½ cupful milk
1½ cupfuls sugar	½ teaspoonful vanilla

Melt butter in a pan and add sugar and milk. Stir to make certain that the sugar does not adhere to the pan, heat to the boiling point, and boil without stirring until a soft ball forms when a small amount of the syrup is dropped in cold water. Remove from the fire, cool, add the vanilla and beat until the frosting becomes the right consistency to spread. If this frosting becomes too hard before being spread on the cake, it may be stirred over hot water until soft enough to be spread on the cake with the back of a spoon.

Use ½ cup cream instead of milk.

Chocolate Cream Frosting

Add from 2 to 3 squares of chocolate to the Cream Frosting as soon as it reaches the boiling point.

Maple Cream Frosting

Add 4 tablespoonfuls of butter and use ½ cupful of maple sugar and 1 cupful of granulated sugar and make like Cream Frosting.

Creamy Cream Frosting

Use ¾ cupful of thin cream instead of milk in making Cream Frosting.

Use heavy cream instead of thin cream and add no butter.

Chocolate Filling

2 squares chocolate	3 tablespoonfuls milk
1 cupful powdered sugar	1 egg yolk
½ teaspoonful vanilla	

Melt the chocolate over warm water. Add the sugar and milk and stir in the beaten egg yolk. Cook over water until thick and creamy, stirring constantly. Cool slightly and add vanilla just before spreading.

Brown Sugar Filling

2 cupfuls brown sugar	2 tablespoonfuls butter
½ cupful milk	½ cupful nuts

Boil sugar, milk and butter until the mixture forms a soft ball when dropped in cold water. Take from the fire and beat until creamy. Add chopped nuts and mix thoroughly.

Lemon Filling

3 egg yolks	2 tablespoonfuls butter
1 egg white	juice of 2 lemons
1 cupful sugar	½ teaspoonful vanilla

Beat the egg yolks and the one egg white with the sugar until light, add the butter and lemon juice and cook over warm water until thick. Add vanilla and cool.

Caramel Frosting

¼ cupful milk	1 teaspoonful vanilla
1½ cupfuls sugar	½ cupful sugar caramelized
	1 teaspoonful butter

Cook milk and granulated sugar together. When boiling add the hot caramelized sugar, which has been prepared by melting ½ cupful of granulated sugar in a frying pan without adding any water. The sugar must be stirred constantly while being melted to a golden brown color. Cook mixture of milk and sugars to the soft ball stage. Then remove from the stove, add butter and flavoring, and beat the icing until creamy and thick enough to spread.

Lightning Icing

2 squares chocolate	3 tablespoonfuls hot water
1 teaspoonful butter	powdered sugar
	few drops vanilla

Melt the chocolate in a small pan placed over hot water. Add the butter and hot water and stir in the sugar gradually until the mixture is of the right consistency to spread. Then add a few drops of vanilla or some other flavoring.

Use ½ cup cream instead of milk.

See recipe for Fluffy Caramel Frosting at the end of this chapter.

Many women living west of the Mississippi River refer to confectioners' sugar as powdered sugar.

Honey Icing

1½ cupfuls sugar
½ cupful honey

½ cupful hot water
2 egg whites

Boil sugar and water together until it will thread when dropped from a spoon. Add the honey slowly and remove the icing from the stove. Have the egg whites beaten stiff and pour the hot syrup over them slowly, beating until the icing holds its shape.

Marshmallow Icing

1 cupful sugar
¼ pound marshmallows
½ teaspoonful vanilla

⅓ cupful milk
3 tablespoonfuls hot water

Stir sugar in milk, boil slowly 10 minutes. Cut the marshmallows in small pieces with the kitchen scissors. Pour the water over them and cook the mixture slowly until smooth. Then add the sugar syrup in a thin stream, stirring all the time. Beat until smooth and of the consistency to spread. Add the vanilla.

Sour Cream Icing

⅔ cupful sour cream
½ teaspoonful flavoring

2 cupfuls sugar

Boil the cream and sugar together until the mixture threads when dropped from a spoon. Cool until tepid and beat until the mixture is creamy and thick enough to spread.

Fruit Filling

½ pound figs
1 teaspoonful lemon juice

½ cupful sugar

Chop the figs fine and mix with the other ingredients. Cook in a double boiler until thick enough to spread.

Date Filling

½ pound dates
1 cupful sugar

¼ cupful water
2 teaspoonfuls lemon juice

Stone the dates and cut in small pieces. Mix ingredients and cook to a paste.

Revised recipe: Put 2 squares unsweetened chocolate, ¼ cup water, ¼ cup butter and 1 cup cut-up marshmallows in small saucepan. Heat on low heat, stirring to blend. Remove from heat and cool briefly. Beat in 2 cups sifted confectioners' sugar and 1 tsp. vanilla. Continue beating until thick. Stir in another 1 cup cut-up marshmallows and ½ cup chopped nuts. This frosting was called Rocky Mountain frosting in many communities. It was invented before miniature marshmallows were born, but they may be used.

Luscious Orange Frosting. Cream until light 1/3 cup butter with 1 to 2 tsp. grated orange peel. Gradually add 2 cups sifted confectioners' sugar, creaming thoroughly. Blend in 1 egg yolk and 1 tsp. vanilla. Gradually add 2 more cups sifted confectioners' sugar. Add enough orange juice (about 2 tblsp.) to make of spreading consistency. Cakes covered with this frosting in many country kitchens are sprinkled with flaked cocoanut.

Oak Hills Farm Special. Combine 3/4 cup sugar, 2 tblsp. cornstarch and a few grains of salt in a saucepan. Blend in 1 tsp. grated orange peel, 3/4 cup orange juice and 1 tblsp. lemon juice. Cook over medium heat, stirring constantly until boils and thickens. Stir a little of the hot mixture into 2 beaten egg yolks and stir into hot mixture in saucepan. Cook 2 minutes longer, remove from heat and add 3 tblsp. butter. Cool. Great to fill a white layer cake.

Orange Icing

Moisten powdered sugar with orange juice until the mixture is of the right consistency to spread.

Orange Filling

Mix 1/2 cupful sugar, 2 1/2 tablespoonfuls of flour and the grated rind of 1 small orange together and combine with 1/4 cupful of orange juice, 2 teaspoonfuls of lemon juice, 1 egg slightly beaten and 1 teaspoonful of melted butter. Cook 10 minutes in a double boiler, stirring constantly. Cool before using.

Fluffy Caramel Frosting. To double-boiler top add 2 unbeaten egg whites, 1 1/4 cups sugar, 1/4 cup water and 3 or 4 tblsp. Caramel Syrup (see Caramel Cake in cake chapter). Cook over boiling water, keeping the water from touching bottom of double-boiler top, beating constantly with a rotary beater until mixture forms stiff peaks (about 7 minutes). Pour into mixing bowl and beat until of spreading consistency, about 2 minutes. No thermometer is needed. Perfect on Caramel Cake.

CHAPTER 21

FRUITS

THE purpose of cooking fruits is to soften them and to provide a change in flavor. Before cooking dried fruits they are soaked several hours in water. The liquid in which they are soaked is used in the cooking, which should be slow and gentle. Spices may be added to cooked fruit for variety if one wishes.

Baked Apples

Wash, wipe, pare and core tart apples. Put in a dripping pan or baking dish, fill the cavities of the apples with sugar and cover the bottom of the pan with water. Bake in a moderate oven until the fruit is soft, basting every 10 minutes with the syrup in the pan. Serve hot or cold with or without sugar and cream.

Baked Apple Variations

Add 1 drop of lemon juice to the cavity in every apple.

Fill the cavity with chopped nuts, raisins and brown sugar instead of granulated sugar.

Fill the center with small red cinnamon candy instead of sugar and serve with cream.

Use chopped marshmallows in the cavities, adding it just before the apples are tender and after the sugar has melted. Before removing the fruit from the oven, place a marshmallow on top of every apple and have the oven slow enough to brown it without burning.

Raisins and sugar may be used in the centers.

A fruit syrup may be used. To make it, boil 1 cupful of sugar, 2 cupfuls of water, the juice and rind of ½ lemon and 1 tablespoonful of butter together. Add 4 tablespoonfuls of chopped raisins to the syrup after it has boiled 5 minutes and let simmer

125

Pare a strip 1 inch wide around the middle of each apple to prevent skin cracking during baking. Bake in moderate oven (375°) 30 to 35 minutes, or until fruit is tender when pierced with a fork.

until the syrup is thick. Pour this over the apples and bake.
When cold, serve with whipped cream.

Boiled Apples

6 apples	1 cupful water
½ cupful sugar	1 lemon

Put the sugar, water and the juice and rind of the lemon in
a saucepan. Boil until the syrup thickens. Then add the pared
and quartered apples and simmer until they are clear and transparent. Lift them from the syrup carefully and place in a large
dish. Top with whipped cream.

Apple Sauce

8 large apples	¾ cupful sugar
	¾ cupful water

Wash, pare and core the apples. Place them in a crock with
water and sugar. Cover and bake until a pretty red in a slow
oven.

Mammy's Baked Apples

6 large apples	6 thin slices lemon
1 cupful sugar	½ cupful water
1 tablespoonful cinnamon	3 tablespoonfuls butter

Pare, core and quarter the ripe apples. Place in a buttered
baking dish, sprinkle with sugar and cinnamon, add the lemon
slices and butter and pour on the water. Cook on the stove
long enough to form a heavy syrup. This usually requires 15
minutes. Place the cover on the dish and bake in a hot oven
about 30 minutes. Serve with lemon or vanilla pudding sauce.

Apples En Casserole

4 cupfuls sliced apples	½ cupful water
2 cupfuls bread crumbs	1¼ cupfuls brown sugar
¼ cupful butter	1½ teaspoonfuls cinnamon

Melt the butter and stir the bread crumbs into it. Arrange a
layer of this in the bottom of a greased baking dish or casserole.
Add a thick layer of apples, sprinkle with sugar and cinnamon,
cover with a thin layer of the crumb mixture and continue this
process until the material is used up, having the top layer of
crumbs. Add the water and bake 35 minutes.

Stewed Prunes

½ pound prunes
4 cupfuls cold water
1 cupful granulated sugar
2 whole cloves

Wash the prunes and let soak overnight in the 4 cupfuls of water. In the morning cook gently in the same water in which they were soaked, adding the sugar and cloves just before the prunes are tender. Chill before serving.

Orange Flavored Prunes

½ pound prunes
1 orange
4 tablespoonfuls sugar
2 cupfuls water

After washing and soaking the prunes, simmer until they begin to get tender. Add the yellow peel of the orange cut in long, narrow strips. Add the sugar and cook 10 minutes. Remove the fruit from the stove and add the orange juice. Serve very cold.

Baked Rhubarb

2 cupfuls rhubarb
1½ cupfuls sugar

Wash the rhubarb, cut in ½ inch pieces without removing the outer skin. Put into baking dish and sprinkle with sugar. Cover closely and bake in a slow oven until tender.

Stewed Cranberries

4 cupfuls cranberries
1 cupful water
2 cupfuls sugar

Pick over and wash cranberries. Put into a saucepan and add hot water. Cover and boil 10 minutes. Add the sugar and boil up again. Skim and cool.

Fruit Salpicon

Use equal amounts of orange, pineapple, grapefruit and white cherries and ¾ as much banana as any other fruit. Dice, chill, sprinkle with sugar and serve in tall sherbet glasses.

Fried Apples

Wash apples, cut in slices and fry in a skillet containing a little butter. Add salt and sugar to taste.

Too sweet. Add less or no sugar. No need to soak overnight. Just cover with water and simmer until tender. Cook together prunes and dried apricots. Their flavors complement each other.

Too much water. Place 1½ pounds cut-up rhubarb, 1 cup sugar, a dash of salt and 1½ tblsp. water in a 1½-quart baking dish. Bake, covered, 30 to 40 minutes in a moderate oven (375°F.), or until tender. One pint sliced fresh strawberries may be stirred in during last 5 minutes of baking. When adding berries, reduce sugar to ¾ cup.

Use canned fruits, except bananas.

Research in meat cookery has altered many old practices. Searing the roast in high heat to retain the juices fails. It shrinks the meat.

Place roast on rack in a shallow pan. Add no water or other liquid. Cook, uncovered, in a slow oven (325°) to the desired doneness. Use a meat thermometer, an unknown instrument in 1923 kitchens, to determine when meat is rare, medium or well done.

CHAPTER 22

MEATS, POULTRY AND FISH

MEAT is either seared on the outer surfaces or plunged into boiling water when cooked. Then the heat is reduced during the rest of the cookery. In the first part of the process the outer surface is coagulated so the inner juices cannot be lost in the cooking. Since dry heat hardens the connective tissue, tough pieces should be boiled, stewed or cooked some other way in moist heat. Salt is added after the meat has been seared or plunged in hot water. If added before this, it extracts some of the juices which give meat its flavor.

Roast Beef

Choose a compact piece of meat and wipe with a small cloth moistened in water. Place on the rack in a roasting pan and put in a hot oven without covering. When well seared, or in about 15 minutes, remove from the oven long enough to sprinkle with salt and pepper. Put a cover on the roaster and set the meat back in the oven. Finish the cooking at a lowered temperature, allowing 15 minutes for rare meat, 20 minutes for medium and 25 minutes for well done, to each pound. If a roasting pan is not available, one may be made by using a dripping pan and covering it with a smaller pan. A rack may be made of a toaster, cake rack or kettle lid.

Roast Pork

Roast as roast beef, cooking until well done throughout.

Roast Veal

Roast as roast beef, seasoning more highly.

Rump Roast

Sprinkle a 4-pound rump roast with 1 teaspoonful of salt, ¼ teaspoonful of pepper and 3 tablespoonfuls of flour. Put into a roasting pan or earthenware vessel and pour 1 cupful of catchup over it. Cover and bake 3 hours in a moderate oven. When one side becomes browned, turn and brown on the other one. Make gravy from the drippings after the meat is placed on a platter to be served.

This is a pot roast. The meat is covered during cooking and a liquid is added. Catchup substitutes for water.

Baked Hamburg

1½ pounds beef	1½ tablespoonfuls chopped onion
1 egg	1¼ teaspoonfuls salt
	¼ teaspoonful pepper

Grind meat in food cutter, beat egg slightly and mix the ingredients thoroughly. Shape into a compact loaf and bake in an oven as a roast.

Most farm women 50 years ago ground beef as they needed it. Food grinders were busy in country kitchens. Add an egg to bind the ingredients together and additional seasonings.

Swiss Steak

Rub salt and pepper into a piece of round steak cut 1½ inches thick. Then pound flour into the steak with the edge of a saucer, using as much flour as the meat will take up. Place in a frying pan with a small amount of hot fat. Brown on both sides and add water to cover. Cover tightly and simmer until tender. The cooking may be done in the oven after the browning if one wishes.

Roast Loin Pork

Select parts from two loins containing the ribs and trim off the backbone. Shape each piece into a semicircle, having the ribs outside, and sew pieces together to form a crown. Trim ends of the bones evenly, taking care that they are not too long. Sprinkle with salt, dredge with flour and place in a roasting pan on a rack, if one is available, with the bones down. Bake in a hot oven 2 hours, basting every 20 minutes with the fat in the pan which comes from the trimmings of pork fat placed under the meat. When cooked, remove to a platter and surround with baked apples.

The crown roast, a fancy bone-in pork roast, was a company special when pork was plentiful in farm homes.

Braised Heart

Wash a calf's heart weighing 2 pounds and remove the veins, arteries and clotted blood. Stuff with a dressing made by mixing together ¾ cupful of bread crumbs, ¼ cupful of hot water, 1 teaspoonful of ground sage, 1 tablespoonful of chopped onion, 1 teaspoonful of chopped red pepper and 1 teaspoonful of salt. Sew together at the top, sprinkle with salt and pepper, roll in flour and brown in hot fat. Place in a small deep baking dish, fill the pan half full of boiling water, cover closely and bake slowly 2 hours, basting three or four times every hour. Remove the heart from the pan and set it on a platter in a warm place. Thicken the liquor left in the pan with flour mixed to a thin paste with a little cold water, using 2 tablespoonfuls of flour to every cupful of liquid. Season with salt and pepper and pour around the heart before serving.

Irish Stew

5 pounds mutton	½ onion
4 cupfuls potatoes	¼ cupful flour
¾ cupful turnips	salt
½ cupful carrots	pepper

Cut the meat into small pieces, removing the fat. Try out the fat and brown the meat in it. When well browned, cover with boiling water, boil for 5 minutes and then cook at a lower temperature until the meat is done. Add the vegetables, which have been cut in small cubes, and the salt during the last hour of cooking, the potatoes being added 15 minutes before serving. Thicken with flour diluted with cold water. Serve with dumplings.

Scotch Stew

2 necks mutton	2 tablespoonfuls suet
1 onion	2 tablespoonfuls flour
4 cupfuls strained tomatoes	1 bay leaf

Cut the necks into small pieces. Put suet into a kettle and shake on the stove until melted. Remove cracklings, add mutton and sear in the fat. Draw to the back of the stove, add flour to fat and mix, add tomatoes, stir until boiling, add seasonings, cover and simmer gently 1½ hours.

Simmer, do not boil, meats when making a stew. Add vegetables at the end of the cooking just in time for them to get tender.

Veal Jelly

Cover a knuckle of veal broken in small pieces with boiling water and let simmer until tender, together with a few slices of carrot, half an onion and a stalk of celery. Drain, reserving the broth, remove all the meat from the bones and return the gristle and bones to the broth. Simmer until 1 cupful of broth is left. Strain and set aside to cool. When the meat is almost cold, cut in tiny cubes or put through the food grinder. Remove the fat from the broth, reheat and stir the veal into it, adding salt, pepper and any other seasonings desired. Decorate a mold with hard cooked eggs, which have been sliced, pour the veal mixture into this, cover with oiled paper, press down with a weight and let stand until the jelly is cold and firm. Serve sliced very thin.

Beef Jelly

Soak ½ tablespoonful of gelatin in ¼ cupful of cold water 30 minutes. Put enough cold boiled beef through a chopper to make 1 cupful; to this add 1 small tomato peeled and chopped fine or one firm canned tomato cut in bits, ½ tablespoonful of grated onion, ½ teaspoonful of salt and a dash of pepper. Add ½ cupful of boiling water to the gelatin. When it is thoroughly dissolved, add it to the beef mixture. Stir all together well, turn into a mold which has been wet in cold water, and when cold, cut into slices and serve.

Pot Roast of Beef

Wipe a 3 or 4 pound piece of shoulder meat with a piece of soft cloth wrung out of cold water. Rub salt and flour over it and sprinkle with pepper. Sear the entire surface in hot grease from salt fat pork and place in a baking dish or kettle. Add ¼ to ¾ cupful of hot water, cover and cook slowly 4 hours, adding more water as needed and turning three times during cooking. If the cooking is done in a baking dish, set it in the oven; if in a kettle, cook on top of the stove.

Pot Roast with Vegetables

Wash and scrape 4 carrots, cut in 1 inch slices, cook in boiling salted water until tender, drain and season with salt, pepper

A star in summer suppers when served with sliced tomatoes and corn on the cob. An appetizing way to use leftover scraps of cooked meat.

All ham recipes in this book were made with country-cured meat.

Known as Christmas ham in many country kitchens because it was a traditional Yuletide food. Most farmers cured their own hams. The meat was mostly cooked in water or a liquid, such as cider or apple juice, and finished off briefly in a very hot oven. It was the browning in the oven that gave the triumph its name, baked ham.

Oysters were the favorite shellfish throughout the Midwest. Bake in a shallow pan in a moderate oven (375° F.).

and butter. Wash, pare and soak 10 small potatoes of uniform size and cut in fourths lengthwise; cook in boiling salted water to cover. Drain when tender and sprinkle with salt. Remove meat to a hot platter, place potatoes at one end and carrots at the other. Serve with gravy.

Ham Baked in Cider

Scrape the ham with the dull edge of a knife and wash thoroughly in hot water, using a brush if one is available. Soak it in cold water overnight. Rinse carefully in the morning and place on the stove in a large kettle with sufficient fresh water to cover. Bring slowly to the boiling point, skimming off the scum as it appears. Then add 6 whole cloves, 6 allspice berries and 1 small red pepper pod. Simmer, but do not boil rapidly, until the ham is so tender that it may be pierced with a fork. Keep the ham covered with water all the time. When tender, remove the kettle from the stove and let the ham cool in the liquor. Then drain it and trim off the surplus fat, the skin and all uneven pieces. Pour 1½ quarts of sweet cider over the ham and let it soak in this 8 hours or overnight. Wipe dry, stick in whole cloves to make a pattern, brush lightly with beaten egg and sprinkle generously with a mixture made by combining equal parts of brown sugar and bread crumbs. Place the ham in a baking pan, pour cider about it and bake in a slow oven until it is neatly browned. This takes from 1 to 2 hours, depending on the size of the ham. Baste frequently with the cider during the baking.

Pigs in Blankets

Wipe dry large oysters and wrap every one in a slice of thin bacon, fastening the bacon on with a toothpick. Place in a pan and set in the oven and toast until the bacon is brown.

Flank Steak en Casserole

1 flank steak	1 tablespoonful lemon juice
1 cupful buttered crumbs	1½ teaspoonfuls salt
1 cupful strained tomatoes	⅛ teaspoonful pepper
1 teaspoonful onion juice	⅛ teaspoonful nutmeg
2 cupfuls hot water	⅛ teaspoonful cloves

Score the steak closely on both sides, put the seasonings into it and mix the bread crumbs and tomatoes and spread over one side of the steak. Roll and skewer. Sear. Place in a casserole. Pour on water or stock, cover closely and bake in a slow oven 1 hour. Lift up steak, thicken drippings to make gravy and pour over the steak.

Mexican Beef

2 cupfuls boiled rice	1 onion
4 cupfuls tomatoes	½ pound round beef, chopped
1 green pepper	3 tablespoonfuls fat
1½ teaspoonfuls salt	

Add the cooked and strained tomatoes to the rice. Place the fat in a frying pan and brown the chopped onion in this. Then add the green pepper cut in bits and the chopped meat. Stir in the rice and tomato mixture and add the salt. Cook 20 minutes.

Sausage Stuffed Apples

Select large rosy red apples and scoop out the pulp, leaving a thick shell. Chop or grind the apple pulp which was removed, add ½ teaspoonful of salt and mix thoroughly with cooked sausage. Fill the apples with this mixture and bake in a medium oven until the apples are tender. Serve with baked or browned potatoes.

Place apples in shallow pan; add enough water to cover bottom of pan. Bake in moderate oven (375° F.) until apples are tender.

Ham with Potatoes

Wash and pare 8 potatoes and steam or boil in salted water until tender. Cut in tiny cubes and mix with 1½ cupfuls of ham which has been put through a grinder or cut in small pieces. Season with 1 teaspoonful of salt, ¼ teaspoonful of pepper and a dash of onion juice. Beat 2 eggs until light, add 4 cupfuls of milk and 3 tablespoonfuls of melted butter. Place the potatoes and ham in a buttered baking dish and pour on the milk mixture. Bake until set, which requires about 1 hour.

Old-fashioned Scrapple

Add 1 teaspoonful of salt to 4½ cupfuls of rapidly boiling water and add 1½ cupfuls of cornmeal very slowly while stirring constantly. When all the meal has been added, let the mixture boil 3 minutes, then set over water, in a double boiler if one is available, to cook 2 or 3 hours. Stir 2 cupfuls of sausage through this mush. Let cook 20 minutes longer; then empty into a pan first moistened in water. When cold and firm, cut in slices, dip in flour and brown in fat.

Hamburg Balls

Put 1 pound of round steak through the food grinder and season highly with salt, pepper and a few drops of onion juice. Shape into balls and broil in a frying pan.

Dried Beef Gravy

¼ pound chipped beef	4 tablespoonfuls flour
4 tablespoonfuls butter	2 cupfuls milk

Brown the butter lightly in a frying pan and add the beef which has been pulled into small pieces. Stir until the meat is frizzled. Add the flour and stir until it is browned. Stir in the milk and boil gently a few minutes, about 5, stirring constantly. Serve with boiled potatoes, rice or hot biscuits.

Casserole of Ham

Place a slice of ham cut an inch thick in a casserole or a pan. Spread on top a paste made by mixing ½ cupful of brown sugar, ½ cupful of fine bread crumbs, ½ teaspoonful of mustard and ¼ cupful of water together. Pour over this ⅔ cupful of apple cider. Bake 1½ hours in a moderate oven.

Baked Pork Chops

Season pork chops with salt and pepper, dip in beaten egg and roll in bread crumbs. Heat frying pan on the stove, place the chops in it and set in the oven. Bake until the meat is tender. A large spoonful of dressing may be placed on top of every chop.

Baked Spareribs

Trim the rough ends, break ribs across the middle, season with salt and pepper, fold over and stuff with dressing. Sew up tightly, place in a dripping pan with 2 cupfuls of water. Bake

Bake in moderate oven (350°F.).

Place ribs in shallow pan, meaty side down, in a very hot oven (450°F.) for about 30 minutes to brown. Pour off fat; fold over with meaty side on top and add the stuffing. Secure with cord or skewers and bake in moderate oven (350°F.) 1 hour.

in a moderate oven, basting frequently.   Turn the meat so both sides will be browned.

Breaded Pork Chops

Select nice lean pork chops, season with salt and pepper.   Dip in beaten egg and roll in bread or cracker crumbs.   Brown in a frying pan.

Pan Broiled Ham

Soak thin slices of ham 30 minutes in tepid water.   Drain, wipe and broil 3 minutes in a hot frying pan, turning the pieces constantly while cooking.

Fried Ham

Remove part of the outside layer of fat from a slice of ham. Place in a frying pan and cover with tepid water.   Let stand on the back of the range 30 minutes.   Drain and dry.   Heat a frying pan and brown the meat in it, quickly on one side and then on the other.

Beefsteak

Wipe the steak with a soft cloth moistened in water and trim off part of the fat.   Rub a hot frying pan with a piece of suet and place the meat in the pan.   Turn several times a minute during the cooking until the outside surfaces of the meat are seared.   Move to a cooler part of the range and cook until the steak is well browned on both sides.

POULTRY

To Truss a Fowl

When the fowl is dressed and singed, place a small amount of stuffing in the opening in the neck and put the rest in the body. Sew up the openings.   Draw the skin of the neck smoothly down under the back, press the wings against the body and fold the pinions under, crossing the back and holding down the skin of the neck.   Thread the needle with white twine and

Steaks were pan-broiled in heavy iron skillets on wood- and coal-burning and kerosene stoves and often on gas ranges. Women disliked using broiling ovens. Here is the procedure followed: heat skillet until hot, rub with a little suet and add steaks, cut about ¾ inch thick. Brown on one side, turn and brown on the other side and reduce heat. Cook 10 to 20 minutes, or until desired doneness is reached. Frequent turning insured even cooking.

Barnyard poultry was the rule, and the birds varied greatly in quality. Discard elaborate way of trussing even though it does give good results.

Note to Roast Fowl:

Brush chicken with fat, place breast side up on rack in shallow pan. Do not cover or add water. Roast young chickens weighing 3 to 4 pounds in moderate oven (375° F.) 2 to 2½ hours; birds weighing 5 pounds or more in slow oven (325° F.) 2½ to 3½ hours, or until thickest part of drumstick feels soft when pressed with fingers. Or use a meat thermometer to determine doneness.

Place washed chicken in saucepan, cover with hot water and simmer until tender, or cook in slow oven (325° F.) 2 to 4 hours.

Bake in slow oven (325° F.) until fork tender.

Simmer chicken for goulash; do not boil it.

push it through the wing by the middle joint, through the skin of the neck and then through the middle joint of the other wing. Return the cord through the bend of the leg at the second joint, through the body and out through the middle joint of the other leg. Draw the cord tight and tie. This cord will help to give the fowl a shapely appearance when served. The cord is removed before the fowl is served.

Roast Fowl

Dress, clean, stuff and truss a fowl. Lay on back on a rack in a roasting pan. Lay a strip of salt pork on the breast unless the fowl is very fat. Place in a hot oven until it begins to brown, then lower the temperature and cook slowly until tender. Baste frequently with the drippings in the pan. From 3½ to 4 hours is required for baking a fowl properly.

Chicken Fricassee

Wash the fowl and cut in pieces for serving, rub well with a soft cloth moistened in vinegar, and sprinkle with salt and pepper. Roll the pieces in flour and brown in fat. Pour over it 1 cupful of boiling water or warm cream. Cover, set in the oven and bake until the meat is tender.

Smothered Chicken

Split two young chickens through the backs, wash and season with salt and pepper. Roll in flour and brown in a roasting pan, set on top of the stove, in which a few tablespoonfuls of fat have been placed. Add 1 cupful of hot water, cover and bake in a hot oven.

Ford County's Favorite

Split a chicken down the back, sprinkle with salt and pepper and dots of butter. Cook in a very slow oven until tender. Then cover the top of the chicken with strips of baking powder biscuit dough. Bake until neatly browned.

Chicken Goulash

1 chicken	6 small onions
2 cupfuls tomatoes	1 small green pepper
2 teaspoonfuls salt	¼ teaspoonful pepper

Boil the chicken until tender. When cool, remove the bones and cut the meat into small bits. Put this back in the broth, add the canned tomatoes, chopped onions, pepper and seasonings. Simmer slowly 1 hour.

FISH

The way in which fish is cooked depends largely on the kind of fish it is. Oily ones, such as salmon and mackerel, are best broiled or baked, at least not cooked in fat. White fish, such as halibut, cod and haddock, are more dry and may be fried or sautéd. If cooked in water, they are best served with rich sauces, and if baked, they must be basted and larded frequently.

Cleaning Fish

Fish are best when cleaned immediately after being taken from the water. Remove the scales by drawing a knife over the fish, beginning at the tail and working toward the head. Wipe off the knife occasionally and brush off the scales from the fish. Wash thoroughly.

To Skin a Fish

Cut off the fins along the back and then cut off a narrow strip of skin down the entire length of the back. Cut the skin around the head, loosen it below the head and draw it off from one side of the fish by pulling gently with one hand and pushing with the back of a knife held in the other hand. Repeat the process with the other side of the fish.

Boiled Fish

Cook small fish whole but cut the larger ones in thick pieces. Use sufficient water to cover and add to this salt and a little lemon juice or vinegar. Salt improves the flavor and lemon juice or vinegar keeps the flesh white. The fish may be tied in a piece of cheesecloth when placed in the warm water, which is brought to the boiling point quickly, and then simmered until the meat separates from the bones.

Cleaning fish was men's work, but most farm women knew how to do it. It was the custom to depend on the men and boys in the family, the fishermen, to deliver their catch to the kitchen ready to use.

Cook fish until it flakes when tested with a fork.

Cans of salmon were kept on hand in almost all Midwestern kitchens. The fish was plentiful and inexpensive. Canned tuna arrived later.

Pan Broiled Fish

Split a fish down the back, clean and wipe dry. Sprinkle with salt and pepper and place in an oiled broiling or dripping pan. Brown first on one side and then turn and brown on the other. Serve on a hot platter at once.

Sautéd Fish

Clean fish and cut in individual pieces. Dip in flour, corn-meal or fine bread crumbs. Brown in hot fat.

Fried Fish

Cut cleaned fish in individual pieces, sprinkle with salt and bread crumbs, dip in egg and then in bread crumbs. Fry in deep fat until brown on all sides.

Salmon Pie

Blend 2 tablespoonfuls of butter with an equal amount of flour and add it to 1¼ cupfuls of milk. Cook until smooth and thick; add salt and pepper to taste. Then open a can of salmon, drain off the liquor and remove the bones. Flake the fish with a fork and add it to the milk mixture. Butter a baking dish and line with warm mashed potatoes. Pour in the salmon mixture, cover with a layer of baked potatoes and brush the top with melted butter. Brown in a quick oven and serve immediately in the same dish in which it was cooked.

Salmon Fluff

1 cupful salmon	1 cupful milk
1 cupful boiled rice	2 eggs
2 tablespoonfuls shortening	1 teaspoonful salt
¼ teaspoonful pepper	

Remove the skin and bones from the salmon and pull into flakes. Add the milk, boiled rice and beaten egg yolks. Add melted butter, salt and pepper. Fold in stiffly beaten egg whites and bake in a moderate oven 30 minutes.

Creamed Salmon

Combine 2 cupfuls of the white sauce for creamed dishes with an equal amount of flaked and drained canned salmon. Serve hot on 6 slices of buttered toast on a platter surrounded with buttered peas.

One menu that brought rejoicing when peas were ready in the garden was creamed salmon, buttered peas and fresh strawberry shortcake or fresh tart cherries baked in a pie.

All recipes in this chapter were cherished treasures of wives of farmers who liked to hunt. Every recipe was backed by a woman who made it work beautifully for her and a man who bragged about the way the game tasted. Children who tasted these dishes are old men and women now. They remember the occasions on which they sampled them with nostalgic affection.

Brown rabbit, floured and seasoned, in skillet containing 1/8 inch fat. Add 3/4 cup water, cover tightly and cook in moderate oven (350°F.) until tender. Replenish water during cooking if needed, adding no more than 1/4 cup at a time.

After browning, bake, covered, in a slow oven (325°F.) until fork tender. Length of cooking depends on age of rabbit.

CHAPTER 23

WILD GAME

Rabbit Chop Suey

1 rabbit	1 small bunch celery
1/8 pound fat salt pork	1 tablespoonful Worcestershire
2 large onions	sauce
1 green pepper	

Cut rabbit meat into 1 inch pieces. Cut fat pork into 1/2 inch cubes. Cut celery, onion and green pepper into small cubes. Cook the pork in a frying pan slowly until crisp, being careful not to scorch the fat. Add the rabbit meat and simmer gently 20 minutes. Then add the onion, cover tightly and cook slowly 20 minutes or until the onion is tender. Add the celery and ground pepper and cook 15 minutes. Stir in the Worcestershire sauce and cook 3 minutes. Serve with boiled rice.

Browned Rabbit

Cut a young, fat rabbit in halves and place these in a greased pan. Dot generously with butter and dredge with flour. Season with salt. Brown on both sides in a hot oven. When cooked, place the rabbit on a warm platter, thicken the drippings with flour and add milk or water to make a gravy. Pour this hot gravy over the rabbit just before serving.

Baked Rabbit

Disjoint a large rabbit. Cut 1/2 pound of bacon in slices and fry to a delicate brown. Remove the bacon and brown the rabbit in the fat. Place the meat in a casserole. Add flour to the fat in the frying pan and then sufficient water to make a gravy. Mince 1 carrot and 1 onion finely and add to the gravy. Add sufficient salt to suit the family's taste and pour the hot gravy

over the rabbit.   Cover the casserole and cook in a moderate oven
2 hours.

Rabbit, Hawaiian Style

1 rabbit	4 large onions
3 large potatoes	½ cupful sour cream
½ cupful tomatoes	salt, pepper and butter

Cut meat from the back and hind quarters.   With a potato
masher flatten every piece and cut into 1 inch sections.   Pare
and slice the potatoes; peel and slice the onions.   Put a layer of
potatoes in an earthenware or glass baking dish, then a layer of
meat and a layer of onion.   Add ½ teaspoonful of salt and ¼
teaspoonful of pepper.   Add a layer of tomato and dot with
butter.   Repeat until all the material is used.   Pour the sour
cream over the top, cover the dish, place it in a pan of boiling
water and cook in the oven for at least 2 hours.

Use a moderate oven (350° F.).

Mrs. Rankin's Quail

6 quail	1 cupful cream
1 teaspoonful salt	water
¾ cupful butter	flour

Dress the birds and leave whole.   Salt well and let stand a few
minutes.   Place the butter in a frying pan on top of the stove,
roll the quail in flour and place in the hot butter, add ½ cupful
of water and cover tightly.   Cook slowly about 2 hours.   Turn
the quail from time to time during the first half hour of cooking; then place them in the oven the rest of the time, adding
water as is needed.   When the meat is tender and is a rich
golden brown, add the sweet cream, simmer 5 minutes and serve
at once.

*This charming farm woman, famed
in her neighborhood for this platter
treat, served it once a year for her
husband and his friends, most of
them hunting companions. The dinner
was a highlight of the Thanksgiving
season.*

Quail on Toast

Dress the quail, cut every bird in halves, roll in flour and
season with salt and pepper.   Place them in a greased baking
dish, add ½ cupful of water and cook until tender, adding more
water as needed.   Remove the quail from the dish and make a
brown gravy from the drippings in the pan, using very rich milk.
When thickened, place the quail on brown toast and pour the hot
gravy over this.   Serve at once.

Roasted Quail

Dress the birds carefully, leaving them whole. Wipe outside and inside with a dampened cloth. Truss, leaving the legs standing up. Tie a thin slice of bacon around every bird. Bake from 15 to 20 minutes in a hot oven. Baste frequently with a small amount of boiling water and butter which are placed in the pan with the quail. Season with salt and pepper. Moisten crisp, brown toast in the liquor and serve the roasted quail on this.

Broiled Quail

Split the dressed birds down the back, brown in a greased pan on both sides, basting frequently with butter. When cooked, spread with butter and season with salt and pepper. Place on moistened toast and set in the oven long enough to melt the butter on the quail.

Prairie Chicken or Grouse

Dress carefully and let stand in a cold place overnight. Put butter in every bird and truss or tie in a good shape. Roast in a hot oven 30 minutes, basting every 5 minutes with melted butter. After roasting 25 minutes, dredge with flour and let brown in the oven the last 5 minutes of the cooking.

Boil the livers of the wild grouse and put them through a food grinder, seasoning them with salt and pepper and making a paste by mixing it with melted butter. Spread this on thin brown toast, pour some of the liquid in the roasting pan over it and serve the grouse on the toast.

Prairie chickens have dark meat, therefore they, like duck, are best when served very hot and rare. Overcooking spoils the flavor.

Wild Ducks

Roast the ducks quickly in a hot oven and serve very hot on slices of browned mush. Do not use a stuffing.

Snipe and Woodcock

Draw the birds carefully and wipe inside and out with a dampened cloth. Cut off the feet and hold the lower part of the

Note to Wild Ducks:

For rare meat, rub birds inside and out with desired seasonings, place on rack in shallow pan and bake uncovered in a very hot oven (500°F.), brushing several times while cooking with a glazing mixture of 2 tblsp. corn syrup with 1 tsp. bottled browning sauce added. For well-done meat, place birds close together, to prevent drying out, on rack in baking pan. Cover and bake in a slow oven (325°F.) 2½ hours, or until fork tender. Baste frequently with butter mixed with lemon juice seasoned with a touch of dried thyme. Or baste with barbecue sauce.

legs in boiling water a few minutes. Then remove the skin from them. Skin the heads and remove the eyes. Press the birds together, draw around the heads, running the little bills like skewers through the legs and bodies. Wrap every bird in a slice of bacon or salt pork and bake in a hot oven 10 or 15 minutes. Baste with butter. Boil the hearts and livers, chop very fine, season with salt and pepper, onion juice and melted butter. Spread this on toast, keep very hot, pour on the juice from the pan in which the birds were cooked and place the game on top of this toast. Serve immediately.

Squabs

Split down the back, dress carefully and break the breast bone with a potato masher. Wipe carefully inside and out and broil like a spring chicken, or roast in a quick oven 1 hour. Serve on fried mush or on toast. Tie a piece of bacon on top of every squab and place a teaspoonful of butter inside before broiling.

Potted Pigeons

Unless the pigeons are very young, they are best stewed. After dressing and trussing the birds, spread a layer of thinly sliced bacon in the bottom of the pan, lay the pigeons on this with breasts up, dice 1 carrot and 1 onion and add them with 1 teaspoonful of salt, 1 teaspoonful of chopped parsley and sufficient water to cover. Cover the pan tightly and simmer until the meat is tender, adding more water if necessary during the cooking. Serve on thin slices of toast with or without thickening the broth to make gravy for an accompaniment.

Partridge

Dress and truss the partridge as chicken. Cover the breast with thin slices of bacon or salt pork. Put into a baking pan and add 2 cupfuls of boiling water. Roast 45 minutes, basting frequently. Place on a hot platter, dot with butter and serve with a gravy made by thickening the drippings in the pan and adding rich milk and seasonings.

To broil partridge, split down the back and rub all the surfaces with butter. Broil 30 minutes, browning on both sides. Sprinkle with salt and pepper and serve on buttered toast.

Almost every country kitchen had a jar in which scraps of homemade bread were stored during the cold weather. The common rule was to dry the bread in the oven (300°F.) before making a stuffing with it.

Recipe for Bread Stuffing makes 4 cups, or enough to stuff a 4- to 5-pound chicken or capon. The recipe was doubled for a 10-pound turkey.

Chop oysters and use oyster liquor for part of liquid needed to moisten bread. Sometimes chicken broth took the liquid role.

Chop onion and celery and cook over low heat in butter to soften, not brown, before adding to stuffing.

CHAPTER 24

STUFFINGS

Bread Stuffing

4 cupfuls bread	1 tablespoonful parsley
1½ teaspoonfuls salt	4 tablespoonfuls butter
½ teaspoonful pepper	hot milk or water to moisten

Mix the salt and pepper and sprinkle over the finely broken bread crumbs. Add the chopped parsley and the melted butter. Pour on the hot liquid gradually and mix thoroughly, stirring lightly. One-half teaspoonful of sage may be used in place of the parsley.

Onion Stuffing

Make as Bread Stuffing, adding 2 tablespoonfuls of chopped onion.

Oyster Stuffing

Make as Bread Stuffing, adding 25 washed and well drained oysters.

Celery Stuffing

Make as Bread Stuffing, adding 1 cupful of chopped celery. If celery is not available, 1 teaspoonful of celery salt may be added to the dressing and only ½ teaspoonful of salt used.

Potato Stuffing

2 cupfuls mashed potatoes	1½ teaspoonfuls salt
1½ cupfuls bread crumbs	4 tablespoonfuls butter
2 tablespoonfuls grated onion	2 tablespoonfuls cream
½ teaspoonful pepper	1 egg

Boil and mash the potatoes and while hot add the other ingredients. If one wishes, 1 teaspoonful of sage and 2 tablespoonfuls of finely chopped salt pork may be added.

Walnut Stuffing

Make Potato Stuffing, omitting the onion, sage and fat pork and adding 1 cupful of chopped black or English walnuts. Use in stuffing tame ducks and rabbits.

Apple Stuffing

2 cupfuls apples   1 cupful raisins

Chop the pared and cored tart apples together with the seeded raisins and use in stuffing a goose.

Peanut Stuffing

Mix together 4 cupfuls of warm boiled rice, ½ cupful of peanut butter, 1 tablespoonful of onion juice, 2 tablespoonfuls of chopped parsley and salt and pepper to taste. If this is not bound together well, add a little rich cream.

Cracker Stuffing

Scald 1¼ cupfuls of milk and pour over 2 cupfuls of cracker crumbs. Add ½ cupful of melted butter, 1 egg well beaten, 1 teaspoonful of salt and ¼ teaspoonful of pepper.

Chestnut Stuffing

4 cupfuls chestnuts	¼ teaspoonful pepper
½ cupful butter	4 tablespoonfuls cream
1 teaspoonful salt	1 cupful cracker crumbs

Shell and blanch the chestnuts by cutting a half-inch gash on the flat sides and putting into a frying pan, allowing 2 teaspoonfuls of butter. Shake over the stove until the butter is melted. Put in the oven and let stand 5 minutes. Remove from the oven and take off the shells with a small knife. The shelling and blanching are accomplished at the same time. Cook the chestnuts in salted boiling water until tender. Drain, mash, add the butter, salt, pepper, cream and cracker crumbs and mix thoroughly.

When a blight destroyed American chestnut trees, one of the favorite stuffings for the Thanksgiving turkey disappeared. After canned water chestnuts came to food stores, some women chopped them up and stirred them into bread stuffings for a crunchy note.

Chocolate Cream Pie

2/3 cup sugar

5 tblsp. flour

3 squares unsweetened
   chocolate, cut up

½ tsp. salt

2 ½ cups milk

3 egg yolks

1 tsp vanilla

1 9-inch baked
   pastry shell

Combine sugar, flour, chocolate and salt in double-boiler top. Stir in milk. Cook over boiling water, stirring constantly, until mixture thickens. Cover and cook 15 minutes longer.

Makes 2 9-inch 2-crust pies.

Bake pastry before adding filling. Women frequently salvaged scraps of pie crust in these pretty tarts.

Stir 1 or 2 tblsp. hot mixture into slightly beaten egg yolks; add to remaining mixture in double boiler. Cook 2 minutes over boiling water, stirring constantly. Cool and add vanilla. Pour into baked pastry shell. Top at serving time with

CHAPTER 25

PASTRY

THE important rules to heed in pastry making are: use ingredients which are as cold as it is possible to have them, avoid handling the pastry any more than is necessary and last, but not least, do not add any more water than is needed to hold the flaky particles of the fat and flour mixture together.

In the cold weather or with the use of a refrigerator in the summer, the flour, salt and fat may be combined in large quantities, placed in covered glass or earthenware jars and kept on hand. Then when pies are desired, water may be added to a portion of this mixture and the pastry may be rolled out quickly. Having this pastry mixture prepared is a great convenience when unexpected guests or crews of men come.

Plain Pastry

4½ cupfuls flour
1½ cupfuls shortening

4 teaspoonfuls salt
cold water to moisten

Mix the flour, salt and shortening together. The fat may be cut in with a knife. Add just enough water to make the particles adhere together. Turn on a lightly floured board, roll thin, handling as little as possible. This makes 3 two-crust pies of ordinary size.

Sweet Pastry

4 cupfuls flour
1 cupful brown sugar

1½ cupfuls butter
½ teaspoonful salt

Mix the flour and salt and cut in the fat with a knife. Roll very thin. Cut with a round cutter, using a doughnut cutter to make half the circles. Use jelly, orange or chocolate filling or jam to fill these tarts, placing the circle with the hole in the center on a plain one to make a tart.

whipped cream, or make a meringue with the 3 egg whites after pouring filling into pastry shell and brown in moderate oven (350°F.) 12 to 15 minutes. Cool before serving.

Dorothy's Pastry

3 cupfuls flour	½ cupful butter
3 teaspoonfuls salt	½ cupful lard
	½ cupful cold water

Mix the dry ingredients, work the lard into them and add the water. Turn this mealy mixture on a lightly floured board and with a knife pat in shape. Roll ½ inch thick. Place the cold butter, which has been washed and chilled, in the center and fold the pastry over it. Roll out, fold over and repeat this process 3 times. Then the pastry is ready to be baked.

Makes 1 9-inch 2-crust pie and 1 9-inch pastry shell.

Raised Pastry

3 cupfuls pastry flour	1 teaspoonful baking powder
1 teaspoonful salt	⅔ cupful shortening
	cold water to moisten

Mix the dry ingredients, cut in the fat and chill the mixture. Then add cold water, roll the crust and bake in a hot oven.

Pastry flour is cake flour.

Apple Pie

Wash, pare and slice thinly tart, easily cooked apples. Cover a pie tin with pastry, arrange the slices of apples in the tin and sprinkle liberally with sugar, either brown or white. Dot with butter. A little cinnamon may be sprinkled over the top if one wishes. Cover with pastry and bake.

Use 6 to 7 tart apples, pared and sliced, combined with ¾ cup to 1 cup sugar, 2 tblsp. flour and spices as desired. Mix dry ingredients before combining with apples. Place in pastry-lined 9-inch pie pan, dot with 2 tblsp. butter, cover with top crust and bake in hot oven (400°F.) 50 minutes, or until top is brown and juices begin to bubble through vents in pie crust.

Berry Pies

Line a pie tin with pastry and fill with berries slightly dredged with flour. Sprinkle with sugar, cover with pastry and bake in a moderate oven.

Pumpkin Pie

2 cupfuls stewed pumpkin	2 tablespoonfuls sugar
1 egg	½ teaspoonful ginger
1 cupful milk	½ teaspoonful cinnamon
1 tablespoonful flour	¼ teaspoonful salt

Combine the ingredients, beating the egg well, and pour in a pie pan lined with pastry. If a brown crust is desired on top of the pumpkin mixture, pour 5 tablespoonfuls of cold milk on top of the pie just before setting it in the oven. This milk will brown. Have the oven rather hot at first to set the crust before

When gardens were yielding pumpkins, women cooked them for pie fillings. Put the pie in a hot oven (425°F.) and bake 15 minutes; reduce heat to 350°F. and continue baking about 35 minutes, or until a knife inserted in center of pie comes out clean.

any of the pumpkin filling can soak into it; then lower the heat and bake rather slowly.

Lemon Whey Pie

1 cupful whey	1 lemon
3 tablespoonfuls cornstarch	½ teaspoonful salt
⅔ cupful sugar	1 tablespoonful butter
	2 eggs

Strain the whey and heat to the boiling point. Mix the sugar and cornstarch together and add to the whey. Cook until the mixture thickens. Then add the beaten egg yolks, the grated rind and juice of the lemon, the salt and melted fat and cook for 3 minutes. Pour into a crust which has been baked and cover the top with a meringue made by beating the whites of eggs until stiff, adding 2 tablespoonfuls of sugar and a few drops of vanilla and beating again. Spread this meringue on top of the pie and bake in a slow oven 20 minutes or until the meringue is browned.

Lucile's Apple Pie

Stew 10 tart apples of medium size in a very little water until tender. Rub through a sieve and add 1¼ cupfuls of sugar, 1 teaspoonful of cinnamon, 4 beaten egg yolks, 1½ cupfuls of cream and 1 teaspoonful of vanilla. Pour in two pastry shells and bake in a hot oven, reducing the heat after the first 10 minutes, when the pastry will be set. Bake 30 minutes longer. Then remove from the oven and cover with a meringue made from the 4 egg whites which have been beaten until very stiff and to which 8 tablespoonfuls of sugar have been added.

English Apple Pie

6 medium-sized apples	1 lemon
6 tablespoonfuls butter	1 cupful sugar
2 egg yolks	1 cupful cream

Make a sauce from the apples. When tender, rub through a sieve and add the butter. Cool and add the beaten egg yolks, sugar and the juice and grated rind of the lemon. Stir in the thick cream. Pour in two pie tins lined with pastry, bake 30 or 40 minutes, then cover with a meringue made from the egg whites, to which 4 tablespoonfuls of sugar are added. Brown the meringue in a slow oven.

Many men praised these pies by saying: "The best reason for making cottage cheese."

Bake in moderate oven (350°F.) 12 to 15 minutes or until meringue browns.

Chocolate Pie

2 eggs	1 tablespoonful butter
4 tablespoonfuls flour	2 tablespoonfuls chocolate or cocoa
4 tablespoonfuls sugar	¼ teaspoonful salt
1 teaspoonful vanilla	2 cupfuls milk

Mix the dry ingredients and stir in the milk, to which the beaten egg yolks have been added. Add butter and cook in a double boiler until smooth and thick. Add vanilla. Fill baked crusts, using stiffly beaten egg whites sweetened with 4 tablespoonfuls of sugar for the top of the pies. Brown in a slow oven. This will make two pies.

See revised recipe, Chocolate Cream Pie.

Butterscotch Filling

2 egg yolks	½ teaspoonful vanilla
3 tablespoonfuls flour	1 cupful brown sugar
2 tablespoonfuls cold water	2 tablespoonfuls butter
	2 cupfuls boiling water

Beat the egg yolks, flour, sugar and cold water together, add the boiling water and let come to a boil. When the mixture begins to thicken, remove from the stove and add the vanilla and butter. Use as a pie filling, covering the top with a meringue.

Use revised recipe, Chocolate Cream Pie, substituting 1 cup dark brown sugar, firmly packed, for white sugar. Add 3 tblsp. butter to cooked mixture before cooling.

Tarts

Bake pastry which has been cut in circles and pricked with a fork over inverted muffin tins. Bake in a very hot oven. When cool, fill with marmalades, sweetened fresh fruit or any pie filling desired.

Highly favored salad accompaniment and a splendid way to use scraps of pie crust. Bake in hot oven (450°F.) 6 to 7 minutes.

Cheese Straws

Roll pastry very thin and sprinkle with grated cheese. Fold over and roll. Repeat three times, every time rolling the mixture very thin. Cut in strips ½ inch wide and 4 inches long. Bake about 8 minutes in a hot oven.

Bake in hot oven (450°F.) 10 to 12 minutes.

Pineapple Pie

1 small can grated pineapple	1 tablespoonful lemon juice
2 egg yolks	½ cupful water
½ cupful sugar	2 egg whites
1 tablespoonful flour	pastry

Beat the egg yolks and add them to the pineapple, sugar, flour, lemon juice and water. Place in a pie pan lined with

See revised recipe.

pastry and bake 30 minutes, reducing the heat in the oven after the pie has baked 10 minutes. Cover with a meringue made by beating the egg whites and adding 2 tablespoonfuls of sugar. Return the pie to a slow oven and brown the meringue.

Prune Pie

1 cupful prunes	1 lemon
½ cupful sugar	3 tablespoonfuls water
2 tablespoonfuls cornstarch	½ teaspoonful cinnamon
1 cupful water	1 teaspoonful vanilla

Wash the prunes and soak 4 or 5 hours in cold water. If all the water is taken up by the fruit, add more and stew until the prunes are tender. Remove the stones, add the sugar and lemon juice and cook slowly 10 minutes. Add the cornstarch dissolved in cold water and cook 3 minutes. Cool, add vanilla and cinnamon and bake in a deep pan between two crusts.

Cut up cooked prunes. Use only juice of 1 lemon, about 3 tblsp. Bake in hot oven (400°F.) until crust browns.

Raisin Pie

Make as Prune Pie, substituting raisins for the prunes.

Orange Pie

1 cupful orange juice	¼ teaspoonful salt
2 eggs	2½ tablespoonfuls flour
⅔ cupful sugar	1½ teaspoonfuls butter

Mix the sugar and flour together and add the well beaten egg yolks and the butter. Stir in the orange juice, adding it very slowly. Cook over hot water until the mixture thickens. Cool and pour in a previously baked pastry shell. Cover with a meringue made by beating the egg whites and adding 2 tablespoonfuls of sugar. Brown the meringue in a slow oven.

Recipe makes 1 8-inch pie.

Custard Pie

Line a deep pie tin with pastry and bake. Pour in a custard filling, same as recipe for Baked Custard, and bake until the custard is set.

Place pie in hot oven (450°F.); bake 20 minutes. Reduce heat to 350°F. and bake 15 to 20 minutes longer, or until knife inserted in center of pie comes out clean.

Lemon Pie Filling

¾ cupful sugar	1 tablespoonful butter
2 tablespoonfuls cornstarch	2 egg yolks
1 cupful boiling water	⅛ teaspoonful salt
¼ cupful lemon juice	grated rind of ½ lemon

Mix the cornstarch and sugar together and stir in the hot water. Cook, stirring constantly, until it thickens, and boil 5 minutes. Add butter, beaten egg yolks, salt, lemon juice and grated rind. Cook 3 minutes. Pour into a previously baked crust; cover with a meringue. Brown meringue in a slow oven.

Mince Meat

½ pound meat	½ tablespoonful cinnamon
1 pound of apples	1 teaspoonful cloves
½ pound raisins	1 teaspoonful mace
½ pound currants	1½ teaspoonfuls allspice
⅛ pound citron	1½ teaspoonfuls nutmeg
½ cupful sugar	water or fruit juice

Boil the meat and cool. Pare and core the apples. Force the meat and apples through the food grinder. Wash the currants, raisins and citron and cut in tiny pieces. Moisten with water or fruit juice. Cook gently until the meat and apples are tender, adding the spices during the cookery. To make mince pies, line a pie tin with plain pastry, fill with mince meat, cover with pastry and bake.

Green Tomato Mince Meat

Chop or grind 8 pounds of green tomatoes. Add 6 pounds of sugar, 1 tablespoonful of cinnamon, 1 tablespoonful of powdered cloves and ¾ tablespoonful of allspice. Cook gently until the tomatoes are tender and clear. Can in sterile jars and combine with meat in making mince meat pies.

Cranberry Pie

To 3 cupfuls of cold cranberry sauce add the yolks of 2 eggs, 1 tablespoonful of butter and 1 tablespoonful of flour which have been mixed into a paste with a few spoonfuls of cranberry juice. Simmer gently 40 minutes. When cool, add ¼ teaspoonful of lemon extract and pour into a deep pie crust which has been baked previously. Cover with a meringue made from the stiffly beaten whites of 2 eggs mixed with 2 tablespoonfuls of sugar. Place in a slow oven to brown the meringue.

Bake pie in hot oven (425°F.) 40 to 45 minutes. Cover edge of pie during last 15 minutes of baking time with 3-inch strip of aluminum foil to prevent browning too much.

To can Green Tomato Mincemeat, process in boiling-water bath 25 to 30 minutes.

All cranberry sauce, 50 years ago, was home-made. Cook it with egg yolks, flour and butter until mixture thickens. Cool. Spoon into baked pie shell, top with meringue and brown in moderate oven (350°F.) 12 to 15 minutes.

Pie shells was what women in the aftermath of World War I called them. Bake in very hot oven (450°F.) 12 to 15 minutes.

See revised recipe for this spring treat.

Best directions for making meringues to top pies. For 2 egg whites, use ¼ cup sugar; for 3 egg whites use ⅓ cup sugar. Beat egg whites with ¼ tsp. cream of tartar until foamy. Beat, adding 1 tblsp. sugar at a time, until stiff, glossy peaks form. Beat in ¼ tsp. vanilla. Be sure to cover pie filling to the edges. Brown in moderate oven (350°F.) 12 to 15 minutes.

Rhubarb Pie

4 cups cut-up rhubarb	Dash of salt
1⅓ to 1⅔ cups sugar	2 tblsp. butter
⅓ cup flour	Pastry for 9-inch 2-crust pie

Use tender young rhubarb from garden. Combine sugar, flour and salt. Spread half of rhubarb in pastry-lined pie pan. Sprinkle with half of the

Pastry Shells

In baking pastry shells use a very hot oven to prevent the pastry from shrinking out of shape. Either line a pie tin with the pastry or place it over the inverted tin, or for small pastry cups or tarts, arrange it over inverted muffin tins. Prick the pastry with the tines of a fork.

Rhubarb Pie

Cut the washed stalks of rhubarb in ½ inch pieces. Cover the tin with pastry, dredge the rhubarb with flour and arrange in the tin. Sprinkle liberally with sugar, cover with pastry and bake.

Meringue

2 egg whites	2 teaspoonfuls lemon juice or
2 tablespoonfuls sugar	¾ teaspoonful vanilla

Beat egg whites until stiff. Add the sugar gradually. Continue beating and add the flavoring. Spread on pies, puddings or desserts and brown slowly in the oven. Use a slow oven so it will take 15 or 20 minutes for the baking.

sugar-flour mixture. Add remaining rhubarb and sprinkle with last half of sugar-flour mixture.

Dot with butter and top with pastry. Bake in hot oven (400°F.) 40 to 45 minutes, or until juices bubble in vents.

Note: For a luscious strawberry-rhubarb pie, use only 2 cups cut-up rhubarb and combine with 2 cups sliced fresh strawberries.

CHAPTER 26

SALADS

THE salad is usually the most attractive dish on the table. It may be made from fruits, vegetables, meats, fish, eggs or combinations of these foods. Many kinds of salad dressings may be served with it; the two general classes are those which contain olive oil or a vegetable oil and those which do not contain oil of any kind.

Salads are made from evenly cut fruits and vegetables. If meat is used, it is freed from bone, skin and gristle and is cut in small cubes. A garnish of some food, such as whipped cream, sprigs of parsley, lettuce, a curl of celery or a strip of pimento, makes the salad more attractive.

As a rule the salad is served on lettuce, which is not only attractive but also edible. To prepare the lettuce for use, it is examined leaf by leaf to make certain that it is free from insects. Then it is washed and placed in a colander to drain. It may be dried between folds of a towel but this process frequently bruises it.

When most of the water has drained off, the leaves are piled lightly in a cloth or paper bag and set in a cold place, such as a refrigerator. If one prefers, the washed lettuce may be placed in a glass fruit jar, covered and set in a cold room. When time to serve the salad, the lettuce is crisp and ready for use.

French Salad Dressing

¾ teaspoonful sugar	½ teaspoonful paprika
1 teaspoonful salt	5 tablespoonfuls vinegar
	10 tablespoonfuls olive oil

Mix the dry ingredients and add the vinegar and olive oil alternately, beating constantly with a silver fork. Lemon juice may be used instead of the vinegar if one wishes.

153

Salads 50 years ago were an after-thought in the minds of menu planners. Tossed green salads had not circulated in country neighborhoods. Countless farmers considered all lettuce salads as fodder.

Plastic bags have assumed the role in lettuce storage once performed by cloth and paper bags and glass fruit jars.

This cooked salad dressing — it never was boiled — enjoyed great prestige in farm meals during the 1920 era.

A hostess special.

Boiled Salad Dressing

3 eggs	½ cupful water
1 teaspoonful salt	½ cupful vinegar
2 tablespoonfuls sugar	2 tablespoonfuls butter
1 tablespoonful flour	⅛ teaspoonful white pepper

Add the sifted dry ingredients to the beaten egg and mix thoroughly. Add the vinegar and water and cook over hot water, stirring constantly until thick. Add the butter, salt and pepper. If one wishes, ½ teaspoonful of ground mustard may be added.

Whipped Cream Salad Dressing

3 egg yolks	½ teaspoonful mustard
2 tablespoonfuls sugar	½ cupful hot vinegar
¼ teaspoonful salt	2 teaspoonfuls butter
½ cupful heavy cream	

Beat the egg yolks until thick and lemon colored. One and one-half eggs may be used instead of the egg yolks. Beat in the sugar, salt, and mustard which have been mixed together. Heat the vinegar and melt the butter in it. Combine the two mixtures and cook over hot water until the dressing is thick, stirring constantly. Add the whipped cream just before serving. Use with fruit salads.

Mayonnaise

1 egg yolk	½ teaspoonful mustard
2 tablespoonfuls lemon juice	¾ teaspoonful salt
2 teaspoonfuls vinegar	½ teaspoonful powdered sugar
¾ cupful olive oil	speck cayenne

Chill the ingredients. Place the egg yolk and the dry ingredients in a cold mixing bowl. Add a few drops of vinegar and then the oil, drop by drop, until 1 teaspoonful has been added. Add alternately with the oil the vinegar and lemon juice, drop by drop, until all the lemon juice and vinegar are used. Add the remainder of the oil more rapidly. Constant beating is necessary throughout the entire process.

Thousand Island Dressing

To 1 cupful of mayonnaise add 6 tablespoonfuls of chili sauce, 2 chopped pimentos and ½ tablespoonful chopped chives.

Russian Salad Dressing

To 6 tablespoonfuls of mayonnaise add 1½ tablespoonfuls of chopped pimentos, 6 sprigs of chives, chopped, 3 tablespoonfuls of chili sauce, ½ teaspoonful of chopped capers, 1½ teaspoonfuls of tarragon vinegar and 1½ tablespoonfuls of whipped cream.

Cabbage Salad

1 small cabbage	1 green pepper
1 small onion	salad dressing
2 small carrots	cabbage leaves

Put the onion and carrot through the food grinder, shred the cabbage finely or grind it, remove the seeds from the green pepper and cut it in shreds. Mix lightly with salad dressing and serve on cabbage leaves.

Salad Dressing for Cabbage

½ cupful cream	2 teaspoonfuls mustard
½ cupful vinegar	2 tablespoonfuls hot water
	1 teaspoonful salt

Whip the cream until stiff and gradually add the vinegar. When well mixed, add the other ingredients, first dissolving the ground mustard in the boiling water.

Potato and Egg Salad

2 cupfuls cabbage	2 cupfuls cooked potato
2 eggs	2 tablespoonfuls green pepper
2 tablespoonfuls pickle	½ teaspoonful onion juice
	1 tablespoonful parsley

Cut the boiled potatoes in cubes, shred the cabbage finely, slice the hard cooked eggs and combine with the chopped pickles, pepper, parsley and onion juice. Celery may be used in place of the cabbage and cucumbers instead of the pickles. Mix these ingredients together with a boiled salad dressing.

Cabbage and Pineapple Salad

4 cupfuls shredded cabbage	2 cupfuls marshmallows
2 cupfuls sliced pineapple	1 cupful of nuts

Cut the canned pineapple and marshmallows in small pieces, mix with the cabbage and nut meats and combine with salad dressing.

Cabbage had only one rival for supremacy in the salad bowl. It was the apple. Juicy, ripe tomatoes, peeled and sliced, were a top summer selection. They commonly were served on lettuce-lined salad plates.

Canned pineapple chunks have eliminated the work of cutting up the slices.

Skip soaking cabbage in cold water and save the vitamin C. Fresh, crisp heads almost always are plentiful in the autumn.

Waldorf salad has been a base on which countrywomen have built new salads ever since the recipe for it arrived in their kitchens before World War I. It still rates high.

The cherries were canned; the grapes were fresh or canned, the choice depending on the season.

Fall Salad

Line a bowl with shredded cabbage which has been soaked in cold water until crisp. Sprinkle with salt and pepper. Arrange alternate layers of thinly sliced beets and carrots which have been cooked until tender in salted water in the nest of cabbage. Add salad dressing and serve.

Apple and Celery Salad

6 apples	2 tablespoonfuls lemon juice
1 banana	2 cupfuls celery
	salad dressing

Pare the apples, remove the cores and cut in dice. Slice the banana and mix with the apples, sprinkling the mixture with lemon juice to prevent discoloration. Add the salad dressing and the diced celery just before serving.

Date Salad

1 cupful dates	1 cupful diced celery
4 tablespoonfuls cheese	1 cupful diced apples
4 tablespoonfuls nut meats	1 tablespoonful lemon juice
	salad dressing

Remove the stones from the dates and fill the cavities with the cheese and nut meats which have been ground together. Let stand several hours in a cold place. Mix the apples and celery together, sprinkle with the lemon juice and add the dates which have been cut in thin slices. Top with salad dressing and serve on a bed of lettuce.

Banana Salad

Arrange slices of bananas on lettuce leaves, sprinkle with chopped nut meats and add salad dressing.

White Salad

For an individual salad arrange a slice of pineapple on a lettuce leaf, place 6 white cherries or grapes on top and add the salad dressing. The pits are removed from the cherries and the seeds from the grapes. A marshmallow may be used for decoration.

Fruit Salad

Cut canned pineapple in small cubes and add an equal quantity of white or green grapes or canned white cherries. Cut the grapes in halves and remove the seeds, or if cherries are used, remove the pits. Cut canned pears in small pieces and combine with the other fruits and salad dressing. Chopped nut meats may be sprinkled over the top if one wishes.

Chicken Salad

Cut cold boiled or roasted chicken in ½ inch pieces and add an equal quantity of celery, cut in small pieces, chilled in cold water and dried in a towel. Just before serving moisten with salad dressing and garnish with the yolks of hard cooked eggs pushed through a fine sieve.

Vegetable Salad

Cut 4 hard cooked eggs lengthwise and remove the yolks. Mash the yolks, season with salt and pepper and toss them in a pan containing melted butter. Mix with 1 cupful of cold, cooked peas. Slice the egg whites and sprinkle with salt. Place the egg and pea mixture on them and add salad dressing.

Spinach Salad

Arrange lettuce leaves on salad plates. On these place left-over spinach which has been molded in small molds. Decorate with tiny balls made from seasoned cottage cheese. Serve with salad dressing.

Turkey Salad

Use either chicken or turkey meat. Take 3 cupfuls of the shredded meat, which has been cooked, and combine with 1 cupful of nut meats, 1 cupful of chopped celery or olives and 1 cupful of apple pulp. Mix with salad dressing and serve garnished with bits of cranberry jelly.

Jellied Chicken

Place the scraps of roast turkey or chicken in a saucepan, add any left-over gravy and a little hot water. Cut up and add to

Hard-cooked egg yolks, pressed through a sieve, were revered as a garnish for salads. Sometimes they formed the centers of daisies, with slices of the whites forming the petals.

Spinach was flying high in the twenties on the wings of a wide promotion of its nutritional assets. Featuring the cooked vegetable in salads never won acceptance.

the meat mixture 1 onion and 3 stalks of celery. Cook until these vegetables are tender. Keep them well covered with water during the cookery. Cool, remove the bones and skin and put the meat through a food grinder. Strain the liquid and to every 2 cupfuls add 1 tablespoonful of gelatin, soaking the gelatin first in ½ cupful of cold water. Add the meat to the gelatin and broth mixture and pour into a square dish which is wet first in cold water. Let stand in a cold place until firm. Slice and serve this jelly on a platter surrounded with spoonfuls of cranberry jelly and green olives, or if one wishes, it may be served on salad plates with salad dressing.

Celery Salad

Select large red apples, cut in halves and scoop out the centers, leaving sufficient pulp next to the skin so that the apple cups thus made will stand up. Cut the apple scooped out into bits and combine with an equal amount of diced celery and a few chopped nut meats. Mix with salad dressing and pile in the apple cups.

Salmon Salad

2 cupfuls canned salmon	3 pickles
1 hard cooked egg	salad dressing

Mix salmon, chopped pickle and salad dressing together and serve on lettuce leaves and garnish with slices of egg.

Asparagus Salad

Cut rings from a green pepper or from a lemon about ¼ inch wide. Slip stalks of cold boiled asparagus through every ring and arrange on lettuce leaves. Serve with salad dressing.

Tomato Salad

Peel medium-sized tomatoes and chill. Cut in slices or in eighths, sprinkle with salt and garnish with a spoonful of salad dressing. Serve on a bed of lettuce.

Potato Salad

3 cupfuls cold boiled potatoes	1 small pickle
2 hard cooked eggs	few drops onion juice

Cut the potatoes in small cubes. Chop egg whites and mix with the potatoes and chopped pickle. When cucumbers are in season, use a sliced cucumber instead of the pickle. Mix lightly with salad dressing, arrange on lettuce and garnish with the egg yolks rubbed through a sieve.

Cole Slaw

Select a small, firm head of cabbage and slice very thinly. Soak in cold water until crisp. Then drain and mix with a salad dressing made by combining ½ teaspoonful of salt, ½ teaspoonful of mustard, 2 teaspoonfuls sugar, 1 egg lightly beaten, 3 tablespoonfuls of melted butter, ¾ cupful of cream and ¼ cupful vinegar. Mix the ingredients in the order given, adding the vinegar slowly, and cook over hot water, stirring constantly, until the mixture thickens. Strain, cool and add to the crisp cabbage.

Hot Slaw

Soak ½ firm cabbage head in cold water until crisp. Then cut in thin shreds and heat in a salad dressing made by combining 2 egg yolks, ¼ cupful of water, 1 tablespoonful of butter, ¼ cupful of vinegar and ¾ teaspoonful of salt.

Molded Salmon Salad

2 cupfuls canned salmon	¼ cupful cold water
1¾ teaspoonfuls salt	1 tablespoonful sugar
½ teaspoonful flour	1 teaspoonful ground mustard
¾ cupful milk	2 egg yolks
1 tablespoonful gelatin	4 tablespoonfuls lemon juice
1 tablespoonful butter	

Soak the gelatin in the cold water. Mix the dry ingredients, add the beaten egg yolks, lemon juice or vinegar and the milk. Cook over water, stirring constantly, until the mixture thickens. Remove from the stove, add the butter and the softened gelatin and stir constantly until the gelatin is dissolved. Add the finely flaked salmon, freed from bones and skin, pour into a mold which has been wet in cold water or into individual molds, chill and serve on lettuce leaves.

Women changed the pace of cabbage salad in their meals by a variation in temperature. Hot cabbage tastes quite different from cold and crisp cabbage.

Men called sweet, rich salads like this one perfect "she-food." That was their way of saying it belonged in the refreshments for women's parties.

The canned cherries and pineapple now come in 1 pound, 13 ounce cans. Some people called it Overnight Fruit Salad because they made it one day to serve the next. It was stored in a crock, covered with a plate, in a cold room when there was no icebox in the kitchen. A big bowl of it often made the rounds of the tables in church suppers and company meals. Everyone spooned out his own serving.

Pineapple Salad

Arrange slices of canned pineapple on a salad plate and place three balls made from seasoned cottage cheese on every slice. Sprinkle with chopped nuts and serve with salad dressing.

Mattie's Fruit Salad

2 cupfuls marshmallows	2 tablespoonfuls sugar
1 cup walnut meats	¼ teaspoonful salt
1 cupful whipped cream	1 tablespoonful lemon juice

Cut the marshmallows in halves, mix with the broken nut meats and fold in the stiffly whipped cream to which the sugar, salt and lemon juice have been added. Serve on lettuce leaves.

Dreamland Salad

1 pound shelled walnuts	1 large can of pineapple
1 pound marshmallows	1 large can white cherries

Cut the marshmallows in halves, drain and cut the pineapple into small pieces, drain and seed the cherries. Mix the fruit with the nut meats and serve with Dressing of the Fairies. This salad may be made a day before it is served.

Dressing of the Fairies

1 tablespoonful flour	¼ teaspoonful salt
1 teaspoonful ground mustard	1 egg
1 cupful milk	2 cupfuls heavy cream
1 lemon	

Mix the flour, mustard and salt and dissolve in a little of the milk. Add to the rest of the milk, stir in the egg and cook until thick in a double boiler. Cool and add the whipped cream and the juice of the lemon. This dressing with Dreamland Salad will make 15 servings.

Apple and Cabbage Salad

2 cupfuls shredded cabbage	1 cupful diced apples
1 cupful chopped celery	½ cupful nut meats

Make a nest of the cabbage, combine the other ingredients and arrange on top. Serve with salad dressing.

Farmers' Favorite

3 cupfuls shredded cabbage 1½ cupfuls ground carrots
2 cupfuls chopped celery salad dressing

Combine the ingredients and moisten with salad dressing.

Cucumber Salad

Peel and cut cucumbers in halves lengthwise, then crosswise. Wash little red radishes and slice thinly. Cut slits ¼ inch deep in every section of cucumber and slip the radish slices into these. Serve on lettuce leaves with salad dressing.

Finger Salad

4 bananas 1 lemon
¾ cupful chopped nuts powdered sugar

Skin the bananas and cut the fruit into halves crosswise, then in 4 pieces lengthwise. Roll in powdered sugar and then in the finely chopped nut meats. Cut the lemon in thin slices, dip in sugar and use to garnish the salad. Serve on lettuce leaves with salad dressing.

Cottage Cheese Salad

Moisten cottage cheese with cream. To every 2 cupfuls add 1 small onion chopped fine and 1 crisp cucumber cut in small pieces. Shape into balls and serve on lettuce leaves with salad dressing. Garnish with slices of hard cooked eggs.

Simple but colorful, and always welcome when fried fish or fried chicken occupied the platter.

The delight of children, who almost never had their fill of bananas. Home-grown fruits monopolized the choices for farm homes.

Covering sandwiches with a damp cloth to keep them fresh until serving time no longer is considered desirable. Wrap them in waxed paper and store in the refrigerator.

Most of the sandwiches on this page are surprisingly nourishing. Maple sugar sandwiches may be an exception. They are an outgrowth of slices of homemade bread, spread with butter and sprinkled with brown sugar, which grandmothers for generations made for children who were hungry between meals.

CHAPTER 27

SANDWICHES

THERE are two kinds of sandwiches—those which are cold and those which are hot when served. A sandwich consists of two thin slices of bread or cake, such as angel food or gingerbread, spread with butter and a filling. Usually the filling spreads more easily if it is put through a food grinder and combined with salad dressing, cream or some liquid to make it a paste.

Bread which has been baked 24 hours cuts better than newly baked loaves. Before spreading the butter, it may be placed in a mixing bowl and creamed with a spoon just as it is in cake making. Creamed butter spreads smoothly and easily.

When sandwiches must be made ready several hours before they are to be served, they will keep fresh and moist if placed in a large earthenware or stone crock which is covered with a dish towel wrung as dry as possible from warm water. The wet cloth should not touch any of the sandwiches. In case the towel becomes dry, it should be wrung from hot water the second time. For packing sandwiches in lunch boxes, a wrapping of paraffin paper keeps them fresh for several hours.

SANDWICH FILLINGS

Bean

Mash cold baked beans and mix with a little tomato catchup or salad dressing.

Peanut and Banana

Scrape the pulp of a banana and to every banana used add ¼ cupful of chopped peanuts.

162

Prune

Use thick, cooked prune pulp to which a few chopped nut meats and a few drops of lemon juice are added.

Salmon

Flake the salmon, add a few chopped pickles and moisten with salad dressing.

Egg

Mash yolks of 4 hard cooked eggs with ½ cupful of cottage cheese.

Date

Remove stones from dates, grind the fruit and moisten with jelly.

Beef

Grind 1 cupful of roasted beef with 1 small onion.

Ham

Grind cooked ham with pickles and moisten with salad dressing.

Spinach

Chopped, cooked spinach may be seasoned with lemon juice or a few drops of vinegar and used for a sandwich filling.

Maple Sugar

Use wafer-like slices of maple sugar.

Fruit

Thicken stewed fruit with cornstarch and cool before using.

Celery

Mince celery and combine with seasoned cottage cheese.

Always welcome in school lunchboxes. Frequent accompaniments were cucumber pickles, wrapped in waxed paper, an apple and homemade cookies.

Raisins and Nuts

Chop raisins and nuts together.

Cottage Cheese

Mix cottage cheese, which is seasoned, with nut meats.

Frosting

Use cake frosting mixed with chopped raisins, nuts, dates or figs.

Chopped Date

Use chopped dates moistened with cream.

Raisin Sandwiches

Place the seedless raisins in a double boiler and steam them 5 minutes. Run them through a food grinder, mix with a little lemon juice or cream and spread between thin slices of buttered bread.

Sponge Cake Sandwiches

Spread thin slices of sponge cake with butter and jelly or fruit preserves.

Bean Sandwiches

| 1 cupful baked beans | 1 tablespoonful celery |
| 1 tablespoonful horseradish | 1 teaspoonful onion juice |

Mash the beans and add the prepared horseradish, minced celery and onion juice. Spread between buttered slices of white or Graham bread.

Chicken Sandwiches

| 1 cupful cooked chicken | 1 cupful celery |
| | ¼ cupful salad dressing |

Put the chicken and celery through the food chopper, add the salad dressing and place between buttered slices of bread.

The hostess liked to serve this dessert sandwich with hot tea when neighbors stopped in for an afternoon of visiting.

Chicken Sandwiches

Put cold cooked chicken through a food grinder and moisten with salad dressing. Add a few drops of celery extract or a dash of celery salt.

Fig Sandwiches

Chop 1 cupful of figs and the same amount of nut meats in fine pieces. To this mixture add 1 cupful of cream and 2 tablespoonfuls of lemon juice. Mix thoroughly and spread between thin slices of bread. Dates may be used instead of the figs.

Ice Cream Sandwiches

Bake either a devil's or angel's food cake in loaf form and when cool cut in long strips. Slice through the center and insert a layer of ice cream for filling. Use a warm sauce for covering instead of an icing. Pudding sauces or those used on ice cream are used for this purpose.

Whipped Cream Sandwiches

Spread between thin slices of cake a filling made of whipped cream which has been sweetened and flavored. Chopped nuts or candied fruit may be added to the whipped cream.

Lemon Sandwiches

Mix together 1 cupful of sugar and 2 teaspoonfuls of cornstarch. To this mixture add 1 cupful of water, 1 beaten egg, 2 tablespoonfuls of butter, and the juice and grated rind of 1 lemon. Cook until thick and when cool spread between slices of buttered bread or cake.

Hot Chicken Sandwiches

Stew a chicken until tender. Then remove the meat from the bones and break or clip with the scissors into tiny bits. Run the giblets through the food grinder. Add sufficient broth to the chicken to make it moist. Season well with salt and pepper. Thicken the other portion of the broth with flour, using 1½ tablespoonfuls of flour to every cupful of broth. Boil, season

There was quite a vogue in the early 1920's for chocolate ice cream sandwiches served with coffee for evening refreshments. The cake was chocolate and the filling generally was vanilla ice cream. Hot chocolate sauce was poured over the sandwiches at the last minute.

Lemon filling was kept on hand in the refrigerator in some households, but it never lasted long.

The meat-and-potato tradition was so firmly established that mashed potatoes and gravy usually were served with hot chicken and beef pot roast sandwiches.

All the sandwiches on this page are substantial and were the kind men liked. Hot ham sandwiches, cream of tomato soup and baked apples composed a supper menu that won approval.

with salt and pepper and add a dash of celery salt. Place the warm chicken on a slice of bread, cover with another slice of bread and then add some hot gravy. This served on a plate with mashed potatoes and a pickle makes good refreshments for a social or party. A large hen will make at least 36 sandwiches.

Pork Sandwiches

Arrange thin slices of broiled bacon on thinly sliced bread. Cover this with slices of cold roast pork. Drain a piece of firm canned tomato and place on top of the pork and cover with a thin slice of buttered bread.

Sausage Sandwiches

Cut cooked sausage cakes in thin slices and spread on buttered bread. Place minced celery over the sausage and add the covering of buttered bread.

Pork Chop Sandwiches

Bone the chops and dip in a batter made by thickening a little milk with flour. Sauté until thoroughly cooked and brown. Then place between buttered slices of bread. Onions, sliced thinly, may be inserted in the sandwich if one desires.

Hot Ham Sandwiches

Take small pieces of cooked ham or pork and force through the food grinder. Mix with sufficient salad dressing or mustard to hold the mixture together and spread thinly on slices of buttered bread. Dip every sandwich in a batter made by beating an egg and adding ½ cupful of milk. Season this with ½ teaspoonful of salt. Brown the sandwiches on both sides in a hot frying pan. Serve while hot with syrup.

Ham and Egg Sandwiches

On a slice of buttered and toasted bread place a thin slice of fried ham. Add a little mustard and cover with a slice of buttered toast. Place a fried egg on top of the sandwich and serve hot for supper or breakfast.

CHAPTER 28

SAUCES

An old saying which has considerable truth in it is: "A cook is known by the sauces she makes." It takes effort to prepare a smooth, properly blended sauce, but of all culinary creations it can do more toward making the ordinary dish toothsome than anything else.

White sauces to combine with different foods are of great value, as are sweet sauces, sometimes colored with fruit juice, which are served with puddings, ice cream and other desserts. Many a meat and fish dish is lifted above the commonplace by the use of a savory sauce.

White Sauce for Cream Soups

1 cupful milk	½ teaspoonful salt
1 tablespoonful flour	1 tablespoonful butter

Scald the milk and stir into it the butter and flour which have been blended together. Add the salt and cook, stirring constantly, until the sauce thickens. Combine equal portions of this sauce and the pulp of the vegetable or food to be used in making cream soup.

White Sauce for Creamed Dishes

1 cupful milk	½ teaspoonful salt
2 tablespoonfuls flour	2 tablespoonfuls butter

Scald the milk and stir into it the butter and flour which have been blended together. Add the salt and cook, stirring constantly, until the sauce thickens. Use equal portions of sauce and food to be creamed. Pour the sauce over the food and if necessary, reheat.

The badge of a good cook 50 years ago depended on the smoothness of her white sauce.

White Sauce for Scalloped Dishes

Use the white sauce for creamed dishes and an equal amount of food. Place alternate layers of the sauce and food in a greased baking dish. Cover with buttered crumbs and brown in the oven.

White Sauce for Soufflés

1 cupful milk	½ teaspoonful salt
3 tablespoonfuls flour	3 tablespoonfuls butter

Scald the milk and stir into it the butter which has been mixed thoroughly with the flour. Add the salt. Cook, stirring constantly, until the sauce thickens. Use equal portions of sauce and food for a soufflé, using 3 eggs to every cupful of sauce. Add the egg yolks to the sauce, stir in the food and fold in the stiffly beaten egg whites. Bake in a buttered baking dish set in a pan of water.

White Sauce for Croquettes

1 cupful milk	½ teaspoonful salt
4 tablespoonfuls flour	4 tablespoonfuls butter

Scald the milk and stir into it the butter which has been mixed thoroughly with the flour. Add the salt. Cook, stirring constantly, until the sauce thickens. In making croquettes use equal portions of the sauce and food. Mix and cool. Shape, roll in crumbs, and then in egg and crumbs. Fry and drain.

Parsley Sauce

4 tablespoonfuls butter	4 teaspoonfuls chopped parsley
4 teaspoonfuls lemon juice	½ teaspoonful salt

Cream butter with a spoon, add parsley and salt. Add the lemon juice slowly. Place on steak or other food and allow the butter to melt.

Egg Sauce

Make the white sauce for creamed dishes and add to it 2 hard cooked eggs chopped in fine pieces and 2 teaspoonfuls of minced parsley. Serve with fish.

Decorative and delicious on sizzling hot steak. Sauce adds just the right touch to hot, boiled new potatoes, which many countrywomen used to start serving when the tubers growing in the garden were the size of large marbles.

Cucumber Sauce

Grind 2 cucumbers, after washing and peeling them, drain, season with salt, pepper and vinegar and serve with fried fish or meat.

Tomato Sauce

2 tablespoonfuls butter	½ teaspoonful salt
1 tablespoonful chopped onion	½ teaspoonful sugar
3 tablespoonfuls flour	¼ teaspoonful pepper
2 cupfuls strained canned tomatoes	

Melt the butter, add the onion and cook gently a few minutes; add the flour and seasonings and gradually stir in the tomato. Bring the mixture to the boiling point, stirring occasionally. Let boil a moment or two and serve with meat.

Tomato Sauce

When tomatoes are ripe, this recipe may be used. Mince fine or put through the food grinder a slice of salt pork. Fry this until it is a light brown. Then add 1 small onion, finely chopped, and 1 tablespoonful of chopped carrot, 2 teaspoonfuls of chopped turnip and 1 tablespoonful of chopped sweet pepper. Brown the vegetables lightly and add to them 6 cupfuls of un-peeled, but sliced, tomatoes, 2 cloves, a sprig of parsley, ½ bay leaf and a small stalk of celery cut in bits. A little celery salt may be used if the vegetable itself is not available. Simmer 45 minutes. Rub through a sieve or colander and thicken with 1½ tablespoonfuls of flour dissolved in a little water.

Chocolate Sauce

2 squares chocolate	1 cupful boiling water
1½ cupfuls sugar	2 tablespoonfuls butter
1 teaspoonful vanilla	

Melt the chocolate over hot water, add butter and gradually add the water. Boil 15 minutes, add the vanilla and serve while warm or when cold on ice cream.

Hot Cocoa Sauce

2 tablespoonfuls cocoa	½ teaspoonful salt
1 cupful sugar	1 teaspoonful vanilla
1½ cupfuls water	1 tablespoonful cornstarch

For a glossy sauce, include corn syrup in the ingredients. Over low heat cook 2 squares unsweetened chocolate and ½ cup water, stirring constantly until thick, about 2 minutes. Remove from heat; gradually add 1½ cups light corn syrup and a dash of salt. Simmer 10 minutes, stirring frequently. Remove from heat, stir in 1 tsp. vanilla. Serve warm or cold on ice cream or slices of unfrosted cake.

Boil the water and sugar together 2 minutes, add the cornstarch mixed in a little cold water. Add the cocoa which has been mixed with a little warm water and boil 3 minutes. Add salt and vanilla. Remove from the fire and serve while hot on ice cream.

Date and Nut Sauce

4 tablespoonfuls dates	½ cupful sugar
4 tablespoonfuls nuts	1 teaspoonful vanilla
1 cupful water	½ teaspoonful salt

Chop the dates and boil them with the sugar and water until the liquid makes a syrup. Remove from the stove, cool, add nuts and vanilla and serve on ice cream.

Brittle Nut Sauce

1 cupful sugar	1 cupful nut meats

Caramelize the sugar by placing it in a pan and heating on the stove, stirring constantly. Do not add any water. When the mass becomes light brown in color and is melted, add the nuts and pour into an oiled pan. When cold, roll until very fine and sprinkle on top of ice cream.

Hot Fudge Sauce

2 squares chocolate	1 tablespoonful butter
2 cupfuls water	2 tablespoonfuls cold water
1½ cupfuls sugar	1 teaspoonful vanilla
2 teaspoonfuls cornstarch	⅛ teaspoonful salt

Mix the grated chocolate, water and sugar together and cook until the sugar is dissolved and the chocolate is melted. Then add the cornstarch which is mixed with the cold water and butter. Boil 3 minutes, stirring constantly. Add the salt and flavoring. Serve either warm or cold on ice cream or pudding.

PUDDING SAUCES

Vanilla Sauce

1 cupful boiling water	½ cupful sugar
1 tablespoonful cornstarch	1 teaspoonful vanilla
2 tablespoonfuls butter	⅛ teaspoonful salt

Every woman had her own tricks in altering this basic sauce. Sometimes a dash of grated nutmeg was added with the vanilla. Another custom was to omit vanilla and add sherry wine to taste.

Combine the cornstarch, sugar and salt and mix thoroughly. Gradually pour in the boiling water, add the butter, stirring constantly, bring to the boiling point and boil for 5 minutes. Then add vanilla and serve hot.

Lemon Sauce

1½ cupfuls boiling water	¾ cupful sugar
1½ tablespoonfuls cornstarch	2 tablespoonfuls butter
2 tablespoonfuls lemon juice	grated rind of ¼ lemon

Combine the dry ingredients, add the boiling water, stirring constantly, the melted butter and the lemon rind. Boil 5 minutes. Remove from fire, add lemon juice and serve hot.

Nutmeg Sauce

1¼ cupfuls boiling water	⅔ cupful sugar
1¼ tablespoonfuls flour	½ teaspoonful nutmeg
1½ tablespoonfuls butter	⅛ teaspoonful salt

Combine the flour, sugar and salt and stir constantly while adding the boiling water. Add the melted butter and boil 5 minutes. Remove from the stove and add the nutmeg. Serve while hot.

Chocolate Fudge Sauce

2 squares chocolate	1½ cupfuls milk
2 tablespoonfuls butter	2 tablespoonfuls flour
2 cupfuls sugar	1 teaspoonful vanilla
	⅛ teaspoonful salt

Melt the butter and stir in the flour and salt. Gradually add half of the milk, stirring constantly. Melt the chocolate over water, add the sugar and the rest of the milk to it, stir and cook together until a syrup is made. Then combine the mixtures and cook gently for 5 minutes or until the mixture is quite thick.

Caramel Sauce

1 cupful sugar	1 tablespoonful cornstarch
2¼ cupfuls boiling water	½ teaspoonful vanilla
1 tablespoonful butter	⅛ teaspoonful salt

Caramelize the sugar in a frying pan, that is, melt it over the fire by stirring it until light brown in color. Do not add any water until the sugar is melted. Then add the boiling water and

Revised recipe. Combine in saucepan 1 cup sugar, ½ cup butter, ¼ cup water, 1 well-beaten egg, ¼ tsp. grated lemon peel and 3 tblsp. lemon juice. Heat to a boil, stirring constantly. Two favored ways to serve this sauce in the twenties were on gingerbread and angel-food cake. Puffs of whipped cream were dropped on top of each dessert serving when there was company.

Perfect on apple dumplings.

For an easier, delectable butterscotch sauce, bring ½ cup light corn syrup, 1½ cups brown sugar, firmly packed, and ¼ cup butter to a boil over low heat, stirring constantly. Remove from heat and stir in ½ cup heavy cream and 1 tsp. vanilla. Stir before serving. Delightful topping for vanilla ice cream.

Make this with strawberries and you have Strawberry Hard Sauce. Delectable on piping hot waffles.

cook until the sugar is dissolved. Add the melted butter, cornstarch and salt which have been creamed together. Boil 3 minutes, add the vanilla and serve hot.

Brown Sugar Sauce

¼ cupful cream	1 cupful brown sugar
¾ teaspoonful vanilla	½ cupful butter

Cream the butter and sugar together and add the cream gradually. Add the vanilla, heat slightly and beat thoroughly before serving.

Fruit Sauce

4 tablespoonfuls butter	1 cupful fruit
1 cupful powdered sugar	1 teaspoonful lemon juice
2 tablespoonfuls cream	¼ teaspoonful vanilla
⅛ teaspoonful salt	

Cream the butter and beat in the sugar and cream alternately. Add the salt and slowly stir in the fruit. Then add the lemon juice and flavoring. Crushed berries or peaches or canned berries, pineapple, peaches, berries or apricots may be used, but they should be cut in small pieces before being added.

Hard Sauce

6 tablespoonfuls butter	2 tablespoonfuls cream
3 cupfuls powdered sugar	¾ teaspoonful vanilla

Cream the butter with a spoon and add the sugar, a little at a time, then stir in the flavoring and the cream. Chopped nuts or shredded cocoanut may be added. Serve on a hot pudding or apple pie.

Berry Butter

4 tablespoonfuls butter	1 cupful powdered sugar
¼ cupful crushed berries	

Cream the butter with a spoon and add the powdered sugar gradually, stirring constantly. Add the berries, a few at a time, beating all the while. Set in a cold place until used. Strawberries and red raspberries make a delicious butter, as do crushed peaches.

Foamy Egg Sauce

1 egg	½ cupful whipped cream
½ cupful powdered sugar	1½ tablespoonfuls milk
¾ teaspoonful vanilla	⅛ teaspoonful salt

Beat the egg white until stiff and dry and beat in the powdered sugar. When smooth, add the vanilla and the egg yolk, beaten until light and lemon colored. Then stir in the milk and serve at once.

Cider Sauce

1 cupful sweet cider	2 tablespoonfuls lemon juice
½ cupful sugar	

Boil the ingredients together 3 minutes. Serve hot with any plum pudding.

Soup kettles bubbled frequently in country kitchens when the first *Farm Cook and Rule Book* was published. Women made their own soups from scratch. Steaming bowls came to the table when the first frosty evenings arrived in autumn and appeared frequently until lettuce, green onions and tiny radishes were ready in the spring garden.

Heat 2½ cups canned tomatoes with 1 small bay leaf, 1 slice onion, 2 whole cloves and salt and pepper to taste. Simmer 10 minutes; strain. Make white sauce with 2 cups milk, 2 tblsp. each flour and butter. Just before serving soup, slowly pour hot tomatoes into hot White Sauce, stirring constantly. Do not reheat.

CHAPTER 29

SOUPS, CHOWDERS AND DUMPLINGS

THE two most commonly used soups are those made from meat stock and those including white sauce (thickened milk) for a foundation. Broth is the liquid in which meat is cooked after it is strained and seasoned. A chowder is a very thick soup; it is in reality an unstrained stew made by combining cut fish, meat and vegetables with milk.

Stock soups and broth are best adapted to use as the first course in a meal, while the cream soups and chowders, on account of their great food value, should be served as the main dish in an otherwise light meal. Cream soups are of great value in the diet of the child because they contain so much milk.

Cream Soups

Use equal portions of the White Sauce for Cream Soups, the recipe for which is given in the chapter on Sauces, and the pulp of the vegetable or food to be used in making the soup. Combine and heat.

Cream of Tomato Soup

1½ cupfuls white sauce	speck baking soda
1½ cupfuls tomato juice and pulp	2 cloves
	1 bay leaf

Add the cloves and bay leaf to the tomatoes and bring to a boil. After boiling a minute or two, add a tiny speck of soda and strain. Pour the tomato juice and pulp into the white sauce, stirring constantly. Reheat at once. Avoid bringing to a boil. Whip with a Dover egg beater and serve at once. Use the recipe for White Sauce for Cream Soups which is given in the chapter on Sauces.

174

Oyster Stew

2 cupfuls oysters
1 quart milk
¼ cupful butter
salt
pepper

Clean and drain oysters. Add liquor to the scalded milk and stir in the butter and seasonings to taste. Bring to the boiling point, add oysters and serve.

Chili Con Carni

2 cupfuls chili beans
¾ pound lean beef
½ cupful suet
2 teaspoonfuls salt
4 cupfuls tomatoes
3 small onions
1 tablespoonful chili powder
4 cupfuls water

Cook the beans in water and when tender, mash slightly. Force the onions, meat and suet through the food grinder. Place the suet in a frying pan on the stove and when the fat is rendered, add the onions, meat and chili powder. Fry 5 minutes, Then turn into a kettle with the beans and canned tomatoes, add the salt and the boiling water. Let cook slowly 4 hours. One may use more chili pepper if a hotter dish is desired.

Peanut Butter Soup

4 cupfuls milk
½ cupful peanut butter
2 teaspoonfuls salt
⅛ teaspoonful pepper

Scald the milk, add the peanut butter and seasonings and serve.

Pea Soup

3 cupfuls peas
1 quart milk
2 tablespoonfuls flour
2 tablespoonfuls butter
1 teaspoonful salt
⅛ teaspoonful pepper
few drops onion juice

Press the stewed peas through a sieve. Thicken the milk with flour, add the butter and seasonings and the peas.   Serve piping hot.

Potato Soup

3 potatoes
2 cupfuls water
1 slice onion
½ cupful chopped celery
2 tablespoonfuls butter
1 bay leaf
⅛ teaspoonful pepper
1 quart milk
2 tablespoonfuls flour

Girls studying home economics in the aftermath of World War I included this soup in many of their menus to provide protein. They influenced their mothers back on the farm to do the same.

Pare the large potatoes and cut in cubes. Cover with the boiling water, add the onion, chopped celery or ½ teaspoonful of celery salt, the bay leaf and pepper. Cook until the vegetables are tender. Press through a colander. Heat the milk and add the flour and butter which have been mixed together. Add the potato mixture and cook until the soup thickens slightly. Stir constantly after the flour is added.

Sweet Potato Soup

Use sweet potatoes instead of Irish potatoes and follow the directions for Potato Soup.

Pumpkin Soup

Use pumpkin instead of potatoes and follow the directions for Potato Soup.

Squash Soup

Use Hubbard squash instead of potatoes and follow the directions for Potato Soup.

Vegetable Soup

2 tablespoonfuls chopped onion	1 quart milk
1 tablespoonful butter	2 tablespoonfuls flour
1 small carrot	1 level teaspoonful salt
2 cupfuls diced turnips	speck pepper

Cook the onion in the butter until it is a delicate yellow in color, then add the chopped carrot and turnips. Cover and cook on the back of the range 30 minutes. Force through a colander. Thicken the heated milk with the flour dissolved in a little of the cold milk, add the salt and pepper and the vegetable mixture.

Lima Bean Soup

2 cupfuls beans	1 bay leaf
1 quart milk	2 teaspoonfuls grated onion
2 tablespoonfuls cornstarch	1 teaspoonful salt
¼ teaspoonful pepper	

Cook the beans in a little water until they are tender. Press them through a colander. Place the milk in a double boiler and add the cornstarch dissolved in a little of the milk. Add the

Use dried lima beans. They were a staple in most country kitchens.

other ingredients and cook in the double boiler until the soup thickens.

Cabbage Soup

1 quart chopped cabbage	speck pepper
2 tablespoonfuls chopped onion	1 quart water
1 teaspoonful celery salt	2 cupfuls milk
1 teaspoonful salt	2 tablespoonfuls butter
	2 tablespoonfuls flour

Chop the cabbage and cook in the quart of boiling water until tender. Rub through a sieve. Add the other ingredients, the butter and flour having been mixed together, and cook until the mixture thickens a little.

Spinach Soup

1 quart spinach	2 tablespoonfuls flour
½ cupful water	2 tablespoonfuls butter
1 tablespoonful chopped onion	½ teaspoonful celery salt
1 quart milk	dash of pepper

Steam the spinach in the water 15 minutes. Chop and push through a colander. Return to a kettle with the liquid in which it cooked and add the other ingredients, having the butter and flour mixed together. Cook until the mixture thickens slightly and serve piping hot.

Onion Soup

4 onions	2 cupfuls cold water
2 slices bacon	1½ cupfuls milk
1 tablespoonful flour	1 teaspoonful salt
	⅛ teaspoonful pepper

Select medium-sized onions, slice and cook gently with the bacon until the onions are a very light brown. Then add the cold water and boil until the onions are so tender that they may be mashed with a spoon. Add the salt, pepper, flour and milk, dissolving the flour in a small portion of the milk. Boil 3 minutes and serve.

Celery Soup

2 cupfuls milk	2 cupfuls diced celery
1 tablespoonful flour	2 cupfuls water
1 large slice of onion	1 teaspoonful salt

Boil the celery in the water 40 minutes, heat the milk to which the onion has been added and stir in the flour and butter which

To sell this soup to their families, many farm women scattered plenty of grated cheese over the tops of the hot soup in bowls. The rule was to use scraps of hard cheese which otherwise might be wasted.

have been blended together. Add the celery and the salt. Strain and serve.

Brown Beef Stock

5 pounds shin of beef	½ cupful carrots
3 quarts cold water	½ cupful turnips
6 cloves	½ cupful onions
½ bay leaf	½ cupful celery
2 sprigs parsley	1 cupful tomatoes

Wipe the beef with a damp cloth and cut the lean portion in 1-inch pieces. Brown half of the meat in a hot frying pan in a little butter, and put the other half with the bone and fat in the soup kettle with the cold water. Let stand 1 hour. Then place on the cool part of the range, add the browned meat and heat gradually to the boiling point. Cover and cook 6 hours. Keep below the boiling point during the cooking. Add the vegetables cut in small pieces, cook 1½ hours and strain. Before serving add salt to taste.

Tomato Soup

2 cupfuls beef stock	2 tablespoonfuls flour
2 cupfuls stewed tomatoes	⅛ teaspoonful celery salt
1 green pepper	1 teaspoonful salt
2 tablespoonfuls butter	⅛ teaspoonful pepper

Add the strained tomatoes to the seasoned stock and then stir in the thinly sliced pepper. Simmer 20 minutes. Add the butter and flour mixed together and stir in the seasonings. Cook until the mixture thickens, stirring constantly.

Chicken Soup

2 quarts chicken broth	1 sprig parsley
1 slice carrot	6 egg yolks
1 slice onion	1 teaspoonful salt
1 stalk celery	¼ teaspoonful pepper
	1 cupful hot cream

Cook the chicken broth with the vegetables 15 minutes. Strain over the slightly beaten egg yolks and stir over hot water until the mixture thickens. Add the other ingredients just before serving.

Stir 3 to 4 tblsp. hot broth into slightly beaten egg yolks and then slowly add hot broth to them, stirring constantly. This helps to make smooth soup.

Corn Chowder

1 quart potatoes	1½ cupfuls corn
1 quart boiling water	1 cupful milk
¼ pound salt pork	⅛ teaspoonful pepper
1 medium-sized onion	salt

10 crackers

Pare and slice the potatoes and parboil them in water. Try the fat from the pork. Chop the onion into bits and brown in the fat. Add the fat to the boiling water, stir in the potatoes and corn and cook until the vegetables are tender. Add either cream or milk and season to taste. Reheat and pour over the crackers.

Boston Chowder

¼ pound salt pork, diced	4½ cupfuls milk
1 medium-sized onion, sliced	2 tablespoonfuls butter
2 cupfuls potatoes, diced	8 crackers
2½ cupfuls water	2 teaspoonfuls salt
1½ cupfuls parsnips, diced	½ teaspoonful pepper

Try the fat from the salt pork and cook the onions in it. Then add the potatoes, parsnips and boiling water and cook until tender. Add the milk and seasonings and pour over the crackers.

Fish Chowder

1 cupful fish, diced	4 cupfuls potatoes, diced
¼ pound salt pork, diced	1 cupful milk
1 medium-sized onion, sliced	2 teaspoonfuls salt
4 cupfuls fish stock	½ teaspoonful pepper

8 crackers

Clean and bone the fish and cut in small pieces. Boil in water, saving the stock. Parboil the potatoes and drain. Try the fat from the pork. Brown the onion in the fat and add to the stock. Add the potatoes and fish and cook until tender. Then add the milk and seasonings and pour over the crackers.

DUMPLINGS

Plain Dumplings

2 cupfuls flour	½ teaspoonful salt
4 teaspoonfuls baking powder	⅔ cupful milk

2 tablespoonfuls fat

Sift the dry ingredients together, work in the fat and add the milk gradually to make a soft dough. Roll out ½ inch thick

Use bacon instead of salt pork and canned whole-kernel corn, unavailable when this book first appeared, or leftover cooked corn cut from cobs.

No need to roll out dough. Make it soft enough to drop from spoon on to vegetables, meat, chicken or other solid food in hot soup. New way to cook dumplings is to leave the kettle uncovered the first 10 minutes, then cover and cook 10 minutes longer.

Combine 1 egg, beaten, 2 tblsp. milk, ½ tsp. salt and enough flour to make a stiff dough. Knead 3 minutes. Roll paper-thin and place between towels until partially dry. Roll up like Jelly Roll and cut crosswise to make strips of the desired width, usually ⅛ to ¼ inch wide. Shake out and let dry at least 2 hours. When ready to cook, break in pieces.

and cut with a biscuit cutter. Cook about 15 minutes with soup stock or with a meat stew. Do not lift the kettle lid during the cooking.

Cornmeal Dumplings

1 cupful cornmeal	½ teaspoonful salt
1 cupful white flour	1 beaten egg
4 teaspoonfuls baking powder	milk

Sift the dry ingredients, add the beaten egg and sufficient milk to make a soft dough. Let stand a few minutes. Then drop by spoonfuls into a boiling stew or soup, cover and cook 20 minutes.

Noodles

2 eggs	1 teaspoonful salt
	flour

Beat the eggs and add flour enough to make a very stiff dough. Knead thoroughly 3 minutes, divide the dough into two parts and roll each one into a thin sheet. Cover and let stand until dry. Then cut in narrow strips, drop in broth or stock and boil rapidly 20 minutes.

CHAPTER 30

VEGETABLES

VEGETABLES should be firm and crisp when made ready for cooking. If they are wilted, they may be freshened by soaking in cold water a few hours or by being wrapped in a damp cloth and set in a cold place. The method of cooking varies with the different varieties, so no general rules can be given.

The water or liquor in which vegetables are cooked should always be saved and used. If it is not possible to boil down the liquor so that it can be served with the vegetable dish, it may be drained off and used in soup or gravy. This liquid contains much food value since the soluble food substances in the vegetables dissolve into it during the cookery and are lost if thrown away.

Oven Fried Potatoes

Wash and pare small potatoes. Cut in eights lengthwise and place in an oiled dripping pan. Sprinkle with salt and pepper and dot with small pieces of lard or other cooking fat. Set in a hot oven and cook until tender.

Pickled Beets

12 medium-sized beets
3 cupfuls vinegar

1 teaspoonful salt
⅔ cupful sugar

Heat vinegar to the boiling point, add the sugar and salt and pour the mixture over the boiled beets. Let stand until ready to serve.

Boiled Beets

Cut tops from beets, leaving 1½ inches of stem. Wash, boil until tender and drain. When cool, remove the skin and cut off the roots. Serve with butter, adding salt to taste.

181

Cook in water to cover from ½ to 1 hour, or until tender. Cooking time depends on age of vegetable.

Vegetable cookery has changed greatly during the last 50 years. Cooking time has been shortened and less water is used to boil vegetables. The general rule is to pour 1 inch of water into the saucepan, add ½ tsp. salt for every cup of water, bring to a boil, add prepared vegetable and cook only until tender. With some vegetables, such as cauliflower, broccoli, green beans and carrots, cook only until tender-crisp.

Soak potatoes cut in thin strips 1 hour in cold salted water. Drain and dry thoroughly. Spread in greased shallow pan and brush with melted butter or drippings. Bake in a very hot oven (450° F.) about 25 minutes, basting occasionally with extra fat. Season with salt and serve.

Combine in saucepan 1 cup water, 1 cup vinegar, 2 tblsp. brown or white sugar, ½ tsp. salt, 1 tsp. ground cinnamon and ¼ tsp. ground cloves. Heat to boiling and pour over 1 quart cooked, sliced beets. Cool and cover. Let stand overnight in refrigerator before serving.

String Beans Vingrette

Melt 1 tablespoonful of fat and add 1 tablespoonful of flour, 1 teaspoonful of salt and ¼ teaspoonful of pepper. When thoroughly mixed, pour on ¼ cupful of vinegar and ½ cupful of the liquor from canned beans or the liquid in which fresh beans were cooked. Add 1 teaspoonful of sugar and boil. Stir in 2 cupfuls of canned or cooked string beans and serve while hot.

Buttered Asparagus

Cut off the lower parts of the stalks as far down as they snap. Wash and cook in boiling salted water 20 minutes or until the asparagus is tender. Drain and spread with butter, using 1½ tablespoonfuls of butter to every cupful of asparagus.

Cook 6 to 10 minutes, or until tender.

Buttered Spinach

Remove the roots, pick over and wash the spinach, making certain that all the sand is removed. Place in a saucepan and let the spinach cook in its own juices 25 minutes, or if there is not sufficient juice for this purpose, add a small amount of water. Cook until all the water or liquid has evaporated and then season with salt, pepper and butter. Buttered spinach is made attractive by garnishing with slices of hard cooked eggs.

Cook, covered, 5 to 10 minutes, stirring occasionally.

Buttered Peas

Drain canned or stewed peas and season with salt, pepper and butter.

Creamed Potatoes

Boil or steam the potatoes until tender. Cool and cut in dice. Melt some butter in a saucepan and place the potatoes in this. Toss until the cubes are coated thoroughly with the butter. Then pour over a white sauce made by thickening milk with flour, using 2 tablespoonfuls of flour to every cupful of milk and 1 cupful of milk to the same amount of potatoes. Add salt and pepper to taste.

Stuffed Green Peppers

Cut off the stem end of large green peppers and parboil 10 minutes in boiling water. Drain, cool and stuff with creamed potatoes. Sprinkle bread crumbs over the top and brown in the oven 15 minutes.

Remove all seeds and membranes from inside of peppers. Parboil in boiling salted water to cover 5 minutes. Heat potatoes before adding to parboiled peppers to shorten baking time. Bake in moderate oven (350°F.) until heated throughout.

Turnips Delicious

Select young turnips, pare and boil whole in meat stock until tender. Drain and save the stock. Place the turnips in a buttered casserole, sprinkle with sugar, salt, nutmeg and dots of butter. Boil down stock and pour into the casserole. Bake until the turnips are slightly browned.

Cook whole turnips in boiling salted water 20 to 30 minutes, cubes or slices 9 to 20 minutes, or until tender.

Sweet Potatoes en Casserole

5 large sweet potatoes	3 tablespoonfuls butter
4 ripe apples	½ cupful brown sugar
1½ teaspoonfuls salt	½ cupful hot water

Boil the sweet potatoes until tender. Cool and remove the skins. Cut in thin slices. Slice the ripe apples thinly, after paring and removing the cores, and arrange alternate layers of the apples and sweet potatoes in a buttered casserole. Sprinkle every layer with brown sugar, salt and dots of butter. After adding the last layer, which should be of potatoes, add the hot water and bake in a hot oven until the apples are cooked and the top is neatly browned.

Cover and bake in moderate oven (350°F.) about 50 minutes.

French Fried Potatoes

Pare the potatoes, cut them in halves lengthwise, and then in pieces like the section of an orange. Let stand in cold water an hour or longer, then dry on a soft cloth. Fry in hot fat until a rich straw color on both sides and tender throughout. Drain on soft paper, sprinkle with salt and serve at once. The fat is hot enough to use when a small cube of bread browns in it in 20 seconds.

Two-step method. Fry a small amount of potatoes at a time in deep fat heated to 375° until very light brown. Drain, on paper towels, cool and refrigerate. When ready to serve, reheat potatoes in deep fat heated to 375° until golden brown and crisp, 3 to 5 minutes. Drain, sprinkle with salt and serve at once.

Beets in Sour Sauce

12 small beets	½ tablespoonful cornstarch
½ cupful sugar	½ cupful vinegar
	2 tablespoonfuls butter

No need to let stand before serving, a custom followed on wood- and coal-burning stoves.

Cover pan and bake in moderate oven (350°F.) 45 to 60 minutes, or until tender. Remove cover during last part of cooking to brown.

Remove any layers of loose skin from onions. Cook in 1 inch salted water until just tender, about 10 minutes. Drain. To the hot sauce made with remaining ingredients, add 1 cup shredded process American cheese. Stir until cheese melts. Place onions in serving dish, pour on cheese sauce and sprinkle with bits of crisp bacon, buttered bread crumbs or chopped peanuts.

Wash beets and cook in boiling water until soft or use canned beets. Remove skins and cut beets in small cubes. Mix sugar and cornstarch, add vinegar and boil 5 minutes. Pour over beets and let stand on the back of the stove 30 minutes. Just before serving add the butter.

Stuffed Cabbage

Select a medium-sized head of cabbage and wash thoroughly. Separate the leaves and remove the center. Fasten into shape or tie in a piece of cheesecloth and steam or simmer until tender. Fill the center with cooked hamburg balls and surround with tomato sauce.

Bessie's Potatoes

8 medium-sized potatoes	2 tablespoonfuls hot water
2 onions	½ teaspoonful salt
4 tablespoonfuls butter	¼ teaspoonful pepper

Wash, pare and quarter the potatoes. Make an incision in each potato and fill with onion. Put in a baking pan and pour the water and butter mixture over them. Cook in a hot oven, basting frequently.

Creamed Onions

8 medium-sized onions	2 tablespoonfuls butter
1½ tablespoonfuls flour	1 cupful milk
½ teaspoonful salt	⅛ teaspoonful pepper

Peel the onions and put in a pan, covering them with salted boiling water. Boil 5 minutes, drain and again cover with boiling water. Cook until soft, drain and break into small pieces. Add to a sauce made by melting the butter in a small pan and adding the flour, salt and pepper, stirring the mixture until it is thoroughly blended. The milk is poured in gradually, having been scalded previously, and the mixture is stirred constantly. Beat until smooth and glossy and serve at once.

Escalloped Tomatoes

3 cupfuls canned tomatoes	1 teaspoonful salt
1 tablespoonful onion juice	¼ teaspoonful pepper
1 cupful bread crumbs	2 tablespoonfuls butter

Cover the bottom of a buttered baking dish with a layer of tomato, then add salt, butter and cover with buttered bread crumbs. Repeat until all the ingredients are used, having the top layer of bread crumbs. Bake in a hot oven until brown or about 15 minutes.

Glazed Carrots

6 medium-sized carrots	4 tablespoonfuls butter
	4 tablespoonfuls sugar

Wash and scrape 3 medium-sized carrots; cook in boiling salted water, allowing 1 teaspoonful of salt to 4 cupfuls of water and using a small amount of liquid and a covered utensil in order that the natural flavor be retained. When cooked, drain and cut in slices. For the glaze melt the butter in a frying pan, add the sugar and when it is melted, toss the cooked carrots in it until slightly browned and glazed.

Wash and scrape 6 medium carrots, not 4. Slice and cook in boiling salted water 10 to 20 minutes, or until tender. Drain and glaze.

Steamed Squash

Steam or boil squash cut in small pieces. Drain and dry. Mash and put through a sieve or ricer. To every cupful of squash add 1 teaspoonful of butter, ¼ teaspoonful of salt, ⅛ teaspoonful of pepper and 1 tablespoonful of cream. Beat until light and fluffy.

Cook serving-size pieces of Hubbard squash in 1 inch boiling salted water, 25 to 30 minutes, or until tender. Drain.

Glazed Sweet Potatoes

6 large sweet potatoes	½ cupful sugar
2 tablespoonfuls butter	3 tablespoonfuls water

Wash and pare potatoes. Cook 10 minutes in boiling salted water. Drain, cut in halves lengthwise and put in buttered pans. Make a syrup by boiling the sugar and water 3 minutes; add butter and brush the potatoes with it. Bake 15 minutes, basting twice with some of the syrup saved for this purpose.

Place cooked sweet potatoes, cut lengthwise in half, in single layer in greased pan. Make a syrup by combining ½ to 3/4 cup brown sugar with ¼ cup water and heating to boiling. Pour over sweet potatoes and bake in slow oven (300°F.) until potatoes are glazed, about 40 minutes. Turn once while baking.

Sweet Corn Delicious

8 ears corn	2 cupfuls milk
4 tablespoonfuls butter	1 teaspoonful salt
	⅛ teaspoonful pepper

Cut the kernels from the cobs and place in a frying pan with the butter. Cook 12 minutes, then add the milk, salt and pepper. As soon as the milk is hot, the corn is ready to be served.

Reduce milk to 1½ cups.

Once a great favorite of Wisconsin and Minnesota lumberjacks, who used dried corn. This recipe calls for canned cream-style corn.

Badger Squaw Dish

½ pound bacon	½ teaspoonful salt
1¾ cupfuls canned corn	¼ teaspoonful pepper

Cut the sliced bacon in tiny squares and brown in a frying pan. When delicately browned, pour off some of the fat, leaving 5 or 6 tablespoonfuls in the pan. Add the corn, salt and pepper and cook 5 minutes. Serve hot.

Corn with Ham

1 cupful corn	1 egg
4 cupfuls chopped ham	⅛ teaspoonful pepper

Combine the ham and corn and mix the egg and pepper into the mixture. Form into little cakes and brown on both sides in a frying pan containing a little bacon fat.

Lima Beans Delicious

2 cupfuls lima beans	1 cupful milk
¼ pound sliced bacon	1 teaspoonful salt
2 medium-sized onions	½ teaspoonful pepper

Brown the bacon, remove from the frying pan and cook the chopped onions in the fat until tender. Then combine all the ingredients, place in a greased casserole and bake in a slow oven until the beans are tender, adding more milk if it is needed.

Baked Cabbage

2 cupfuls boiled cabbage	1 cupful milk
1 tablespoonful flour	1 teaspoonful salt
2 tablespoonfuls butter	¼ teaspoonful pepper
¾ cupful bread crumbs	4 tablespoonfuls cheese

Place a thin layer of the chopped cabbage in a baking dish, sprinkle with a little of the flour, salt and pepper, dot with some of the butter and cover with a layer of bread crumbs. Repeat this process until the dry ingredients are used, having the top layer of bread crumbs. Pour on the milk and sprinkle the grated cheese over the top. Bake in a slow oven until the top is browned nicely.

Sweet Potato Balls

5 sweet potatoes	1 teaspoonful salt
1 cupful nut meats	⅛ teaspoonful cinnamon
4 tablespoonfuls butter	⅛ teaspoonful nutmeg

Boil the sweet potatoes and mash. Add the other ingredients and shape into balls. Roll these in flour and brown in butter.

Place in a single layer in greased shallow pan. Heat in moderate oven, 25 to 30 minutes.

Baked Carrots

Select small, tender carrots, allowing two or three for each person. Scrape them and boil or steam until tender. Stack them in a baking dish in cord-wood fashion, sprinkle them with salt and pepper and lay thinly sliced bacon over them. Place in a hot oven and bake until the bacon is crisp.

Hashed Potatoes

Put 2 tablespoonfuls of drippings in a frying pan. When hot, add cold boiled potatoes cut in small cubes. Add sufficient cold milk to cover. When the milk begins to simmer, season with salt and pepper and hash or cut the potatoes very fine with a knife. Turn frequently to prevent burning. Brown on the bottom and turn on a hot platter.

An old-fashioned way of salvaging leftover boiled potatoes.

Lyonnaise Potatoes

| 4 cupfuls boiled potatoes | 1 onion |
| | 4 tablespoonfuls fat |

Cook the chopped onion a few minutes in 1 tablespoonful of fat. Then add the sliced potatoes and the rest of the fat. Let cook until all the fat has been taken up; season with salt and pepper and brown.

Potatoes with Sausage

Mix 3 cupfuls of ground sausage with 3 finely chopped boiled potatoes of medium size. Add ½ cupful of cream. Form into cakes and brown on both sides in a frying pan. Serve with griddle cakes.

Vegetable Garnish

Boil equal amounts of carrots, parsnips, potatoes and turnips separately. When tender, rub through a sieve, season with salt and pepper and butter and serve hot with a pot roast of beef.

Boiled Lettuce

Wash the leaves and cook in an abundance of boiling salted water 10 or 15 minutes. Drain, pour over cold water and let stand a few minutes. Then drain again, chop in small pieces and heat in a pan with sufficient butter, salt and pepper to taste. This boiled lettuce may be heated with a cream sauce made by thickening 2 cupfuls of milk with 3 tablespoonfuls of flour. Two well beaten egg yolks are added to the cream sauce just before the lettuce is stirred into it.

Unacceptable today.

Escalloped Asparagus

3 cupfuls asparagus	1½ teaspoonfuls salt
1½ cupfuls milk	⅛ teaspoonful pepper
2 tablespoonfuls flour	½ cupful grated cheese
2 tablespoonfuls butter	1 cupful bread crumbs

Cut the asparagus in small pieces and stew until tender in a little water. Thicken the milk with the flour and season with the salt, pepper and butter. Add the grated cheese and cooked asparagus to the milk mixture and arrange alternate layers of this mixture and the bread crumbs in an oiled baking dish.

Bake in moderate oven (375°F.) about 25 minutes.

Spinach en Casserole

Season 2 cupfuls of hominy grits with butter, salt and pepper and spread 1 cupful of it in the bottom of a greased baking dish. Add a layer of cooked spinach seasoned to taste. Cover with the other cupful of hominy and sprinkle with ½ cupful of grated cheese. Bake in a slow oven until the top is browned.

Garden Greens

Select leaves of mustard, horseradish, beet tops, radish tops or lambs quarter and place in a kettle partly filled with hot water.

Add a piece of fat smoked meat and boil until tender. Serve hot on a platter with slices of lemon and hard cooked eggs.

Creamed Spinach

1½ cupfuls cooked spinach	1 tablespoonful butter
1½ cupfuls milk	1 teaspoonful salt
1 tablespoonful flour	⅛ teaspoonful pepper
	slices of toast

Thicken the milk with the flour and add the salt, pepper and butter. Stir in the cooked spinach and serve on slices of toast.

Marie's Asparagus

2 cupfuls asparagus tips	1 tablespoonful butter
1½ cupfuls milk	2 egg whites
1 teaspoonful salt	2 egg yolks
⅛ teaspoonful pepper	1½ tablespoonfuls flour

Cook the asparagus tips in a little water until they are tender. Make a cream sauce from the milk, salt, pepper, butter and flour. Pour the tender asparagus on a hot platter and cover it with the thickened and seasoned milk to which the finely chopped whites of the hard cooked eggs have been added. Press the yolks of the cooked eggs through a fine sieve and sprinkle them over the top of the dish.

Vegetable Oysters

Grate the pulp from ears of cooked corn, or use the canned vegetable, and to every cupful add 1 egg beaten until light and foamy and 1 tablespoonful each of sweet milk, flour and melted butter. Add salt to taste. Stir the ingredients together and drop from a spoon on a hot griddle. Brown on both sides. Serve hot with or without syrup.

Corn on the Cob

Remove the husks and silk from freshly gathered corn and pack the ears together closely in a kettle of rapidly boiling water, using as little water as possible. Cook the corn no longer than 8 minutes.

One favored way of cooking "roasting ears" in Iowa and other states in the Corn Belt: Cover corn in large kettle with cold water. Bring to a rolling boil and drain. Serve at once.

All snap or green beans had strings
50 years ago. Today most of them
have very few or no strings. Long,
slow cooking is frowned upon by
nutritionists. Cook in a little salted
water 10 to 20 minutes or until
tender.

Cook, uncovered, in ½ to 1 inch boiling
salted water 5 minutes. Cover and cook
3 to 7 minutes, or until tender. Drain
if necessary, add butter or cream, heat
and serve.

Make White Sauce with 3 tblsp. butter,
2 tblsp. flour, 3 cups milk and 1 tsp.
salt. Add to hot sauce 2 tblsp.
chopped onion and 6 medium potatoes,
pared and sliced thin. Pour into greased
baking dish, cover and bake in moderate
oven (350° F.) 1 hour. Uncover and
bake until potatoes are tender and
brown.

String Beans with Pork

String beans may be cooked with a slice of salt pork. Their flavor is most delicious if the beans are placed in a kettle of rapidly boiling water with the pork and left to simmer 2½ or 3 hours at the least. A small pinch of soda, sugar and salt may be added when the beans are placed on the stove to cook.

New Peas

New peas are best when cooked 25 or 30 minutes in just barely enough water to cover. The pods are washed before the peas are shelled and for an especially delectable dish they are boiled 3 minutes in the water which the peas are cooked in later. Seasonings are added just before taking the peas from the stove.

Festive Sweet Potatoes

Boil 3 sweet potatoes of medium size until tender. Mash and add ½ cupful of sugar, 4 tablespoonfuls of butter, 4 tablespoonfuls of chopped raisins and 2 tablespoonfuls of broken nut meats. For seasoning use ½ teaspoonful of salt and a few grains of cinnamon. Place this in an oiled baking dish and cover with ¼ pound of marshmallows. Set in a slow oven until the marshmallows are browned.

Escalloped Potatoes

Peel the potatoes and slice very thin. Put a layer in a greased baking dish, sprinkle with salt, pepper and flour and repeat this process until the dish is full. Dot the top with bits of butter and bake in a hot oven for an hour or until the potatoes are brown on top. Keep covered for the first half hour and then uncover.

Fried Eggplant

Pare an eggplant and cut in very thin slices. Sprinkle with salt and pile on a plate. Cover with a weight to press out the juice. Let stand 1½ hours. Dredge with flour and brown slowly in butter until crisp and brown.

Favorite country supper in autumn:
platter of fried eggplant bordered by
sliced tomatoes. Serve with plate of
sliced Cheddar cheese.

Baked Beans

Pick over 1 quart of beans, cover with cold water and soak overnight. In the morning drain, cover with fresh water and heat slowly, keeping the water below the boiling point. Cook until the skins burst. Drain beans. Scald rind of ¾ pound of salt pork, mostly fat, scrape, remove ¼ inch slice and place it with a small onion in the bottom of the bean pot or pail in which the beans are to be baked. Cut through the rind of the remaining pork every half inch, making the cut at least an inch deep. Put the beans in the pot or pail and bury the pork in them, leaving the rind exposed. Mix 1 tablespoonful of salt, 1 tablespoonful of molasses, 3 tablespoonfuls of sugar, 2 teaspoonfuls of ground mustard and 1 cupful of boiling water. Pour this over the beans, cover the utensil holding them and bake until the beans are tender and brown. This requires about 8 hours. If they are uncovered the last hours of cooking, they will brown evenly.

Chopped Turnips

Chop hot boiled turnips very fine, add parsley, salt, butter and lemon juice to season.

Potatoes au Gratin

3 cupfuls diced potatoes	2 tablespoonfuls butter
1½ cupfuls milk	salt
1 tablespoonful flour	pepper
3 tablespoonfuls grated cheese	buttered crumbs

Cook the potatoes in boiling water and cut in dice. Arrange a layer of them in an oiled baking dish, cover with the milk which has been thickened with the flour and seasoned with the butter, salt and pepper and sprinkle with the grated cheese. Repeat until all the ingredients are used, covering the top with buttered bread crumbs. Set in a moderate oven to brown the top nicely and to heat the potatoes.

Stuffed Baked Potatoes

Bake 6 medium-sized potatoes; remove from the oven and cut in halves. Scoop out the inside; mash and beat it with a spoon. Add 2 tablespoonfuls of milk and 3 tablespoonfuls of melted

Instead of soaking beans overnight, cover them with cold water, bring to a boil and boil 2 minutes. Remove from heat, cover and let stand 2 hours. Then combine with other ingredients and bake in a 2-quart bean pot or baking dish with lid in slow oven (300°F.) 3 hours. Remove cover during last part of cooking, adding a little boiling water if beans appear dry.

Use leftover cubed boiled potatoes, or mashed potatoes. Spread in greased shallow baking dish and sprinkle with 3/4 cup shredded process American cheese (enough for 3 to 4 cups potatoes) and with 1/4 cup buttered bread crumbs. Bake in moderate oven (350°F.) 30 minutes, or until heated and lightly browned.

butter. Then fold in the whites of 2 eggs which have been beaten until stiff. One teaspoonful of salt is stirred in and the potato mixture is piled in the skins. Just before serving the potatoes are baked 10 minutes in a hot oven.

Grandmother's Succotash

2 cupfuls shelled lima beans	2 cupfuls young corn
1 cupful water	1 teaspoonful sugar
1 teaspoonful salt	2 tablespoonfuls butter

Cook the lima beans in the water until they are tender. Add the corn cut from the cob and stir in the salt, sugar and butter. Cook 5 minutes and serve piping hot.

Vegetable Combination

2 cupfuls string beans	1 teaspoonful sugar
2 cupfuls lima beans	¼ teaspoonful pepper
2 cupfuls young corn	2 cupfuls tomato sauce
1 teaspoonful salt	3 tablespoonfuls thick cream
	water

Cut the string beans in small pieces, place in a kettle and add boiling water to cover; add the salt and sugar and cook 20 minutes. Then add the lima beans and cook until the vegetables are tender. Drain and add the tomato sauce. When this boils, add the corn cut from the cob and cook 5 minutes. Add the cream and pepper and serve at once.

Make with fresh lima or green beans and corn cut from the cob during the summer, canned whole kernel or frozen corn when gardens are not bearing.

CHAPTER 31

VINEGARS

THE art of vinegar making which our grandmothers knew so well is becoming extinct in most American homes. On farms where an abundance of fruit is available, the revival of this work is a matter of thrift. In some cases customers may be secured for this product and a profitable trade developed.

Fruits used for making vinegar should be sound and ripe. Since ripe fruits contain more sugar than underripe ones, they produce a stronger vinegar. Care should be taken to have all the utensils used clean and to wash the fruit carefully before crushing it.

Cider Vinegar

Wash ripe apples and remove all the decayed spots. Crush in a cider mill or run through a food chopper. Squeeze out the juice in a press and strain into a clean jar, keg or barrel. For every 5 gallons of juice add 1 cake of yeast which is softened by soaking in a cupful of the liquid. Stir the juice after the yeast is added. Then cover it with a clean cloth to keep out insects and allow to ferment. Fermentation is accomplished in less than a week if the temperature of the room in which the juice is kept is from 80 to 90 degrees Fahrenheit. A second fermentation is necessary to make vinegar. This is called the acetic acid fermentation. Before this starts, the juice will cease bubbling. When this occurs, it is wise to add 1 gallon of a good, strong vinegar to every 5 gallons of the fermented juice, but this is not necessary. The addition of the vinegar gives more satisfactory and uniform results.

After adding the vinegar, the juice is covered with a clean cloth and set in a dark place having a temperature of from 70 to 90 degrees F. Air should be allowed to enter but the film which forms on top should not be disturbed. By tasting of the

193

When bumper fruit crops ripened on farms, keeping the surplus from wasting challenged thrifty women. Making vinegar helped to conserve it.

Homemade vinegars varied in acid content. Women judged their acidity before adding them to foods. "It's mild," they sometimes said. Or they exclaimed: "This vinegar really is sour." They made the other ingredients in the dish they were making give in some to the vinegar. Frequently all they needed to do was add a little water to the sour vinegar, lemon juice to the dish when the vinegar was very mild.

vinegar every week one can tell when it is sour enough or when it ceases getting more sour. Then it should be strained off in jugs or bottles and stoppered tightly. If air gets to it, the vinegar will become weak and will lose its strength or sour taste in time.

Other Fruit Vinegars

Grapes, oranges, blackberries and pineapples may be used in the place of the apples in the recipe for Cider Vinegar.

Peach Vinegar

Crush ripe, sound peaches with a potato masher. To every bushel of peaches use 1 cake of yeast, first dissolved in a little lukewarm water. Place in a clean barrel or keg, cover with a clean cloth and allow to ferment in a room having a temperature of from 80 to 90 degrees Fahrenheit. Stir the fruit every day to keep it from molding. After 3 days, squeeze out the juice and let it ferment until it stops bubbling. Then add 1 gallon of a strong, good vinegar for every 4 gallons of peach juice. Cover with a clean cloth and set in a dark room having a temperature of from 70 to 90 degrees F. Taste of the vinegar every week and when it is sour enough, strain it into bottles and jugs and stopper them tightly. If the vinegar is cloudy, allow it to stand in stoppered kegs until the sediment sinks to the bottom. Then pour it off carefully without disturbing the sediment.

Raspberry Vinegar

Crush 5 pounds of raspberries and add 10 cupfuls of vinegar. Allow to stand in an earthenware jar a week, stirring thoroughly every day. Then strain through a muslin bag and add 1 cupful of sugar to every cupful of juice. Boil this 3 minutes, cool, bottle and seal.

Nasturtium Vinegar

Cut the flowers, leaves and seeds of nasturtium plants in small pieces with kitchen scissors and place 3 cupfuls of them in a quart fruit jar. Cover with strong cider vinegar and let stand 2 weeks Then add ½ ounce of ground cloves and ¼ ounce of red

Some homemade vinegars were not produced with "from-scratch" recipes. Seasonings from gardens, such as nasturtiums, cucumbers and horseradish were added to homemade or commercial cider vinegar.

pepper. Let stand 5 days, shake every day, then strain through muslin. Bottle and seal.

Gooseberry Vinegar

Crush ripe berries and add three times as much cold water as there are berries. Bring them to the boiling point, cool and let stand 24 hours. Then strain through muslin and to every quart of the liquid add 2¼ cupfuls of brown sugar. Stir well and put into a barrel or jar. Add ¼ pound of honey and bung up or cover tightly.

Cucumber Vinegar

Wipe cucumbers clean and slice them without peeling into clean glass fruit jars. Add sufficient vinegar to cover. For 1 quart of vinegar add 1 clove of garlic, 1 teaspoonful of white pepper and 1 teaspoonful of salt. After standing 2 weeks, drain the vinegar into clean bottles, straining it through muslin.

Horseradish Vinegar

Grate 1½ ounces of horseradish and add to it ½ ounce of cayenne pepper and ½ ounce of minced shallots. Pour 2 cupfuls of vinegar on this and let stand a week. Strain through a fine cloth and bottle for use.

Molasses Vinegar

Fill a large jug or keg with a mixture made by combining 1 quart of New Orleans molasses with 2 cupfuls of homemade yeast and 3 gallons of rain water. Tie a cloth over the top to keep out the dust and insects. Place outdoors in the sun in the summer or let stand near the stove in the winter. In a month, or sooner, the vinegar will be made.

Quick Cider Vinegar

For every gallon of cider add 2 cupfuls of New Orleans molasses and 1 cupful of homemade yeast. Place in a jug and leave out the cork to admit air. In about a week the vinegar will be made. Pour into bottles and cork tightly.

Gooseberry bushes grew in the woods and along fence rows on many farms. Some years they yielded a bounty of berries free for the picking. The problem was what to do with them after the family had its fill of gooseberry pie and an adequate amount of gooseberry jam and conserve was in the fruit closet. Vinegar offered another outlet for the surplus.

White Raisin Vinegar

Cut 4 pounds of raisins in small pieces and add 2 gallons of strained rain water. Place in a jug, leaving out the cork and stand it in a warm place. In a month, strain through cheesecloth and bottle for use.

Corn Vinegar

Boil 4 cupfuls of corn in 1 gallon of rain water until the kernels break. Then pour this mixture into a stone jar and add another gallon of warm rain water, making certain that there is approximately 2 gallons of liquid in all. Dissolve 2 cupfuls of sugar in 2 cupfuls of boiling water and pour this in the jar. Cover the top of the jar with 3 thicknesses of cheesecloth and let stand in a warm place, where the temperature will be about 80 degrees Fahrenheit. In a month pour off the vinegar into a jug, being careful not to get any of the sediment in the jug. Cover the mouth of the jug and store in a warm, dry place.

Corn Vinegar was made by pioneers who frequently had to wait a few years for the orchards they planted to bear fruit.
Corn was one of the first crops planted and it produced food fast. Rain water was saved, especially in localities where the water was hard. It was used in many ways in addition to vinegar making, as for shampooing hair and washing clothes. Air pollution was not yet in the American dream.

CHAPTER 32

COOKING IN LARGE QUANTITIES

EVERY farm homemaker is called on to prepare meals for large crews of men or many guests at some time during the year. In addition there are community picnics, socials at the church and other gatherings where food is cooked in large quantities. It is for such occasions that the recipes in this chapter are given.

Spice Cookies (10 dozen)

6 eggs	6 teaspoonfuls salt
1 cupful buttermilk	2 teaspoonfuls soda
4 cupfuls sugar	2 teaspoonfuls baking powder
7 cupfuls flour	1¾ cupfuls melted lard
7 teaspoonfuls cinnamon	2 pounds chopped and seeded
5 teaspoonfuls cloves	raisins

Mix the fat, sugar, salt and spices together. Beat until the mixture is creamy and light. Then add the eggs and beat again. Sift the flour, soda and baking powder together and add this mixture alternately with the buttermilk. Stir in the slightly floured raisins, roll out and cut. Bake in a hot oven.

Cabbage Salad (2 gallons)

9 pounds cabbage	1 cupful sugar
1 quart sweet pickles	½ ounce celery seed
1½ pounds English walnuts	2 cupfuls rolled cracker crumbs
18 hard cooked eggs	1 small can Spanish peppers
1 quart salad dressing	2 teaspoonfuls pepper
½ cupful whole mustard seed	1 small bunch celery
salt to taste	

Put the ingredients through a food grinder after shelling the nuts. If the salad dressing fails to make the salad moist enough, add the vinegar from the pickles. Serve on lettuce leaves.

Hot Chocolate (25 servings)

1½ cupfuls grated chocolate	3 cupfuls boiling water
¾ cupful sugar	1 gallon milk
¾ teaspoonful salt	2½ teaspoonfuls vanilla

If an urn is not available for making coffee for a crowd, use a large kettle. Tie 4 cups regular-grind coffee into a clean cloth bag, filling bag only half full. Bring 8 quarts cold water to a rolling boil in kettle; reduce heat. Drop coffee into it, but first tie bag shut with cord. Leave cord long enough to tie to the kettle's handle to make removal easier. Push bag of coffee up and down in water with a spoon to submerge it and stir frequently while brewing to get a high extraction of coffee. Simmer 7 to 8 minutes, but do not let boil. Lift out coffee bag and let drip over the kettle. This will serve 25 people.

Mix the dry ingredients with the boiling water and boil until the mixture is smooth and glossy. Add the scalded milk and cook from 10 to 20 minutes. Add vanilla just before serving.

Coffee

If a large coffee pot is not available, use an enamel kettle or boiler. In a cheesecloth bag place 1 pound of coffee for every 50 cupfuls of coffee desired, and use 8 quarts of rapidly boiling water for every pound of coffee. Drop the bag of coffee in the boiling water and use a cup to pour the water on the bag until it is thoroughly soaked. Then remove the coffee from the fire and stir the bag in the hot, but not boiling, liquid 5 minutes. Lift up the bag and let it drain, then remove it entirely and keep the coffee hot, but do not boil. Serve as soon as possible after being made.

Oyster Stew

2 gallons milk	2 tablespoonfuls salt
2 quarts oysters	1 teaspoonful white pepper
	1 cupful butter

Scald the milk and add the oysters, butter and pepper. Cook until the edges of the oysters begin to curl. Add salt just before serving. This makes 30 servings.

Potato Salad

5 pints boiled potatoes	¼ teaspoonful white pepper
2 cupfuls celery or sliced cucumber	3 cupfuls salad dressing
1 tablespoonful salt	1 pimento
	1 tablespoonful chopped onion

Dice the potatoes, chop the celery, onion and pimento. Combine with the other ingredients. This makes 15 servings.

Salad Dressing

¾ cupful cornstarch	2 tablespoonfuls paprika
¾ cupful sugar	1 teaspoonful salt
3 pints milk	2½ cupfuls vinegar
1 tablespoonful mustard	8 egg yolks

Mix the cornstarch, sugar, mustard, salt and paprika together and stir in the scalded milk. Beat the egg yolks and add the vinegar to them. Stir this into the thickened milk and cook 5 minutes, stirring constantly. This makes a little more than 2 quarts of salad dressing.

Scalloped Potatoes

1 gallon potatoes	3 tablespoonfuls salt
1½ quarts white sauce	½ cupful buttered crumbs
4 tablespoonfuls butter	

Grease a pan, cover with a layer of sliced boiled potatoes, then with white sauce to which the onion and salt have been added. Add another layer of potatoes and white sauce. Cover with the buttered crumbs and bake until brown. This serves about 20 persons.

White Sauce

2 quarts milk	1 tablespoonful salt
1 cupful flour	¾ cupful butter

Make a paste from the flour and a small portion of the milk. Scald the rest of the milk and add this paste to it. When the sauce is thickened, add the butter and salt. This makes about 2 quarts.

Chicken Salad

2 quarts cooked chicken	1½ quarts diced celery
3 cupfuls salad dressing	

Cut the chicken in dice and mix with the celery and salad dressing. This may be garnished with slices of hard cooked egg and served on lettuce leaves. This makes 25 servings.

Biscuits

12 cupfuls flour	2 tablespoonfuls salt
¾ cupful baking powder	1½ cupfuls shortening
1½ quarts milk	

Mix and sift the dry ingredients and rub in the shortening. Add the milk gradually, mixing to a soft dough. The amount of milk required will vary somewhat with different flours. Roll the dough ¾ inch thick and cut. If small biscuits about 2½ inches in diameter are cut, this will make 90 of them.

Use recipe for Baked Beans in chapter on vegetables, which yields about 10 servings. It's easy to bake three pots at a time for 30 servings.

Revised Table Giving Approximate Amounts for 50 Servings

Bread for sandwiches — 2 3-pound loaves

Butter for sandwiches — 1 to 1¼ pounds

Ice Cream — 2 to 2¼ gallons

Sundae Sauce — 1½ pints

Lemonade — 6 quarts

Oysters for stew — 5 to 6 quarts

Chicken, to cook and cut up for
    salad or creaming — 20 to 25 pounds

Chicken, to roast — 33 to 40 pounds

Turkey, to roast and slice — 38 to 40 pounds

Chicken Salad — 6¼ quarts

Lettuce, to line salad plates — 6 heads

Salad Dressing or Mayonnaise — 1 quart

Pies, 9-inch — 9

Potatoes for salad — 15 pounds

Potatoes for scalloping — 14 pounds

Coffee, regular grind — 1¼ pounds

Rolls or Biscuits — 5 to 6½ dozen

Butter for breads, in pats ½ inch thick — 1¼ pounds

Ham Sandwiches

1½ pounds ham   ¾ cupful pickles
1½ cupfuls salad dressing

Chop the ham and pickles together and combine with salad dressing. Put between slices of bread. This amount of ham filling makes 25 sandwiches.

Baked Beans

2 quarts beans   1½ teaspoonfuls mustard
1½ tablespoonfuls soda   1 teaspoonful paprika
½ cupful molasses   3 tablespoonfuls salt
4 tablespoonfuls sugar   1 pound bacon

Soak the beans overnight in cold water. Add the soda and boil until almost tender. Drain, add the seasonings and the bacon. Bake in a moderate oven until the beans are tender and browned. This serves about 30 persons.

Table of Quantities

Sandwiches—Sixteen sandwich slices may be cut from a one pound loaf of bread.

Butter—One pound will make 50 sandwiches or serve 25 persons.

Cake—A medium-sized cake will serve 20 persons.

Ice Cream—One gallon will serve 20 persons.

Oysters—One-half gallon of oysters, escalloped, will serve 20 persons.

Lemonade—Five quarts serve 25 persons.

Chicken Salad—One chicken weighing 3 pounds will serve 20 persons.

Whipped Cream—One-half pint will yield 12 heaping tablespoonfuls.

Potato Chips—One pound serves 20 persons.

Chicken Pie Dinner—To serve 250 persons the following ingredients are required; 50 chickens, 50 pounds flour, 8 pounds butter, 24 dozen pickles, 3 quarts lard, 2 bushels potatoes, 4 gallons cooked cranberries and 10 large heads of cabbage with 4 gallons of salad dressing for slaw.

Cakes, 2-layer — 4

Potato Chips — 3 pounds

Cream, to whip for dessert garnish — 1 quart

Cream for coffee — 1 quart

CHAPTER 33

RECIPES FOR LITTLE GIRLS

When having a tea party for the dolls or when cooking for the family, little girls like to have recipes of their own to use in preparing the food. The recipes in this section have been designed for this purpose and therefore produce smaller amounts than those mother uses. All the measurements are level.

Spice Cake

½ cupful shortening	1 tablespoonful hot water
1 cupful sugar	2 cupfuls flour
1 egg	1 cupful sour milk
1 teaspoonful soda	1 teaspoonful powdered cloves
1 teaspoonful powdered cinnamon	

Cream the butter or other shortening, if butter is not used, with a spoon. Gradually add the sugar, beating the mixture with a spoon. When it is light and creamy, add the egg yolk which has been beaten until it is a light lemon color. Sift the flour and spices together and add them alternately with the milk. Then fold in the stiffly beaten egg white. Last of all, stir in the soda which has been dissolved in the hot water. Bake in layers or as a loaf.

Raisin Cake

Use the recipe for Spice Cake only add 1 cupful of chopped and floured raisins to the batter.

Nut Cake

Use the recipe for Spice Cake only leave out the spices, and add ½ cupful of chopped and floured nut meats and 1 teaspoonful of vanilla.

Instead of giving little girls exciting new recipes of their own, many mothers gave them miniature versions of some of their favorites. Everyone expected girls to develop into good cooks. No special lures, other than compliments from many fathers, were provided. The wonder is, from today's vantage point, how the youngsters ever met with success. The recipes they followed would keep most adults guessing. Mothers did stay nearby during their daughters' first attempts for consultation if needed. They considered that their duty. Practically all girls learned to cook at their mother's side, a mother-daughter relationship that prevailed 50 years ago in country kitchens.

Butter Frosting

⅓ cupful butter   1½ cupfuls powdered sugar

Beat the butter and sugar together, adding strong coffee or vanilla drop by drop until the frosting will spread on the cake.

Tea Cake

1 cupful sugar	2 cupfuls flour
½ cupful butter	3½ teaspoonfuls baking powder
1 egg	1 teaspoonful vanilla
1 cupful sweet milk	1 small pinch soda

Cream the butter and sugar together with a spoon and beat until light and creamy. Add the beaten egg yolk. Sift the flour, baking powder and a small pinch of soda together and add them alternately with the milk. Stir in the vanilla and fold in the stiffly beaten egg white. Place in an oiled dripping pan, spread melted butter over the top and sprinkle with sugar and cinnamon. Bake in a hot oven 10 minutes, then reduce the heat and finish baking. This should be about 1¾ inches thick when baked.

Drop Cookies

6 tablespoonfuls shortening	1½ cupfuls flour
¾ cupful sugar	2 teaspoonfuls baking powder
1 egg	¼ teaspoonful salt
3 tablespoonfuls milk	1 teaspoonful vanilla

Cream the shortening, add the sugar, beaten egg, milk, salt, vanilla and the flour and baking powder sifted together. Beat the batter thoroughly, then drop by spoonfuls 3 inches apart in oiled pans and bake 10 minutes in a hot oven.

Nut Cookies

Add ½ cupful of chopped and floured nut meats to the batter for Drop Cookies and drop by spoonfuls in oiled pans. Bake in a hot oven.

Fruit Cookies

Add ½ cupful of chopped and floured raisins, currants or dates to the Drop Cooky batter and bake in the same way.

Muffins

4 tablespoonfuls butter	3 teaspoonfuls baking powder
2 tablespoonfuls sugar	1 egg
¼ teaspoonful salt	1 cupful milk
2 cupfuls flour	

Cream the butter with a spoon, add the sugar and the well beaten egg. Sift the baking powder with the flour and add to the first mixture alternately with the milk. Bake in buttered muffin tins 25 minutes. One-half cupful of chopped dates, raisins or currants may be added with the flour.

Smothered Potatoes

4 potatoes	¼ teaspoonful pepper
1¾ cupfuls sweet milk	¼ small onion
2 tablespoonfuls butter	3 tablespoonfuls flour
1½ teaspoonfuls salt	4 tablespoonfuls bread crumbs

Cut pared potatoes in thin slices. Arrange a layer of the potatoes in the bottom of a buttered baking dish. Sprinkle with salt, pepper, flour and chopped onion and dot with butter. Add milk and cover with buttered crumbs. Bake in a moderate oven until the potatoes are tender.

Rarebit

Heat 1 cupful of milk and add to it 1 tablespoonful of flour blended with 1 tablespoonful of butter. Add 6 tablespoonfuls of cheese cut in bits and cook over water until the cheese melts, stirring constantly. Serve on toast or crackers.

Sandwiches

Cut thin slices of brown or white bread. Spread with butter and a paste made by chopping or cutting raisins in small pieces and moistening them with cream.

Spiced Prunes

8 prunes	½ inch stick cinnamon
1 whole clove	1 tablespoonful sugar

Wash prunes and soak them overnight in cold water. Cook in the water in which they soaked. Add spices, cover and simmer gently until they are tender. Then add sugar and cook 5 minutes. Take out the prunes and if the syrup is not thick, boil it longer. Discard the pits and pour the syrup over the prunes.

Goblin Salad

Remove the pits from cooked prunes and stuff the centers with cottage cheese. Fasten the prunes together with toothpicks to represent goblins or men. Serve with salad dressing or whipped cream.

Fancy Sandwiches

Cut thin slices of bread and butter them evenly. Use fancy cooky cutters to obtain pretty shapes.

Peach Snow

Wipe and remove the skin from two large ripe peaches. Force the pulp through a sieve and drain if there is much juice. Beat the whites of 2 eggs stiff and add the peach pulp gradually while beating. Sweeten with powdered sugar. Chill and serve with cream.

Baked Rhubarb

1 cupful rhubarb	¾ cupful sugar

Wash rhubarb, cut in ½ inch pieces without removing the outer skin. Put into baking dish and sprinkle with sugar. Cover tightly and bake in a slow oven until tender.

Apple Sauce

1 large apple	¼ cupful water
2 tablespoonfuls sugar	Few drops lemon juice or 3 whole cloves

Wipe, pare, quarter and core apple. Make a syrup by boiling water and sugar together. Add the lemon juice or cloves. Place the apple in a pan and add barely enough water to cover. Simmer until tender. Cook the syrup until it thickens slightly. Then pour it over the apple.

Fudge

2 cupfuls sugar	1 tablespoonful butter
1 cupful milk	1 teaspoonful vanilla
1 square chocolate	1 cupful nut meats

Melt the butter in the kettle and add the finely cut chocolate to it. Cook, stirring constantly, until the chocolate is melted. Add the sugar and cook while the chocolate is being mixed into the sugar. Then add the milk and cook until the mixture reaches the soft ball stage. Cool. When lukewarm, beat until the mixture is creamy and begins to harden. Pour into pans and cut in squares.

Maple Divinity

3 cupfuls sugar	1 cupful boiling water
1 cupful maple syrup	3 egg whites

Put sugar, syrup and water in kettle. Cook without stirring until it forms a firm soft ball when a small portion is tried in cold water. Beat whites of egg in a gallon crock. When the syrup is cooked so that it forms the firm soft ball, almost a hard ball, in cold water, pour it over the egg whites, beating vigorously with a stiff spoon. Continue beating until the candy is stiff and fine-grained. Spread and cut in squares.

When a farm woman realized the meal she was getting would be late, she set the table before the men came from the barn to the house for dinner. She found it assured the men that the meal soon would be ready. The common belief was that a good cook not only gets appetizing meals, but she also serves them on time.

Note to Raisin Custard:
The custard was served hot from the oven. Women were great menu jugglers, and the dessert might have been home-canned cherries or apricots with cookies previously baked.

CHAPTER 34

QUICK MEALS

ON wash day, when returning home from a trip to town or whenever time is limited, it is helpful to have in mind pattern meals which can be prepared in 30 or 60 minutes, depending on the time available. The following menus for 30-minute and 60-minute meals can be made ready in the allotted time, provided the fire is built or a kerosene stove is used. Recipes for making the dishes used are found in this book.

30-Minute Meals

Pan Broiled Ham		Creamed Potatoes
	Apple and Cabbage Salad	
Bread	Butter	Fruit Preserves
	Raisin Custard	
Milk		Coffee

The potatoes are pared, cut in small cubes and set on the stove to cook in salted water. Then the custard is made and set in the oven. The cabbage and apples are prepared and combined with the salad dressing which has been made previously. Then the ham is placed in the frying pan to cook. While these foods are cooking, the table is set, the salad, bread, butter, preserves and milk are placed on the table. When this is accomplished, the potatoes are drained and seasoned with milk which is thickened with flour and seasoned with salt, pepper and butter. The ham which has been turned occasionally is now ready. The custard will be baked by the time the dessert is needed. If cookies are available, they may be served with it. When coffee is desired, it is set on the stove to cook just before the potatoes are drained.

Creamed Salmon on Toast

Buttered Peas   Oven Fried Potatoes

Bread   Butter   Jelly

Stuffed Canned Pears

Coffee   Milk

Place the potatoes in the oven to cook, then make the white sauce for creamed dishes and add the flaked salmon to it. Open the can of peas and place them with the seasonings in a kettle to heat. Put the coffee on to cook. Open the can of pears, place them in serving dishes and fill the cavities in them with thick jam and shredded cocoanut. Cut the bread and butter and set the table. By the time the toast is made for the salmon, the rest of the meal will be ready.

Pork Chops

Boiled Potatoes   Buttered Spinach

Cornbread   Butter   Horseradish

Sliced Peaches with Cookies

Coffee or Tea   Milk

Pare the potatoes and place on the stove to boil. Stir up the cornbread and place in the oven to bake. Then put the pork chops on to cook. Open the can of spinach and place it in a kettle with seasonings to heat. Set the table and place the milk, horseradish, butter and canned peaches and cookies on it. If coffee is to be served, prepare it. After draining the potatoes, season them with salt, butter and pepper.

Badger Squaw Dish

Buttered Asparagus   Pickled Beets

Dropped Biscuits

Butter   Jam

Pineapple and Marshmallow Dessert

Prepare the Squaw Dish first, then make the biscuits, placing them in the oven to bake. Put the canned asparagus on the stove to heat with the butter and seasonings. Set the table and arrange the dessert, which consists of chopped canned pineapple and marshmallows cut in bits, on the table. If milk is wished, pour it or place the glasses and pitcher on the table. By this time the food will be cooked and ready for serving.

Scrambled Eggs with Peas

Pickles   Muffins   Jelly   Butter

Apple Betty with Cream

Stir up the muffins and place them in the oven to bake; then prepare the Apple Betty and set it in the oven. Next scramble

Where are the salads? In the 8 menu plans, only 3 include a salad. And where are the hamburgers and frankfurters?

the eggs and bacon and set the table. If coffee is used, place it on the stove to cook. Let the Apple Betty bake until it is almost time to serve it.

One-Hour Meals

Baked Potatoes   Breaded Pork Chops
Cabbage Slaw
Bread   Butter   Jam
Date Pudding with Cream
Coffee   Milk

Select mediumly small potatoes and place them in the oven to bake. Brown the pork chops, after dipping them in egg and bread crumbs, then pour a little water in the frying pan, cover tightly and set in the oven to finish cooking. Prepare the date pudding and set in the oven to bake. Make the cabbage slaw, set the table and put the coffee on to cook. Leave the pudding in the oven until time to serve it, unless it is baked before this time.

Fried Ham
Scalloped Potatoes   String Beans Vingrette
Bread   Butter   Jelly   Chili Sauce
Peach Shortcake

Place the potatoes in the oven to bake, put the ham on to fry and then prepare the dough for the shortcake, setting it in a cool place. Then prepare the beans and the sauce for the shortcake and set the table. Just before sitting down to the table, place the shortcake in the oven to bake.

Creamed Ham with Potatoes
Pickled Beets   Buttered Spinach   Bread   Butter
Chocolate Pie
Coffee   Milk

Set the ham and potatoes in the oven to bake, make the pie crust and then the filling. Set the table, prepare the spinach and then brown the meringue of the pie in the oven. Set the coffee on the stove to cook.

Beef Steak
Fried Potatoes   Scalloped Tomatoes
Bread   Butter   Jam
Apples en Casserole
Coffee   Milk

Prepare tomatoes and place in the oven, then prepare the apples and place them in the oven to bake. Set the table, then fry the potatoes, put the coffee on to cook and fry or broil the steak.

Rarebit on Toast
Baked Potatoes   Olives or Pickles   Pineapple Salad
Berry Dumplings with Cream

Give potatoes first attention, then prepare the salad and set the table. Then make dumplings and set them in the oven to bake. While they are baking, prepare the rarebit and toast.

In looking over the menus for quick meals, the question arises: Did ovens in wood- and coal-burning and kerosene stoves accommodate the combinations of foods assigned to them? Could Muffins and Apple Betty bake successfully at the same temperature? The answer is that a good farm cook 50 years ago made her recipes give and take. She worked out a compromise between the foods she baked together; both gave a little.

This chapter was included in the first _Farm Cook and Rule Book_ mainly for men. They did the butchering, divided the carcass into cuts and took an active role in the curing. During the half-century since then, these activities have just about vanished from farms. The arrival of locker plants and freezers had much to do with the change.

Now a farmer delivers an animal, beef, pork or lamb, to professionals at any time of the year the family's meat supply needs replenishing. After the slaughtering, much of the meat is cut, frozen or cured. The sausage is made and the lard rendered. The cuts commonly cured are the hams, pork shoulders and bacon sides.

The meat returns to the farm ready to cook. Many farm women have a meat market in the freezer near the kitchen.

Some men and women, largely as a hobby, frequently cure a couple of hams, pork shoulders and sides of bacon. They make a little sausage to get the seasonings they especially like, but they are the exception to the rule, and some of them use the convenience mixtures for curing meats.

CHAPTER 35

BUTCHERING

MEAT should be cooled at least 24 hours after butchering before it is cured. It should not be frozen when placed in the brine, for if it is, the brine will not be able to penetrate it evenly. As a result, the meat will not have a uniform flavor throughout.

Any clean and tight hardwood barrel may be used to hold the brine, but a thoroughly washed and scalded molasses barrel is preferable. In case a vinegar barrel is used, it must be burned out on the inside as well as scalded and washed. If the barrel has any trace of bad odor after this treatment, a small lump of quicklime may be placed in a dish and set in it and a gallon of boiling water poured over it. The barrel is then covered while the fumes of the slacking lime sweeten it. After this, the barrel is washed and rinsed again.

Salt, molasses or sugar and saltpeter are the preservatives commonly used in curing meat. Salt has an astringent action, that is, it draws the moisture from the meat and hardens the muscles somewhat. Sugar and molasses have the opposite effect and are therefore used with salt. They help keep the muscles tender and the meat from becoming too dry. Saltpeter is used to retain the natural color of the meat and is always added in small quantities.

Sugar Cured Pork

Sprinkle a layer of salt on top of a clean table and pile the bacons, tongues and hams on this, sprinkling every piece with salt. This table should be in a cool and dry room. After the meat has stood for 10 days, the pieces are washed off with lukewarm water.

Make a pickle by dissolving 2½ pounds of brown sugar, 2 ounces of saltpeter and from 8 to 10 pounds of salt in 4 gallons of warm water. This amount of pickle is sufficient for 100 pounds of meat. Pack the meat in the barrel, after trimming off all the rough and hanging pieces, placing the heaviest hams and shoulders in the bottom and the bacons and tongues on top. Pour the cool brine over the meat, weight it down with a heavy block of wood, making certain that it is kept submerged all the time. Leave the bacons and tongues in this pickle from 4 to 5 weeks, the lighter hams about 6 weeks and the heavy hams from 6 to 8 weeks. Wash the meat in lukewarm water when it is taken from the brine to remove the scum and crust which may have formed on it. Dry 2 hours, hang in the smokehouse, let stand overnight and the next day smoke.

If at any time during the curing the brine does not cover the meat, more water should be added. In case it shows any sign of fermentation, it should be drained off, boiled, cooled and then poured back over the meat. If the brine becomes ropy, the barrel should be washed out with scalding water while new brine is being made.

Dry Cured Pork

Weigh out 2½ pounds of granulated sugar, 6 pounds of salt, 2 ounces of saltpeter and 4 ounces of black pepper. This is sufficient for curing 100 pounds of meat. Divide the sugar, salt and saltpeter mixture into equal parts, rub one portion over the cooled meat and pack it in a barrel. At the end of three days, take the meat from the barrel, rub with a second portion of the salt, sugar and saltpeter mixture, and repack. After standing 3 more days, the meat is removed from the barrel and rubbed with the last portion of the mixture and then it is repacked. Let stand in the brine formed 2 weeks. Then take from the barrel, wash off with lukewarm water, dry 1 hour and smoke.

Pickled Salt Pork

Mix together 2 ounces of saltpeter, 8 to 10 pounds of salt and 4 gallons of boiling water. Cool and pour over the meat which has been packed in a clean barrel. This is sufficient pickle for 100 pounds of meat. Weight the meat down with a heavy block and keep every piece submerged all the time. Although fat

Use medium granulated or flake salt in curing meats. Do not use iodized salt.

Some farmers like to cure a few hams, pork shoulders and sides of bacon, but they commonly use commercially prepared mixtures, following the manufacturer's directions.

Seasonings for sausage vary from 1 family to another and in different parts of the country. For 5 pounds meat, a mixture of 5 tsp. salt, 3 or 4 tsp. rubbed sage and 2 tsp. black pepper pleases many people.

pieces of backs are usually cured in this way, any piece of meat may be, provided it is cut in narrow strips or 6 inch squares. The meat is left in the brine and is taken out as needed.

Virginia Cured Hams

Place the hams on a table covered with salt and sprinkle them with saltpeter until quite frosty. Use about 5 ounces of saltpeter for 100 pounds of meat. Salt and pile for 3 days, then salt again and leave in salt a day for every pound of meat. Wash with warm water, partially dry and rub the entire surface with finely ground black pepper. Smoke for 30 or 40 days, watching the color so as to get a uniform tobacco brown color. Hickory wood is best for smoking. Re-pepper the hams after they are smoked.

Pickled Pigs' Feet

Soak the feet from which the toes have been removed overnight in cold water. Cover with fresh water in the morning and boil slowly until the meat is very tender. Salt is added for seasoning during the cooking. Remove the pigs' feet from the kettle, split them and pack in a stone jar. Pour on sufficient hot vinegar to cover. Spices may be added if one wishes. To 1 quart of vinegar, 1 tablespoonful of whole cloves, the same amount of peppercorns and 1 teaspoonful of salt are good amounts to use.

Pork Sausage

For every 3 pounds of fresh lean pork allow 1 pound of fat. Grind the meat and fat in a food grinder. Weigh the meat and spread it out in a thin layer on a flat surface and sprinkle with the seasonings. For every 5 pounds of ground meat, use 1½ to 2 ounces of salt, ½ ounce of black pepper and ½ ounce of ground sage. Mix the seasonings and meat together and put through the grinder again.

Sausage Casings

Carefully cleaned intestines of sheep, hogs and cattle are used for casings. As a rule pork casings are used for pork sausage, beef rounds from the small intestines are used for bologna and beef bungs from the large intestine are used for large bologna and for ham sausage. These casings may be purchased if one does not wish to prepare them. They are cleaned by being emptied and washed thoroughly inside and out. Then they are soaked in a solution of lye or in water to which wood ashes have been added. They are scraped inside and out until the slime and gat are removed. Then they are washed again and packed in salt until needed.

Narrow muslin bags 20 inches long and 3 inches wide may be used in place of the casings. Melted lard is rubbed over the outer surface of the bags to seal the surface.

Bologna Sausage

To 8 pounds of lean beef use 1 pound of fat pork. Put the meat through a food grinder, spread it out on a flat surface and sprinkle with the seasonings. For every 9 pounds of meat allow 2¼ ounces of fine salt, ¾ ounce of black pepper and ¼ ounce of ground mace or coriander. Mix the seasonings with the meat and regrind. Stuff into casings, dry 1 hour and smoke 8 or 10 hours. Dry before putting away.

Liver Sausage

Add 5 pounds of well cooked pork or beef liver and 1 pound of flour to 8 pounds of well cooked pork from boned hogs' heads or jowls. Cut the meat into small pieces, mix thoroughly with flour and put through a food grinder. Spread out and sprinkle with 6 ounces of fine salt, 2 ounces of finely ground black pepper and 1 ounce of finely ground sage. Regrind, adding 1 onion if the onion flavor is desired. Stuff the meat into round casings or hog bungs and cook in boiling water 10 minutes. Cool in ice, or very cool, water and hang up to dry.

Headcheese

Skin the hogs' heads, remove the brains and eyes and split the heads down the center of the foreheads and noses. Put the pieces in a kettle, cover with water and boil gently until the

Casings for sausage may be purchased in different places. Meat markets frequently have them or will fill orders for them, as will many locker plants. Homemade muslin bags are good substitutes. The size depends on personal preferences, but they usually are made 12 to 20 inches long and 2½ to 3 inches in diameter.

meat comes off the bone easily. Then remove the meat, chop it finely, return it to the kettle and add a part of the liquor in which it was cooked, and boil 15 minutes. While this is cooking, season to taste with salt and pepper. To 12 pounds of meat add ¼ pound of salt, ⅛ pound of pepper and if desired, a trace of allspice and cloves. Put the cooked meat and the liquid that remains in stoneware jars or crocks, place a weight on top and cool. When firm, it is ready to be sliced and used.

Lard

Render the leaf fat, the fat from the sides, trimmings from hams, shoulders and neck and that from the guts separately. The same process is used in rendering the three kinds of fat and if one wishes, the leaf fat and that from the sides, hams, shoulders and neck may be rendered together.

Either run the fat through a food chopper or cut it into 1½ inch cubes. Cook over a very slow fire, never letting the mixture reach the boiling point of water. Stir frequently with a wooden stick. When the cracklings are light brown in color and float on top, remove them and drain. Save the cracklings to make crackling bread, to feed the chickens or for soap making. Stir the lard as it cools. When cool enough, strain through muslin cloths into jars or cans and cover.

Corned Beef

Cut wholesome, fresh beef in pieces about 6 inches square and place a ¼ inch layer of salt, then a 6 inch layer of meat in an earthenware jar or a wooden barrel. Repeat this process until all the meat is used. Be sure to have a good layer of salt on top. Weigh the meat before cutting it and allow 8 pounds of salt to 100 pounds of meat. Let the beef stand overnight in the salt.

The next morning make a brine by dissolving 3 ounces of saltpeter, 2½ ounces of baking soda and 5 pounds of sugar in 4 gallons of boiling water. Pour through muslin and cool. When thoroughly cooled, pour the brine over the meat and salt and if the meat is not covered, add sufficient cold water that the meat will be submerged. Weight it down with a heavy block of wood. After 5 days, overhaul the meat and repack, putting the pieces previously on top in the bottom.

At any time, especially in the warm weather, that the brine shows signs of fermentation or becomes ropy, it should be drained off, boiled, strained through a clean cloth, cooled and poured back on the meat. Scald the barrel or jar and wash the meat before the brine is poured back. Keep the meat in a cool, dark place. It will be ready for use after standing in the brine one month. If kept 2 months, soaking the meat before cooking it will be necessary to remove some of the salt. The parts of the beef usually selected for this purpose are plate, rump, cross ribs and brisket. Best results are obtained by removing the bone before putting the meat in the brine.

Dried Beef

Use the round for this purpose. To 50 pounds of cooled meat, weigh out 3 pounds of salt, 1½ pounds of brown sugar and 1 ounce of saltpeter. Mix these ingredients and divide into three portions. Rub one portion on the meat and place it in an earthenware jar. Let stand 3 days, then take the meat from the jar, but leave the syrup formed during the curing in it, rub the second portion of the mixture on the meat, return it to the jar and let stand 3 more days. Then take out the meat and rub the third portion on it and put back in the jar with the syrup. After standing 3 days, hang it up in the smokehouse. Smoke until dry and then keep in a dry place.

Vienna Sausage

Grind very fine 4 pounds of lean beef and 2 pounds of fat pork. Sprinkle with 1½ ounces of salt, ½ ounce of black pepper and ¼ ounce of sage. Regrind until very fine. Stuff in cleaned casings of any desired size. Smoke until they take on a rich orange color, then cook in hot, but not boiling, water from 10 to 15 minutes, depending on the size of the sausages. The use of too hot water or too much fire in the smokehouse will cause the sausages to split and be wasted.

To smoke hams, pork shoulders and slabs of bacon, let meat dry overnight to avoid streaking. Hang so pieces do not touch. Build a fire under them with any hard wood available or with corncobs and sawdust. Do not use resinous woods like pine. Leave ventilator open the first day to permit moisture to escape. Then close it and smoke meat until it is the desired shade of brown. Two or 3 days usually is enough. It is important not to overheat the meat. A temperature of 80 to 90° F. is right for the smokehouse.

See revised directions at end of this chapter.

Smoking Meat

After meat has been in the brine or pickle long enough, it is removed, soaked in lukewarm water 20 minutes and then washed in fresh lukewarm water. The pieces are then strung with heavy twine and hung in the smokehouse so that no two pieces touch. Allow to dry 24 hours. Then smoke, beginning with a very low fire. The fire should make as little heat and as much smoke as possible. Too hot a fire dries the outside of the meat and prevents the smoke from penetrating it.

Any hard wood may be used for smoking meat, although hickory smothered in sawdust is a favorite. Maple is also satisfactory and when wood cannot be obtained, corncobs are an excellent substitute.

Length of Time to Smoke

Meat is smoked until it is of an even light or medium brown color. The shortest time meat is smoked is 2 days, but the flavor is usually much better if smoked slowly a much longer time. If meat is frozen, it should be thawed out before being smoked. In warm weather the fire should be allowed to die out every other day until the meat is smoked. This keeps the temperature from becoming too high.

When the meat is of the right color, the door and ventilators of the smokehouse are opened. The meat is left hanging until it is cool. It is then wrapped in heavy newspapers and sewed up in stout muslin bags.

Wash for Keeping Meat

The United States Department of Agriculture gives the following recipe for a wash to be applied to the muslin bags holding the smoked and cured meat. For 110 pounds of meat use 3 pounds of baryates, 0.06 pound of glue, 0.08 pound chrome yellow, which is a poison, and 0.40 pound flour. Half fill a pail with water and mix in the flour, dissolving all the lumps. Dissolve the chrome in a quart of water and add it and the glue to the flour mixture. Bring to the boiling point and add the baryates slowly, stirring constantly. Make this wash the day before it is needed. Stir frequently while applying it with a brush to the outer surface of the muslin bags around the meat.

Grandma's Mince Meat

8 pounds meat	4 tablespoonfuls allspice
6 pounds currants	4 pounds suet
6 pounds raisins	2 pounds citron
12 pounds sugar	20 pounds raw apples
12 tablespoonfuls cinnamon	12 gallons cider
8 tablespoonfuls mace	4 tablespoonfuls salt

4 tablespoonfuls grated nutmeg

Use either boiled beef or pork for this purpose and put through the food grinder with the currants, seedless raisins, citron and apples. Add the spices and sugar. Bring the cider to the boiling point and add the other ingredients. Boil 1 hour, stirring frequently. Can while hot in air tight and sterilized glass fruit jars. These jars may be sterilized by boiling in water 15 minutes.

To can mincemeat, spoon hot mixture into clean, hot jars, adjust lids and process at 10 pounds pressure in pressure canner for 60 minutes.

Storing Smoked Meat. Pack the cooled, cured hams, pork shoulders and bacon in tightly woven cloth bags. Put at least 6 inches of crumpled newspaper in the bottom of each bag. Stuff more newspaper around the meat to hold it away from the bag. Close bag and tie shut to keep out insects. If packed airtight, the meat may spoil. Hang in a dry place to avoid the formation of mold. Different directions for storage of cured meats were advocated 50 years ago when huge quantities often were cured during winter months to last a family the remainder of the year.

PART II

CHAPTER 1

HOUSEHOLD RECIPES

Toilet Soap

PLACE 10 pounds of double refined 98 per cent caustic soda powder in an earthenware jar or in a can with 4½ gallons of water. Stir a few times with a stick. The powder will dissolve immediately and become hot. Let it stand until the lye thus made is cool.

Weigh out and place in any utensil convenient for mixing 75 pounds of linseed oil, cottonseed oil or any vegetable oil, clean grease or tallow. If grease is used it must be melted slowly until it is liquid and just barely warm, not hot. When oil is used, it is not heated at all.

Pour the lye into the oil slowly, stirring with a wooden stick, and continue to stir gently until the oil and lye are combined thoroughly and have the appearance of honey. Do not stir the mixture longer or it will separate. The time of stirring varies with the temperature and the atmospheric conditions but ordinarily from 15 to 20 minutes is long enough.

Dampen the sides of pans or boxes with cold water and pour the soap into them. Allow this to stand in a warm room for 24 hours. Then cut in squares.

The addition of a few drops of oil or mirbane, artificial almond oil, just after the oil and lye are mixed provides perfume. Other pleasing odors are supplied by a few drops of real almond oil, citronella or oil of cloves. The precautions to heed in making this soap are: allow the lye to cool before using it, use exact weights of double refined 98 per cent caustic soda and grease or oil and stir the lye into the grease, not the grease into the lye.

Destroying Weavils in Beans

Place the beans in a box with a tightly fitting lid or in an old trunk if one is available. Pour carbon bisulphide in a saucer and

221

Reading the recipes in this chapter explains why women's work never was done.

Soap making rated enough importance in the two decades before 1920 to be taught in home economics classes.

Many farm families purchased a winter's supply of dried beans in autumn to last through the winter. Baked beans and bean soups were great favorites.

Tin foil was used for many purposes before aluminum foil was manufactured.

The mercury moves around in little bubbles on glass and is not easily controlled, but many old-timers managed it successfully.

set this on top of the beans. Close the lid of the box or trunk and do not open for 24 hours. Since carbon bisulphide is explosive, care must be taken not to use it near a fire.

Re-silvering Mirrors

Spread a sheet of tin-foil corresponding to the size of the plate of glass evenly on a smooth and solid table, and carefully rub down every wrinkle on its surface with a brush. Pour a portion of mercury and rub it over the tin-foil with a piece of very soft woolen cloth. Apply rulers to the edges; then pour mercury on to the depth of a dime. Carefully remove any oxide on the surface, remove the old coating from the glass and be sure it is clean and dry. Then slide the glass over the surface of the liquid metal so no air, dirt or oxide can possibly remain or get between them.

When the glass has reached the proper position, apply gentle pressure and slope the table a little to carry off the waste mercury. Cover the glass with a flannel cloth and load it with heavy weights. After 24 hours slant the glass a little. Keep slanting it a little more every day until at the end of a month it becomes perpendicular. It is then ready to be used.

Fly Killer

An inexpensive and effective fly killer which can be used on the farm without danger to the children and livestock is made by mixing ½ cupful of milk, 1 teaspoonful of formaldehyde and 1½ cupfuls of water together. This is poured into shallow pans and is especially effective if set in places where water is scarce.

Cleaning Silverware

Place the tarnished silver in an old aluminum pan or kettle which contains boiling water. Add 1 teaspoonful of baking soda and an equal amount of salt to every quart of water used. The silver should be covered by this solution. As the water boils the tarnish is dissolved.

Paste for Wall Paper

Mix 1 quart of flour with sufficient cold water to make a stiff paste or batter and then add 1½ gallons of boiling water. Stir

Wallpapers that could be applied without brushing on paste were not even in the imagination.

the mixture until the flour is cooked. When this has stood a few hours, but not overnight, it is ready for use. If the paper is being hung on walls which have been painted, the paste is thinned with ½ cupful of molasses. When very heavy paper is being hung, the addition of 2 teaspoonfuls of Venetian turpentine will help make it stick.

Re-sizing Rugs

To re-size rugs which have become flimsy, dissolve 1 quart of powdered dry glue in 1 gallon of boiling water. Keep this on the stove until the glue is dissolved. Tack the rug wrong-side down on the floor, spreading old newspapers around the edges to protect the floor. Use a brush to apply the glue solution, taking care to cover every inch of space. Cover the edges of the rug with the solution. Do not move the rug for 24 hours or until the sizing is dry.

Laying Linoleum

Spread a layer of heavy paper, frequently called builder's felt, or some other heavy paper on the floor. Using a brush, paste this to the floor with linoleum paste. This lining should fit closely to the baseboard, and if there is a molding, it should be removed.

Next the strips of linoleum are laid on the floor; they are matched at the seams and cut to fit the room. Then by rolling one strip back half-way paste is applied to the underside to within three inches of the edges. Linoleum cement is then spread on the edges. The purpose of the linoleum paste and cement is to fasten the floor covering firmly to the floor so water cannot get underneath to rot the fiber. The paper lining keeps the expansion and contraction of the wood, due to atmospheric conditions, from causing the linoleum to bulge or crack.

Weights are needed until the cement and paste are dry. A good way to secure the necessary weight is to fill a wooden box with bricks, fasten a rope to it for a handle and then pull this back and forth over the surface, particularly up and down the seams. A board weighted down can be laid over the seams for 24 hours to hold the cement firm. Then the molding is replaced.

Men performed this task, but women stood by to offer suggestions, if necessary, and to help.

Today's freezer holds butter much more successfully. If made with pasteurized cream, butter, when frozen, keeps up to 9 months.

Freezers keep unfrosted cakes 4 to 6 months, frosted cakes 2 to 3 months.

In cold weather the rolls of linoleum should be left in a warm room at least 48 hours before being laid.

Putting Down Butter

Before the grass is gone in the fall and while cream is plentiful, butter may be put down for winter use. Work the butter as for immediate use, making certain that all the buttermilk is removed. Pack the butter in earthenware jars to within 5 inches of the top. Make a brine from coarse salt and water strong enough that an egg will float in it. Strain through fine cloth and pour over the butter, filling the jar. Cover the jar tightly and set in a cave or cellar. This butter will keep through the winter.

Keeping Cake Fresh

If several layers of cake are baked at one time and placed in a tightly covered earthenware jar, they will stay fresh many days. Just before using two or three of the layers, cover them with a cooked icing, the warmth of which steams and freshens the cake. By using different kinds of icings, the taste of the different cakes made from the same batter will be varied. Or the batter may be divided before being baked and the different layers flavored with a variety of extracts. Having this cake on hand when guests or crews of men come is very helpful.

Keeping Cider Sweet

The fermentation of cider may be retarded greatly by the addition of sodium benzoate, but it is doubtful if the addition of this substance or any chemical preservative at all permissible for this purpose will prevent fermentation under all conditions. Apple juice treated with 0.1 to 0.2 per cent sodium benzoate will, however, probably not undergo any fermentation within a considerable period of time if it is kept cool during storage. Benzoate of soda in amount not to exceed one-tenth of one per cent is permitted by the Pure Food and Drug's Act in juices to be sold, but its presence in the material must be indicated on the label.

Making Hominy

Dissolve 4 tablespoonfuls of lye in 1 gallon of boiling water. Boil the corn rapidly in this solution 30 minutes. Then drain and wash the kernels thoroughly several times in cold water to remove the lye. Rub with the hands until the husks, or covering of the kernels, are removed. Then place the corn in an enamel kettle and boil in a little water until tender. Wash again, pack in glass jars and sterilize by the cold pack method of canning, following the directions given in the chapter on canning.

Salt Rising Bread

2 cupfuls milk
½ cupful cornmeal
4 teaspoonfuls sugar
2 teaspoonfuls salt
2 cupfuls water
flour

Scald the milk and mix it with the cornmeal, sugar and salt. Let stand several hours, or overnight, in a very warm place. After standing it should be light. Add warm water and enough flour to make a drop batter. Keep at a very warm temperature, 167 degrees Fahrenheit, until light. Then add sufficient flour to make a stiff dough and shape into 2 loaves. Allow to rise and double its bulk, and bake. Care should be taken to keep the temperature higher than for ordinary bread. The milk should always be scalded before mixing the batter, as more uniform results may be obtained, and a product secured which does not have the unpleasant odor frequently associated with salt rising bread.

Making Sauerkraut

Remove the outside leaves and hard core of cabbage. Cut into fine shreds and pack in layers, 3 to 6 inches deep, in a crock or keg. Sprinkle every layer with salt, repeating the process until the cabbage is within a few inches of the top. For every 100 pounds of shredded cabbage use 10 to 12 cupfuls of salt. Press the cabbage down until the brine covers it, place a few leaves over the top, arrange a clean board or plate over the leaves and weight it down with a heavy block. Lime stones should not be used for weights since they are attacked by the

When canning, hominy, cook the kernels in water 30 to 40 minutes, or until tender, and drain. Pack hot in hot jars to within ½ inch of jar top. Add salt, (½ tsp. to pints, 1 tsp. to quarts) and fill with boiling water, leaving ½-inch headspace. Adjust lids and process at 10 pounds pressure 60 minutes for pint jars, 70 minutes for quart jars. Do not use water bath in canning hominy.

To can sauerkraut when cured, fill canning jars, leaving ½-inch headspace. Adjust lids and place in water-bath canner holding cold water. Water should extend to shoulders of jars. Bring slowly to a boil and process quart jars 30 minutes.

When eggs were plentiful on the farm in autumn, they were preserved in this way for use in cooking during the cold months when the hens usually were lazy.

Farmers and their sons were enthusiastic trappers in their neighborhoods, but by 1920 they rarely tanned the hides. They sold them and hides from beef they slaughtered to put a little jingle in their pockets.

acid of the brine. Remove the scum which forms on top when it is noticed and see that the kraut is kept covered with brine. Keep a clean cloth over the top of the crock to make certain that dust, dirt and insects cannot get in. When the kraut is cured, which will be from 2 to 3 weeks in warm weather and from 6 to 8 weeks in winter, it may be canned.

Preserving Eggs

Eggs are most abundant and lowest in price during the spring and early summer months. Therefore it is best to put them up at this season for winter use. Use only good, fresh eggs for this purpose. Six quarts of solution in a 3-gallon jar will preserve 10 dozen eggs. Use 1 part, about a pint, of waterglass to 9 parts of boiled water which has been allowed to cool. Stir the mixture thoroughly and pour it into a crock and put in the eggs. Store in a cool place, such as a cellar, and be certain that the tops of the eggs are covered with 2 or 3 inches of the liquid. Add fresh water to replace the liquid which evaporates. Buy fresh waterglass from the druggist every year instead of keeping a supply on hand. The solution is not good for a second year's use. Infertile eggs are better for preserving than fertile ones.

Keeping Cellar Free from Dampness

A large open box or pan filled with fresh lime helps to dry and purify the air in a cellar. When the lime becomes air-slacked, it should be discarded and fresh lime added.

Tanning Hides

Wash the skin with strong soap suds to remove dirt from the wool, soak overnight in soapy water and tack down over a barrel to dry. Have the flesh side down. When nearly dry, remove the hide and clean off any pieces of flesh or fat that remain. Rub prepared chalk over the skin until no more can be rubbed in and then rub with powdered alum and sprinkle this all over the skin. This is the method used for treating sheepskins and goatskins.

In preparing coon and squirrel hides for caps, sheepskins and goatskins for rugs and lambskins for coats and vests the hides may be rubbed with alum and saltpeter. Then they are folded with the flesh sides together, rolled tightly and stored in a dry place a week. The flesh side is then rubbed down with a damp cloth dipped in rotten stone until it becomes smooth and acquires a polish.

Bleaching and Re-sizing Straw Hats

Mix the juice of 1 lemon with 1 tablespoonful of sulphur and apply this thick paste with a brush to the hat. It is best to remove the hat band before the mixture is applied. Rub the paste into the straw, then rinse by moistening the brush in clear water, taking care not to use any more water than is necessary to remove all the paste. If the straw hat is flimsy, re-size by beating up the white of an egg and applying this to the straw with a fine brush.

Waterproofing Leather

An old-fashioned recipe for waterproofing leather is to melt by gentle heat 4 ounces of raw linseed oil, 5 ounces of boiled linseed oil, 4 ounces of suet and 4 ounces of beeswax. This is applied to the leather while warm. A simple method is that of rubbing the leather with equal amounts of mutton tallow and beeswax.

Removing Furniture Blemishes

To remove white spots from varnished surfaces which have been caused by water, fill a small basin with tepid water and add several drops of household ammonia to it. Dip a soft cloth in this, wring quite dry and apply to the unsightly places. It may take three or four applications to remove every trace of whiteness. When they disappear, rub the surface gently with furniture polish.

White stains on dining room tables made by hot dishes may be removed by being covered with baking soda. A hot iron is held near, taking care that the wood is not scorched. Repeating this process two or three times and rubbing the surface with furniture polish will usually restore the desired appearance.

When scratches appear on furniture or woodwork, go over the surface with a cloth moistened in furniture polish to see if the

Men and boys wore straw hats the summer long to protect against sunburn. The hatless craze was years in the future.

dye in it will make the scratch invisible. Another method which may be used is to apply a small amount of water color for wood to the scratch, using a shade which matches the finish of the wood.

Highly polished surfaces which are marred by hairlines or tiny cracks may be improved by being rubbed from day to day with a cloth moistened in oil, 1 part lemon oil to 2 parts of boiled linseed oil.

Bruises or dents may be removed with water and heat. Take four thicknesses of blotting paper and dip in water. When the superfluous water has dripped away, place the paper over the bruise and hold a hot flat or electric iron near it. The heat and moisture cause the wood to expand. More than one treatment of this kind may be required to remove a large dent. After removing the blotting paper, lay a cloth moistened in linseed oil on the surface. Several hours later, remove it and polish with a solution made by combining equal parts of turpentine and linseed oil.

Removing Floor Blemishes

Black, ink-like stains on oak floors are caused by the iron in water reacting with the gallic acid in the wood. They are very obstinate but may be dimmed and frequently are removed by dipping a cloth in weak oxalic acid and rubbing the spot with this. After it is dimmed or disappears, the surface is rinsed two or three times with clear water and wax or oil is applied to restore the finish. Care should be taken not to let the acid touch the hands.

Making Lye

Fill a wooden keg or half-barrel with wood ashes. Holes should be bored in the keg or barrel a few inches above the bottom. Pour water on the ashes and place a wooden trough or pails to catch the lye water which seeps out from the ash barrel or keg.

Making Cider

Only wholesome apples should be used. Bruised fruit need not be discarded but the decayed portions should be cut out or

Area rugs were fashionable in country homes. Frequently they were spread on oak floors. The ink-like spots caused by spilled water were a constant concern.

Only a few grandmothers in 1923 made lye.

Canning Cider or Apple Juice, Sweetened to Taste. The recommended 1976 way is to bring the cider or juice to simmering, not boiling, and pour into pint or quart canning jars, leaving ½-inch headspace. Adjust lids and process in boiling-water bath 10 minutes. The old method of sterilizing cider was too much work.

they will give the cider a disagreeable flavor. Wash the apples, grind them in a cider mill and place them in a press which removes the juice. Drain this in clean vessels, wooden barrels or kegs which have previously been scalded. Store in the coolest place possible.

Since sweet cider sours so rapidly, it usually is pasteurized the next day after it is made. To do this sterilize glass fruit jars or bottles by boiling them in water several minutes. Pour the cider in these sterile containers and set these on a wooden rack in the bottom of a wash boiler. Fill the boiler with cold water which reaches to the necks of the bottles and hang a thermometer half its length in the water. Heat the water until it reaches 175 degrees Fahrenheit, but do not let the water become warmer. Leave the vessels containing the cider in this water bath 30 minutes if quart or half gallon bottles or glass jars are used and 45 minutes if gallon containers are used. Then remove the cans or bottles and tighten the covers on the cans and place corks in the bottles. Place in the cellar, cave or some cool dark place for storage. Watch them for a week or two; if there is a froth at the top of the cider, it is fermenting. The lids of the jars will have to be loosened and the corks of the bottles removed and the containers placed in the water bath and given the same treatment as before. Before placing the cider in the wash boiler, place cotton in the mouths of the bottles and place rubbers and lids which have been sterilized in boiling water on the cans. Do not screw the lids on tightly, but just give it a half turn so it will hold during the sterilization. The lids may be sterilized by being boiled with the cans and the rubbers are dipped in boiling water.

The cooked or boiled taste that usually is not liked when canned cider is served is avoided in this method, provided a thermometer is used and the water is not heated above 175 degrees F. It must be heated this much, however, or it will not keep.

Sizing Walls

Dissolve 1 pound of glue in a little hot water and then add 1 gallon of cold water. Apply this to the wall with a brush before adding new paper.

Leather was plentiful and used extensively in upholstering chairs and sofas.

Since almost all farms kept a flock of chickens, a surplus of eggs sometimes developed. Many enterprising women capitalized on it by selling eggs to buy clothes for the children and articles for the house. A candler came in handy for these country entrepreneurs.

Cleaning Shoes

If a coarse scrubbing brush is kept near the door, the shoes may be cleaned with this much easier than if a knife is used. The knife may cut or scrape the leather. Rubbing leather shoes with milk once a week helps to keep them in a good condition.

Preventing Leather Seats from becoming Sticky

Leather chair seats and upholstered furniture frequently become sticky. This usually is caused by the leather drying out. To prevent it, rub the leather every month or two with a soft cloth moistened in neat's-foot oil. When the stickiness occurs, remove as much of it as possible with gasoline and apply neat's-foot oil. Do not wipe the oil off for a day or two.

Removing Mildew from Leather

Apply vaseline with a soft cloth to remove mildew from leather.

Removing Grease from Leather

Beat the white of an egg slightly and apply to the grease spot. Set in the sun to dry, then brush off.

Making Egg Candler

Before setting eggs under hens or putting them down for the winter, they may be candled to make certain they are fresh. A simple candler consists of a pasteboard shoe box with a hole a little larger than a half dollar cut in one side. Slip the box over the lamp or electric light bulb in a dark room and hold the eggs, large end up, before the opening in the box. Good eggs will look clear and firm and the white spot, or air cell, at the end of the egg is small, not larger than a dime. The yolk can be seen as a dim spot in the center. A large air cell and a dark, freely moving yolk indicates that the egg is not fresh.

Cottage Cheese

Set a quantity of fresh sour milk in a moderately warm room and allow to sour naturally. Unless the milk has been con-

It tastes different from today's commercially produced cottage cheese. There was one bonus, or whey, a by-product, featured in one of the famous pies of yesteryear.

taminated at the barn or by a soiled utensil, the curd will be smooth, even and free from gas bubbles. The best temperature to set milk for cottage cheese is 70 to 72 degrees. As soon as the milk is curdled throughout, stir and break it up; then heat it gradually to 104 degrees Fahrenheit. If you do not have a dairy thermometer, set the milk on the back of the stove so it will not be heated too much. When the whey separates from the curd, pour the curd into a muslin bag and hang up to drain. It takes from 2 to 10 hours to drain the curd, depending on the size and firmness of the curd particles. When drained, it is moist and granular but not sticky.

The drained curd is then salted to taste. About 1 ounce of salt is sufficient for 8 pounds of cheese. Two cupfuls of cream added to this amount of cheese will improve its flavor. Some homemakers also add 2 tablespoonfuls of sugar.

Furniture Polish

To 1 cupful of turpentine add a piece of beeswax about the size of a walnut. Stir into this 1½ pints of paraffine oil. Mix and shake well and apply to the furniture with a soft cloth, being careful not to use too much. Ugly stains may be removed by using rotten stone for scouring along with this polish.

Cleaning the Mattress

To remove stains from a mattress rub the soiled places with dry starch, moistening it with a little soap jelly or soap dissolved in warm water. This will make a paste. Care should be taken that it is not wet enough to soak into the mattress. When dry, brush off the starch. Occasionally more than one application is necessary. When the stains have disappeared, sponge the surface with a little ammonia water.

Making Bags

Housework is made easier by the use of convenient bags. After lettuce is washed, it may be stored in a cheesecloth bag in a cool place, such as a refrigerator. Tomatoes are prepared easily if placed in a tomato bag of cheesecloth and scalded. They can be hung up to drain. By the time they are cool, the

How unfortunate that versatile plastic bags were so far in the future!

skins can be rubbed off and the vegetables returned to the bags to await the serving time. A three cornered jelly bag made of two thicknesses of cheesecloth or of cotton flannel is helpful. If a canton flannel bag is tied over the broom, the walls and ceilings may be brushed down without being scratched. Bags of cheesecloth, net or mosquito netting which are filled with dried sweet clover, rose petals or leaves, rose geranium, lemon verbena, lavender or other summer sweets impart a fragrance to sheets, pillow slips and other household linens if placed among them. Large cheesecloth bags for use in blanching or scalding vegetables before canning them by the cold pack method simplify the work.

Wall pockets which consist of a rectangle of heavy material such as cretonne, Indian head and denim on which pockets of various sizes are stitched, make a home for the odds and ends in a household. Shoe and laundry pockets may be tacked to the clothes press doors. The kitchen wall pocket should hold a ball of twine, wrapping paper, soiled tea towels, corks, rubber bands and other useful articles, a pocket in the bathroom holds the dried and soiled towels and a mending pocket near the sewing machine is never empty long.

Making Old-Fashioned Rose Jar

Gather the rose petals on a dry day after the dew is gone and place these petals in rose jars, which are vases with lids, or in fruit jars. Arrange the petals in thin layers, covering each one with a thin layer of salt. Repeat until the jar is filled. If one wishes, a handful of lavender flowers or rosemary leaves may be added. Add 3 or 4 ounces of pulverized bay salt, 1 ounce of nutmeg, 1 ounce of cinnamon and 1 ounce of cloves. Keep the jar closely covered except when the perfume is wanted in a room. These are especially attractive additions to old-fashioned bedrooms.

Making Money in the Farm Home

The homemaker of the farm household who wishes to make money will find that there are many products which she can sell. The important factor is to find a market for these articles. An exclusive trade of city customers is the most satisfactory for

Some countrywomen and their daughters once again are making rose jars as a hobby and for Christmas gifts.

these people are willing to pay for the word country when applied to a product. Eggs direct from the country, homemade country sausage, horseradish or cottage cheese are worth more to a city dweller than store eggs, sausage, horseradish and cheese. A few of the articles which farm women may sell with profit are poultry and poultry products, homemade jellies and jams, canned fruit and vegetables, horseradish, cottage cheese, vinegars, flowers, ferns, rhubarb and fancy fruit preserves. If the home is large enough, city boarders may be taken during the summer months when vacation season arrives. Occasionally a market for fancy work and other types of hand sewing may be found.

Making Baby's First Bed

Select a stout clothes basket with strong handles. A satisfactory length for this is 36 inches. The easiest way to make this basket attractive is to apply two coats of flat white paint to it, allowing the first coat to dry before the second one is added. For a finish a coat of white enamel is applied. Then the basket is lined so it will make a soft bed. First, take a roll of cotton batting and distribute it evenly on the sides of the basket, tacking it in place with thread. Cover this with a washable material, such as dotted swiss, mull, silkaline, cheesecloth or dimity. A very pretty effect is obtained by using two linings, the under one being of a delicate pink or blue which shows through the white top lining of sheer lawn, dotted net or some other fabric. Usually these baskets are about 10 or 15 inches deep. To line them cut the material, which is 36 inches wide and 2 yards long, in two strips 18 inches in width. Sew these together making one long piece. The raw edges are turned back and the strip is gathered at the top and bottom so it will fit the basket. A heading is allowed at the top for a finish. Then the gathered strip is glued or sewed at the top and bottom of the inside of the basket. To make the bassinet comfortable, as well as pretty, a mattress or pillow is placed in the bottom.

Removing Fish Odors

The odor of fish or cabbage may be removed from dishes by filling them with boiling water and dropping a piece of char-

Some grandmothers and many great-grandmothers remember carrying an adorable baby in a basket they trimmed in blue for a boy, in pink for a girl.

Detergents for dishwashing make fish and other objectionable odors vanish.

These were flatirons, the kind considered antiques and often used for doorstoppers.

coal in the water. After standing a short time the undesirable odor will disappear.

Cleaning Irons

Wipe the flat iron with oiled or wax paper and rub it on a piece of fine sandpaper which is tacked on the ironing board, or on dry salt.

Making Cellars Warmer

Paste heavy paper over the rafters in the ceiling and down over the sills and around the frames of the windows, using the paste which is applied in hanging wall paper. The addition of 2 teaspoonfuls of Venetian turpentine to the paste will help make the paper stick.

Loosening Drawers Which Stick

Rub the parts of the drawers which stick with yellow soap, with paste wax or with tallow.

Filling Cracks in Floors

Putty may be used for filling cracks in floors but it shows through varnish or any finish placed on the surface. Another filling may be made by dissolving 1 ounce of glue in 2 cupfuls of boiling water. While this is hot, tiny bits of newspaper are stirred into it. When the mass becomes as thick as putty, it is placed in the cracks, being pushed in tightly with a putty knife. If a putty knife is not available, a blunt-edged case knife may be used. This filling should be put in the cracks while hot and finished evenly at the top. If one wishes, it may be colored to match the stain in the wood.

Mending Wall Paper

Select the right portion of the pattern in the roll for the patch. Then tear an irregular piece instead of cutting it. Paste this over the tear in the paper on the wall.

Removing Grease Spots from Walls

Fold a piece of white blotting paper and pin French chalk in the fold. Hold this over the grease spot, ironing it with an electric or flat iron, taking care that the wall is not scorched. Change the position of the blotting paper frequently.

Drying Herbs

Among the herbs which may be grown in the garden or in window boxes are sage, parsley, thyme, chervil, basil and mint. The leaves from these plants may be picked, spread on paper and dried in a warm room, but not in direct sunlight, for use in the winter.

Powdering Herbs

The dried herbs may be placed in tightly covered cans for storage. If one wishes, they may be powdered by being pounded in a wooden chopping bowl with a wooden potato masher.

Making Pan Holders

The hands will be saved many burns if hot pan holders are kept in the kitchen for use when one is cooking. Satisfactory holders are made by cutting diamond shaped pieces from heavy table padding and covering these with removable gingham covers which may be washed. If an unbleached muslin pocket is made for these holders and hung near the kitchen stove, one never needs to look for them.

Storing Vegetables

For home use cabbage and root vegetables may be stored in the cellar for early winter consumption and outdoors in pits for late winter use. The great danger of cellar storage for these vegetables is that they may wilt. This can be overcome to some extent by packing them in boxes with alternate layers of sand or earth and setting these boxes in the coolest part of the basement. The outer leaves of the cabbage are removed before the heads are packed in the boxes.

Usually the pits for outdoor storage are made above the

Gardeners are resurrecting the old custom of storing root vegetables for winter use.

ground unless one is certain that the drainage is unusually good. The cabbage is pulled with roots and leaves on and the heads are placed in regular rows on a level stretch of ground. The heads are placed down. The common way is to arrange three heads in a row with two heads on top. Earth is piled against the cabbage until the plants, including the roots, are entirely covered. In cold climates a layer of manure is placed over this pile. Parsnips, salsify and horseradish may be stored in this same way. They are covered with 6 or 8 inches of earth. Turnips, rutabagas, potatoes, beets and carrots may be stored in outdoor pits, but they must be covered sufficiently so they will not freeze. Usually it is more convenient to store these vegetables in the cellar or cave. In case there are not facilities for cellar or basement storage, place the vegetables on the ground and cover them with 8 inches of straw or hay. Then cover the straw with 8 inches of earth. A layer of manure is then placed outside the earth.

Celery may be stored in the cellar or cave if it is cool. The plants are dug with the roots on and are planted in moist earth on the cellar or cave floor. The earth about the plant roots is wet occasionally, but care must be taken not to moisten the leaves.

After onions are pulled, they should be allowed to dry or cure before being stored. If the cellar is cool, the onions may be placed in baskets and hung at the top of the cellar. Attic storage is satisfactory if there is a place near the chimney where it is warm enough to keep the onions from freezing. Darkness keeps them from sprouting.

Sweet potatoes, pumpkins and squashes must be stored in a warm and dry place where there is a free circulation of air. A good way to keep sweet potatoes is to put them in slatted boxes which are set in an upstairs room which is kept warm all the time or in a basement where there is a furnace.

Mending Rugs

Select a piece of soft, flimsy woolen material or burlap and baste this under the hole in the floor covering. Either darn this down with yarn to match that used in the rug or use the yarn double and stick the needle through from the top. bring it up in almost the same place and tie to the end above. Repeat this process until the surface of the patch is covered with loops. Trim these off evenly.

Removing Varnish

Wash the surface with strong lye water, using a scrub brush so the hands will not touch the water. When most of the varnish disappears, rinse the surface two or three times with clear water. The few spots of varnish left may be removed by applying wood alcohol or by being rubbed with sandpaper. The surface should be sandpapered before being refinished.

Sweetening Rancid Butter

Soak the butter in water to which a small handful of baking soda has been added. After soaking some little time, drain off the water and wash the butter with sweet milk. Work the milk out thoroughly and the flavor of the butter will be fresh.

Pigments for Stains

When staining furniture, woodwork or floors, burnt umber may be added to give a black walnut color, burnt sienna for mahogany and yellow ocher for a yellow shade. Three tablespoonfuls of any of these materials are added to a gallon of the stain.

Polishes for Woodwork

A good polish for wood surfaces is made by mixing together 1 cupful of turpentine, 1 cupful of linseed oil and 1 cupful of vinegar. Another excellent polish is prepared by mixing 1 cupful of linseed oil, 1 cupful of turpentine and 1 teaspoonful of ammonia together. Either of these polishes is sprinkled lightly on a soft cloth and applied to the furniture or woodwork with the grain of the wood.

Repairing Plaster

Cut away the edges of the crack or hole with a sharp paring knife, making them straight. Fill the cavity with plaster of Paris mixed with a little vinegar. The vinegar keeps the plaster

There is no excuse for rancid butter today with refrigerators and freezers doing their work efficiently.

of Paris from setting so quickly. A good filling for cracks in plaster is made by mixing 1½ tablespoonfuls of plaster of Paris with 3 tablespoonfuls of fine sand and moistening the mixture with vinegar.

Removing Putty

Putty may be removed from glass by applying a heated iron to the spot and when it becomes soft, scraping it off with a knife. If the putty is on the wood, either soften it with the hot iron, taking care not to scorch the wood, or apply a little dilute sulphuric acid to it with a brush. After using the acid, wash the surface with soapy water and rinse two or three times in clear water.

Renovating Gilt Picture Frames

If pieces of the frame are broken off, use a bit of putty properly shaped to build up the surface. Then apply a coat of gold paint. The putty should be allowed to dry before the paint is added.

Packing Books and Pictures in Moving

Since books are so heavy, pack them in several small boxes or barrels instead of one large one. Wrap the books in small packages, placing a layer of paper between the bindings. Place about 6 books in every package. Use old newspapers for the wrapping paper. Tie every package of books with cord so they cannot rub together. These packages of books are packed in the box or barrel, the open space being filled with crumpled newspaper or excelsior so the books cannot move within the box.

Two pictures are packed together face to face with a blanket or quilt between them. Small ones are placed among clothes in bureau drawers and the large ones are crated.

Clearing Room of Mosquitoes

Mosquitoes may be driven from a room by hanging tender branches of castor beans here and there or by spreading wilted leaves of the castor bean in different parts of the room. The Entomology Bureau of the United States Department of Agriculture recommends sprinkling equal parts of spirits of camphor

In wet seasons the mosquitoes were a real menace. That is why so many homes in irrigated country had tightly screened porches as well as windows.

and oil of citronella and ½ part of oil of cedar on a towel and hanging this at the head of a bed in a room infested with mosquitoes.

Preparing a Dust Cloth

Dust will collect on the furniture if too much polish is applied. A good way to add the right amount is to place 2 tablespoonfuls of the polish in a glass fruit jar, rolling the can until its sides are coated with the polish. Then insert the tightly rolled dust cloth, close the fruit jar and let stand 2 days. The polish will be evenly distributed on the cloth.

Making Whitewash

Place 10 pounds of quicklime in a container and stir in 2 gallons of water. Cover and let stand an hour, stirring occasionally. The addition of 4½ pounds of salt will make the whitewash stick better.

A whitewash which will last longer is made by using 38 pounds of quicklime, 3 pounds of sodium phosphate, 5 pounds of caseine and 9½ gallons of water. Mix the lime and the water and when cool, add the casein dissolved in the solution of sodium phosphate. This is used for exterior purposes.

Another excellent recipe for whitewash is this: mix 50 pounds of hydrated lime in boiling water until a thin paste is formed. Add 1 peck of salt, 3 pounds of rice flour, ½ pound of Spanish whiting and 1 pound of clear glue dissolved in boiling water. The salt should be dissolved in boiling water and the rice flour boiled with water to a thin paste before it is added to the salt solution. After mixing thoroughly, the mixture is allowed to stand several days. When being applied, the whitewash should be hot if possible.

This method of preparing dust cloths for use still is used in many homes with a coffee can substituting for the glass jar.

CHAPTER 2

LAUNDERING RECIPES

Homemade Soap from Cracklings

Pour 2 gallons of water into an iron kettle and empty 3 cans of lye into it. Let cool 1 hour. Place the lye mixture on the stove and add 14 pounds of fryings or cracklings. Let this boil until every particle of grease is dissolved. Add cold water from time to time, adding just enough to keep the quantity of liquid the same all the time. The addition of cold water also keeps the mixture from boiling over.

When all the grease is dissolved, set the mixture aside to cool overnight. In the morning skim off the white crust and brown jelly, leaving the sediment in the bottom. Dispose of the sediment and wash the kettle. Put the white crust and jelly back into the kettle and boil 2 hours. Then add boiling water until the soap becomes the consistency of honey when dropped from a stick. Be careful not to add too much water. Pour into molds or boxes, which have been wet first in cold water, and cover the soap while cooling. Do not let freeze before it is hard.

Laundry Soap from Fat

Use 1½ gallons of water to every 1 pound box of lye and 5 pounds of fat to every pound of lye. Dissolve the lye in the water. As soon as the solution boils, stir in the fat and boil until the mass becomes the consistency of honey when dropped from a stick. When almost done, a small portion should be placed in a saucer and if it solidifies, the mass should be removed from the stove, poured into wet molds and set away in a warm place to harden.

240

Soap without Boiling

Dissolve 2 pounds of soda lye in 6 quarts of water. When cool, add this to 14 pounds of melted, but not heated, fat. Stir the mixture until it resembles the consistency of honey and is creamy. Pour into granite-ware pans, wet first in cold water, or in pasteboard boxes. When almost hard, cut in squares. Pack it with open spaces between pieces and allow to dry for at least a month before using. This makes a hard laundry soap.

Soap Jelly for Washing Woolens

Shave 2 cakes of any mild white soap in 2 quarts of water, add 1 cupful of borax and heat gently until the soap is dissolved. Pour this in fruit jars, cover and use as needed.

Whitening Flannels and Silks

If white woolen or silk garments, such as baby flannels, white serges, silk gloves and hose, become yellowed, they may be whitened with hydrogen peroxide. To every 10 pints of luke-warm water add 1 pint of hydrogen peroxide and a few drops of household ammonia. Soak the clothes in this solution until they are white.

Starch Making

Mix ½ cupful of starch with ¼ cupful of cold water and add ¼ teaspoonful of shaved white wax and 4 cupfuls of boiling water. Boil a few minutes, stirring to prevent sticking, and cool before using. This makes a thick starch. If thin starch is desired, add 4 cupfuls of cold water to the thick starch and stir until the mixture is smooth. Salt added to starch prevents it from freezing in clothes hung outdoors in cold weather. To a quart of cooked starch add 2 teaspoonfuls of salt. Gum arabic may be added to increase the gloss and to provide stiffness. In fact, starch containing gum arabic gives material the appearance and body that new fabrics have.

To prepare the gum arabic for use in starch dissolve 2 ounces of white gum arabic in 2 cupfuls of water. Place the gum

Shaving bars of mild soap and dissolving the shavings in water for quick sudsing was a step toward the packaged soap flakes now on supermarket shelves. The borax was added to soften the water in which the woolens were washed.

Cotton clothing, which dominated country wear before man-made fabrics arrived, often required the addition of starch in the laundering process. Most women had pet theories about making starch with few faults. Everyone agreed it had to be smooth as satin and of the right consistency. Spray starch was not yet on the dream board.

It was uncooked starch, known as "cold starch," that gave men's collars, and sometimes their cuffs, that desired stiffness of boards. The trick was to keep the starch from sticking to the iron. If it did, brown spots appeared and another washing and starching was in order.

arabic in a fruit jar, add the water, cover tightly and shake until it is dissolved. After the solution has stood 2 days, drain through cheesecloth and bottle for future use. Just before taking the boiled starch from the stove, add 1 tablespoonful of the gum arabic solution.

Rice Starch

Add 4 tablespoonfuls of washed rice to 1 quart of rapidly boiling water. Cook until the rice is a pulp, adding more hot water occasionally so the amount will remain the same. When the rice is cooked to a pulp, add 1 quart of boiling water and strain, without pressing, through a flannel bag. Use while hot, diluting with a little cool water if it is too thick.

Tinted Starches

A little tea may be added to the starch used with dark fabrics and a few drops of bluing improve the appearance of the starch used with white and blue materials.

Uncooked Starch

To 3 tablespoonfuls of starch and 1 teaspoonful of borax add 2 cupfuls of tepid water. Stir and use immediately.

Setting Colors

Add 1 pint of salt and 1 tablespoonful of powdered alum to 1 gallon of water and use in soaking fabrics to set the following colors: pink, brown, red, yellow, gray, black and black and white mixtures.

Green is set by soaking the garment in 1 gallon of water to which 1 tablespoonful of powdered alum has been added.

If strong salt water fails to set blue dye in fabrics, 1 tablespoonful of powdered alum, ½ cupful of strong vinegar and 1 tablespoonful of sugar of lead, a poison, may be added to a gallon of water used in the soaking.

Lavender and purple are set by being soaked in a gallon of water to which ½ cupful of strong vinegar is added.

Bleaching Yellowed White Fabrics

To bleach yellowed white cotton and linen fabrics, moisten the material in a solution made by dissolving 2 teaspoonfuls of potassium permanganate in 2 quarts of water. Rinse in a clear warm water. The material will become brown. Then dip it in a dilute oxalic acid solution, made by diluting the concentrated acid in an equal amount of water. Rinse through several waters, one of which is soapy.

If all the white clothes appear a little yellow, use a lemon or oxalic acid rinse when washing. Use ¼ tubful of hot water and add the juice of 4 large lemons or 2 tablespoonfuls of oxalic acid crystals first dissolved in a little warm water. Put the clothes in this rinse a few at a time and let stand 4 or 5 minutes and then put through a clear hot rinse.

Drying the clothes outdoors in the sunshine is the best way to keep them white. Slightly yellowed garments may be wet in water and spread on the grass in the sunshine to bleach.

Washing Pillows and Feathers

Fill a tub almost full of water and add 1 cupful of borax and 1 tablespoonful of ammonia. Place soiled feather pillows in this and boil 20 minutes. Scrub the tick to make certain it is clean. Rinse three times in clear warm water and hang outdoors in the wind, but in a shady place if possible. If one wishes, the feathers may be poured through a small opening in the tick into a muslin bag. Then the feathers and the pillow covering may be washed separately.

Javelle Water

1 pound sal soda or pearl ash   ¼ pound chloride of lime
2 quarts cold water

Mix the ingredients thoroughly and let stand overnight. Pour off the clear liquid and bottle for use. Store in a cool, dark place. To use Javelle Water, stretch the stained article and rub the liquid into it. Then rinse it quickly in clear water and rub a little if necessary. When the stain is gone, rinse in a little ammonia water. Javelle water is used only in removing stains from white cottons and linens.

Before bleaches were bottled for home use, women invented their own methods. With patience and practice some of them were quite successful.

In well-regulated households Javelle Water was made and kept in a dark place ready for treating stains on white tablecloths and napkins.

These were the best-known methods used in homes, but their performance was far from perfect. Some of today's annoying stains, such as ball-point ink, fingernail polish and lipstick, were not common and had no place on the list.

Removing Scorch

Scorch usually can be removed from cottons and linens by being moistened in water and placed in the sun to dry. It may be necessary to repeat this process more than once.

Removing Mucus from Handkerchiefs

Soak the handkerchiefs in salt water or in boric acid and water.

Removing Ordinary Stains

Blood—Soak fabric in tepid water.

Chocolate and Cocoa—Wash in cold water. Bleach white fabrics with Javelle water.

Coffee—Pour boiling water through fabric or cover with water in which borax is dissolved.

Egg—Wash out in cold water.

Fruit—Pour boiling water through fabric or dissolve in alcohol. Use Javelle water on white materials.

Glue—Use white vinegar or acetic acid.

Grass—Dissolve with alcohol or kerosene.

Grease—Soften with lard or turpentine and then wash in soap suds.

Gum—Remove stain with gasoline.

Ink—Soak in milk or bleach with salt, lemon juice and sunshine.

Fountain Pen Ink—Use Javelle water.

Iron Rust—Lemon juice, salt and sunshine or Javelle water.

Iodine—Hyposulphite of soda or chloroform should be used.

Medicine—Dissolve the stain in alcohol.

Mildew—Bleach with lemon juice and sunshine or Javelle water.

Milk or Cream—Wash with cold water, then with cold water and soap suds.

Paint, Varnish and Tar—Soak in turpentine or alcohol or if very dry, soften with lard and wash with soap suds.

Paraffin—Scrape off the excess and wash with hot soapy water.

Perspiration—Wash with soapy water and bleach in the sunshine.

Sugar—Wash in water or alcohol.

Tea—Pour boiling water through the fabric and wash in cold water.

Wax—Scrape off the excess and place a blotting paper over and beneath the stain. Iron with a warm iron.

Mud-stained clothes were a challenge in farm homes. The method of handling them was just getting its start. The techniques that still hold were: let the stain dry, brush well and rinse in cold water until no mud comes out. Then launder. Never plunge mud-stained fabrics in hot, sudsy water. Red and yellow clays produce stains that resemble iron rust; hot water sets them.

New interest in making housework easier flourished in the aftermath of World War I. Homemade work savers, promoted by the extension departments of agricultural colleges, evolved. This chapter presents a sampler of some of them.

CHAPTER 3

LABOR-SAVING DEVICES

Washing Machines

WASHING machines furnish the mechanical force needed to remove soil from clothing. Everything else must be supplied by the homemaker.

Dirt is held in clothing by two substances, grease and albuminous materials, largely skin excretions. The first purpose of washing is to dissolve these substances so the particles of soil will be loosened.

Grease is dissolved by soapy water and for this reason soap is used in washing. The albuminous materials are dissolved most easily in tepid water; they, like the albumin in egg white, are set by hot water.

If the washing machine is to accomplish excellent results, the water placed in it should not be scalding hot, but tepid, and it should contain an abundance of soap suds. A good way to judge the temperature of the water is to have it just hot enough that the hands may be placed in it with comfort. The operation of the machine forces the soapy water back and forth through the meshes of the fabrics, in this way dissolving the materials holding the soil.

Types of Machines

There are four kinds of washing machines, all of which may be driven by hand, electricity or gasoline engines. Vacuum machines have inverted cups or funnels which cleanse by moving up and down, forcing water through the fibers of the cloth. In the cylinder type the garments are placed in the cylinder of metal or wood. As this revolves within the tub, the clothes are lifted out of the water and dropped back into it so the water moves back and forth through the clothing.

The tub of the oscillator machine rocks back and forth like a cradle, this motion forcing the soapy suds through the fabrics being washed. Then there is the dolly type, so called on account of the agitator or disc known as the dolly which fits down on the clothes. This grasps the garments while turning and reversing, accomplishing the cleaning by this movement of the water back and forth through the clothing. The tubs of these machines usually have corrugated sides.

Machines Rinse Efficiently

Clothes are first placed in the machine that the dirt in them may be loosened. After this process, which is commonly called rubbing, the garments are rinsed to remove loosened particles of dirt. Since the water needs to be forced through the fabrics in this process, the mechanical force of the machine gives better results than rinsing the clothes by hand in a tub. Rinsing water should be hot, too warm for the hands to be inserted with comfort.

After the clothes are rinsed, they are put through a bluing water and then they are hung on the line. If considerable moisture is left in them, the clothes will be more nearly white when dry. The water, wind and sunshine provide for the process of oxidation, nature's way of bleaching.

The washing machine is a saver of human strength and the garments. With its use rubbing on the board is not necessary, provided moderately warm or tepid, but not hot, soapy water is used for the washing and hot water is used for the rinsing, which, of course, must be forced back and forth through the clothes until all traces of soil and soap are removed.

Dehydrating Foods

Dehydration is the outgrowth of drying foods. It is an improvement over the older method of food preservation. In drying, foodstuffs are either exposed to the direct heat of the sun or are placed in an evaporator which sets over the kitchen range. In some cases the drying process is hastened by oven heat. All of these methods of expelling the moisture rupture the plant cells. This allows the volatile materials to escape with

Women for generations rinsed clothes by pushing the garments down in water and lifting them up. Letting the washing machine do the work, as well as the washing, was a new idea. After rinsing, the wringer removed the surplus water. Hanging clothes on a line in the yard to dry in freezing weather, as well as on fair, warmer days, was the next step. Women enjoyed the fresh fragrance of clothes so dried.

History repeats. Gardeners now are reviving the old custom of preserving some of their crops by drying them. Some of them are building dehydrators. One rule to heed is: never eat a dried food that has mold on it.

the moisture. It is in this way that the taste and appearance of the foods are changed and in addition all the volatile food value is lost. Dried fruits and vegetables are cooked to some extent in their own juices during the drying.

Dehydrators are constructed so that nothing but the moisture is driven off during dehydration. This device has slots in the bottom through which air is admitted. Above these are several open-mesh wire shelves on which the products to be dehydrated, after being sliced or cut in small pieces, are placed. A kerosene burner at the bottom warms the air, thereby hastening the evaporation of the moisture. To make certain that the right temperature is maintained all the time so the cells will not be broken by too much heat, a thermometer hangs in front of the shelves where it may be seen through the doors. The temperature of this device is no more difficult to regulate than is that of an incubator.

The heated air rises in and around the food on the shelves and escapes through an opening in the top. Fresh air enters through the openings in the bottom and this continual circulation of air makes it possible to dehydrate foods in a sanitary manner in from 10 to 12 hours.

Dehydrated foods are stored in paraffin coated paper cartons, glass fruit jars wrapped in paper or heavy paper bags. The surprising factor is that when the foods are cooked, after being soaked several hours in cold water, they taste and appear much like fresh products. They are a great economy in storage space because the removal of the water decreases the bulk of foods greatly. One pound of dehydrated pumpkin, for example, makes 18 pumpkin pies of ordinary size.

Self-Freezing Ice Cream Freezers

Among the labor-saving devices on the market are the vacuum ice cream freezers which have no crank to be turned. The cream mixture is simply poured into the freezer after the ice and salt have been placed in a separate compartment, and there is no stirring during the freezing process.

The construction of this appliance is similar to that of a fireless cooker. When making ice cream, the freezer is inverted and the ice and salt mixture are placed in their compartment. A

Efforts to eliminate turning the crank of ice cream freezers developed. Someone discovered that a mixture rich in heavy cream makes a fine-grained ice cream without being stirred during freezing. Self-freezing ice cream freezers were hailed as efficient. They did not last long when electric refrigerators and freezers arrived.

cupful of cold water is added to start the melting and then the lid is adjusted. The freezer is turned right side up and the ice cream mixture is poured in its compartment. The lid is adjusted tightly. The walls of the freezer are constructed with a vacuum space so that it is impossible for the cold temperature provided by the melting ice to escape.

An old theory that ice cream will be coarse grained if it is not stirred with a dasher during the freezing has been upset by this appliance. Experience shows that a thin watery cream mixture produces a cream coarse in texture while a rich creamy one is a velvety, fine ice cream when frozen.

Long-handled Plunger

When one does not have a washing machine, a plunger may be used to advantage. This device consists of an inverted funnel or cone, a vacuum cup, fastened on to a handle like a broomstick. The tub partly filled with soiled clothing and soapy, lukewarm water is set on the floor. Then the plunger is pushed up and down on the clothing, the movement being the same as that of a churn dasher. This vacuum cup forces the soapy water back and forth through the fabrics, loosening the dirt in them. In rinsing the process is the same except that the washed clothing is placed in clean hot water, instead of soap suds. The ease with which the plunger is operated depends on how successful the worker is in keeping his back straight. Even strokes cleanse more quickly than uneven ones. This appliance is especially helpful in laundering blankets, quilts, overalls and other heavy articles without a washing machine.

Kerosene Stoves

Although kerosene stoves are used throughout the year, they are especially helpful in the hot weather when the heat of the range is objectionable. If they are given a position in the kitchen where breezes cannot blow upon them very often, they seldom smoke. There are two types of kerosene stoves; those which have wicks and those that are wickless. It is important that those without wicks be placed on a level foundation. When the floor slopes a little, pieces of cardboard or tiny blocks may be placed under the legs of the stove to level it.

For those households without the convenience of a gasoline or electric washing machine, the long-handled plunger was advocated as a valuable helper. Demonstrations on how to stand when operating the hand appliance to produce the least strain on the worker were not uncommon.

Welcome as the kerosene stove was in summer, when the wood- and coal-burning range reigned the remainder of the year, it created problems in the save-work era. Ideas about how to clean the burners, trim the wicks and where to place the stove in the kitchen to avoid drafts, which caused smoking, traveled around the countryside.

Every oil stove gives better satisfaction if kept clean. It takes only five or ten minutes every morning to keep it in this condition. Soap and water are the best cleansing agents, for in a rich suds every part of the stove may be washed. A small brush is helpful in scrubbing the corners a cloth cannot reach.

A small whisk broom is efficient in cleaning the asbestos ring, the metal jackets and spreaders in the wickless stove. By gentle brushing the small particles of dirt which might interfere with the flame are removed. When the stove has a wick, it must be kept smooth and even. Trimming with scissors brings disaster because it is not possible to cut it evenly. If the wick is new, it is well to let the uneven flame burn a few minutes until the edge becomes well charred. The charred surface may be packed down and made even. This is done best by placing a piece of soft tissue paper over the finger and then pressing down gently. Wicks cared for in this way will last much longer and give better results than if they are trimmed with scissors.

If the flame becomes low when there is plenty of oil in the supply tank, the pipe which carries the oil to the burner is clogged. To clean this remove the cap at the end of the pipe and force oil through until it flows freely.

There is a type of kerosene stove with an oven attached. In these stoves the baking is practically the same as in an ordinary cook stove. Most models, however, have separate ovens. These are not heavily insulated, and for this reason they heat and bake rapidly, while when there is insulation to be heated considerable kerosene is burned before the oven is ready for baking. It is advisable to buy the oven made for the particular type of stove being used. The main precaution, of course, is, if the flame comes near the top of the stove, that the floor of the oven be elevated at least six inches to give adequate space for combustion.

Kerosene Water Heaters

Oil heaters for the hot-water tank are a welcome piece of equipment in homes where there is running water. Its care is similar to that of a kerosene stove. Drafts should be avoided and all parts should be kept clean. The wicks will last longer in the heaters and in the stoves if the supply tank is kept well filled with oil. When there is no oil, the wick burns in its place.

Pressure Cookers

The pressure cooker is nothing more than a steam-tight kettle. The enclosed steam creates pressure and the pressure raises the temperature, cooking food quickly. In this kettle any food which is to be boiled or steamed can be cooked rapidly with a great saving of time and fuel. Foods which must be cooked a long time ordinarily, such as chicken and beans, may be steamed or boiled in the pressure cooker in a few minutes and then browned in the oven afterward.

These cookers are not complicated. First, there is a steam gauge which registers the pressure. This must be kept clean and dry. Then there is a pet-cock to let out the steam when the cooking is completed. It is wise to leave the pet-cock open when the food starts to cook, giving the cold air in the cooker a chance to escape, but when the steam starts to come out, it is closed.

The safety valve lets off steam. It works automatically, making the utensil safe. To keep it in order, loosen the valve when not in use so the moisture will not corrode it. If it leaks steam, a good cleaning, scouring and oiling of all the parts is needed. When the cooking begins, the safety valve must be closed. The cooker must always contain water when it is heated or it may crack or bulge. Usually ¼ cupful of water is sufficient. After the food has been cooked long enough, the lid must not be opened until the steam has been let out through the pet-cock.

Since most cookers have two pans which fit into them, different kinds of foods may be cooked at the same time. For instance, meat might be placed in the bottom of the cooker and the two pans, one holding a vegetable and the other rice pudding, could be cooking above. If one wishes to have the meat browned, it can be seared in the bottom of the cooker in a little fat before water is added and the lid is adjusted. Potatoes can be cooked with the meat. It takes from 30 to 40 minutes to cook a meat stew in the cooker while 3 hours are required for the same process on top of the stove. There is a saving of time comparable to this in cooking all foods. Even Boston Baked Beans may be prepared in 50 minutes. The beans are cooked in the pressure cooker 25 minutes and then they are browned in a hot oven the other 25 minutes.

The description deals with the first pressure cookers, which have had an important place in farm kitchens where home canning is practiced. At first, they were such a novelty that many women hesitated to use them for fear they would explode. They learned that following directions led to safety. It is still important to heed them.

Only people in the Golden Age group remember the homemade fireless cookers, which were followed by commercial cookers. They were an attempt to evolve a system of cooking with less pot watching, but the flavor of the food prepared without air circulation doomed their survival.

Entire meals may be cooked in the pressure cooker. Here are some of the combinations which may be cooked at the same time: fried chicken, steamed potatoes and buttered carrots; Swiss steak, steamed squash and potatoes; ham stew and rice pudding; and baked beans, steamed brown bread and apple sauce.

Fireless Cookers

The fireless cooker is a device for conserving the heat of cooking foods; therefore it saves fuel. It also is economical of the homemaker's time and energy. Using it in the summer helps to keep the kitchen cool.

This appliance consists of one or more cooking compartments fitted with utensils and insulated to retain the heat of foods introduced, thus finishing their cooking in their own heat.

It is not difficult to manage a fireless cooker because the foods do not spoil if over-cooked with the constantly lowering temperature. If the food should be underdone, it may be reheated and placed in the cooker again. Less water is used in this type of cookery, since there is little evaporation after the food is placed in the fireless. The radiators of soapstone or metal are heated on the stove and placed in the cooker, then the heated food is added and the lid is closed. Frequently a heated radiator is placed on top of the container holding the food; this is always done when baking. The insulated walls retain the heat of the food and the radiators so that the foods within cook slowly.

A Homemade Fireless

A fireless cooker of considerable merit can be made in the home. A tin lard can, wood candy box, any tightly built box or an old trunk may be used for the outer container in which insulation and a utensil for holding the food are placed. A tin or agate bucket with straight sides and a tightly fitting cover is suitable for holding the food to be cooked.

The packing between the lard can or outer container and the bucket which is to hold the food should be a poor conductor of heat. Among the materials which are usually available in most farm homes for use in this way are: excelsior, shredded newspapers, straw, hay, lint cotton and wool. The lard can is lined with sheet asbestos about 1/8 inch thick. The nest or well, as it is called, in which the bucket of food is to set is also lined with this asbestos. The packing is placed between. If possible, have at least 4 inches of this insulation between the lard can and the bucket. If two wells or nests are to be made, such as is the case when an old trunk is used for the outer container, 6 inches of packing should be placed between the two nests.

First line the lard can or other utensil used in its place with asbestos, then place 4 or more inches of the packing in the bottom. Make the nest of asbestos, being sure that it is large enough so the bucket can be placed in it easily. Set this in the lard can and stuff in the packing firmly between the nest and the sides of the can. Make a collar of sheet asbestos to fit between the sides of the can and the nest, fitting this over the top to hide the packing. This should fit tightly. When this is done, make a cushion of muslin and fill with the packing. This should be 4 inches thick and it is fitted on top of the fireless cooker, filling the space between the top of the bucket and the asbestos collar and the top of the lard can. Place the cover on the lard can or other container and the fireless cooker is made. In this type of cooker the food is heated to the boiling point in the bucket and placed in the nest. The insulation retains the heat which completes the cookery. No radiators are used. The homemade cooker is adapted to cooking cereals, stewed and boiled foods; the commercial devices with their discs which may be heated and placed under and above the foods may also be used for baking and roasting.

Layer Steamers

Steamers on the market nowadays have two pans which fit into them above the water so that two or more kinds of foods may be steamed at the same time. While this is being done, another food may be stewing or boiling in the bottom part of the steamer kettle. When kerosene or gas stoves are used, this type of a steam kettle reduces the amount of fuel used in preparing a meal. In addition, they provide a saving of food value. In boiling foods, especially the vegetables, some of the food value dissolves in the liquid in which they cook. If this liquor is

Iceboxes, or refrigerators, were new enough in many homes to justify programs devoted to their care. Among the helpers advocated was baking soda. Its merits still are promoted.

drained off, it is frequently thrown away so the food elements in it are lost. Steamed foods retain all of their nutritive value because they are not cooked in water.

Care of Refrigerators

Three factors are essential in caring for refrigerators. They must be kept cool, dry and clean. Coolness is obtained in most cases by the use of ice. When ice is placed in its compartment, the air about it becomes cold. Since cold air is heavier than warm air, the cold air falls down around the shelves containing the food, absorbing the heat. The warm air rises and passes into the ice chamber where it becomes cold and heavy. Then it falls to the bottom of the refrigerator. It is this continual circulation of cold and warm air that keeps the food in a refrigerator cold.

The old belief that it is economical to wrap paper or a blanket about the ice in the refrigerator to make it last longer is incorrect. It takes the warm air much longer to reach the ice to be cooled, which interferes with the circulation of the warm and cold air.

Butter, cream, milk and water should be kept on the lower shelf, as should other foods requiring a low temperature. The bottom shelf is the coldest part of the refrigerator. Meats, vegetables and fruits may be placed on the next shelf above and the top shelf should be reserved for cheese and other foods with a strong odor. The warm air takes up these odors as it rises and carries them to the ice chamber from which they should escape through the drain pipe. It is unwise to keep food directly on the ice unless tightly covered for it will absorb these odors. Moreover, it is cooler in other parts of the refrigerator.

Dryness is essential in refrigeration because the micro-organisms which grow in foods causing them to spoil develop best in warm, moist and unclean places. Poor circulation of air or washing the refrigerator with warm water so steam forms on the walls makes the refrigerator moist.

The best way to keep the refrigerator clean is to wipe up every spot with a damp cloth as soon as anything is spilled. Once a week a thorough washing may be given with a little cool water to which a teaspoonful of baking soda has been added. The washed surface is dried with a clean towel. The drain pipe can be taken out and washed with hot soapy water and a long-handled brush. It is cooled before being placed back in the refrigerator.

Making an Iceless Refrigerator

Have a box made 3½ feet high, 2 feet wide and 18 inches deep. The top and bottom should be solid and the sides of screen wire. It is best to use copper or galvanized wire since it does not rust. The front should be hinged to make a door. Put in two adjustable shelves from 12 to 15 inches apart, and have these made of slats or of the wire screening fastened on a wooden frame. On top of this set a bread pan about 16 or 18 inches square or use a shallow dish pan. Stand the whole box in another shallow pan. Paint the pans and box white and, when dry, apply a coat of white enamel.

Then make a covering of white cotton flannel to fit over the box. An old blanket or grain sacks sewed together may be used instead of the flannel. Use the smooth side of the flannel on the outside and fasten the covering with hooks and eyes. Sew one row of hooks on the door near the fastening and another just opposite the door so that the hems will project over and keep out the warm air that otherwise might enter. Fasten the covering at the top as well as at the side. Two double strips one-half the width of the side should be sewed to the top of each side and allowed to extend over two or three inches into the pan on the top which contains water.

Set this refrigerator outdoors in a shady place or in the kitchen under a window where there is a good circulation of air. Keep the wicks in the supply of fresh water in the upper pan. This type of refrigerator gives best results on dry, hot days. It is not good for use in extremely damp weather or at the seashore since there is not enough evaporation to cool the food within on the shelves.

The Kitchen's Dumb Waiter

A dumb waiter between the kitchen and the basement saves many steps. These shelves which are built like those of a cupboard are pulled back and forth. They are operated by a cord and a counter weight. To be of the greatest use the shelves

Ranch homes in arid country made excellent use of iceless refrigerators.

The step-saving device was borrowed from an Early American home, or Thomas Jefferson's country mansion.

Many farm families had sponge boxes, but not the majority of them. When the men in the household were interested in carpentering, the device was easily built. It was especially appreciated in homes without a furnace, where the kitchens often were cold on wintry nights.

should be wide enough so that crocks and other large utensils may rest on them and no farther apart than it is necessary to have them to accommodate the articles to be carried on them.

The shaft which extends into the basement should be provided with a screen door if possible, so the food lowered into the basement in the waiter to be kept cool will be protected. For a woman of average height the upper door for the shelves should be about three feet from the kitchen floor.

Making a Sponge Box

In the cold weather it is frequently very difficult for the housekeeper to find a place to set the bread sponge at night so it will not chill. A sponge box may be made without much expense or labor for this purpose and it is the best way to keep the bread sponge at the right temperature.

A box 26 x 20 x 20 inches is a good size. In this about 10 inches from the bottom a shelf is made of slats which rests on cleats fastened to the sides of the box. Four inches above this a shelf constructed in the same way as the lower one is inserted.

Under the lower shelf a sheet of galvanized iron slightly wider than the shelf is inserted. It is curved in appearance when in position. This helps to distribute the heat from a lamp which sets in the bottom of the box and to keep the heat from scorching the lower shelf. The door is on hinges and is fastened with a hook and staple.

Bore several holes in the top of the box and the upper parts of the sides. In the center of the top, bore a hole and fasten in it securely a cork through which a hole large enough to admit a chemical thermometer has been made. Use a Fahrenheit thermometer, one that will register as high as 100 degrees.

If a kerosene lamp is to be used to heat the sponge box, line the box with sheets of asbestos or tin to avoid danger of fire. A 16-candle power electric light will provide sufficient heat for the box and it will not be necessary to line the box if this is used.

The bread sponge is set on the top shelf, a shallow pan of water on the lower shelf to keep the air moist and a small lamp or electric light bulb below. Keep the temperature around 65 or 70 degrees for sponge standing overnight and at 85 degrees for dough after it has been kneaded in the morning. If the bread is made in the quick way, that is, if the sponge is set in the morning, have the temperature of the box 85 degrees.

Turning the flame of the lamp up or down or placing cold or hot water in the pan on the second shelf changes the temperature if one wishes to do so.

Bread Mixer

A bread mixer in which the dough can be kneaded in 3 minutes by turning a crank instead of 15 minutes by hand is a valuable labor saver. This device consists of a bucket-like utensil with a curved, dull blade which is turned by a handle. This mixes the sponge and kneads the bread. The sponge and dough can be allowed to rise in it and with its use any member of the family can knead the dough just as well as the homemaker can. In buying a mixer the amount of dough to be kneaded in it should be taken into consideration. If large batches of bread are made at a time, a large mixer is desirable, while if small bakings are made, a small one gives better results. It is impossible for a huge mixer to knead dough for one or two loaves efficiently.

Cake Mixers

Cake mixers are constructed much the same as bread mixers only they are smaller in size. There is an electric cake mixer which may be used in stirring up one cake, but those turned by hand are especially adapted to the mixing of more than one cake at the same time.

Self-Heating Irons

By the use of self-heating irons, many steps between the stove and the ironing board are saved. When the house is wired with electricity, of course, the electrically heated iron is desirable. Irons heated by gasoline, alcohol, kerosene and gas are also convenient and they are satisfactory if drafts that might blow the flame are avoided.

Ironing Machines

There are two kinds of ironing machines, those with heated rolls and those with cold rolls. The first kind is made with padded and covered rolls or cylinders which revolve against a

The so-called blade that did the kneading was what today is known as a dough hook. It is an attachment to some of the more powerful home electric mixers.

The hand-turned cake mixer was the forerunner of today's electric mixers which beat most of the cake batters.

Saving steps was a household battle cry 50 years ago. Self-heating irons banished repeated trips between ironing board and the kitchen range to exchange cool flat-irons for hot ones. The worker had to keep a watchful eye on drafts, which would extinguish the flames that provided the heat.

Before polyester fabrics abolished much of the ironing, ironing machines, called mangles, were appliances women with large families dreamed of buying.

heated plate or shoe. The padded roll takes the place of the ironing board and the heated shoe of the iron. Some ironers have special arrangements made for ironing ruffles, but best results on the padded rolls are obtained in ironing flat pieces. The ironer with cold rolls smoothes out the wrinkles by heavy pressure. Ironing machines are operated by hand or electricity and the rolls are heated by gasoline, gas or electricity.

Vacuum Cleaners

Vacuum cleaners suck up fine dust and dirt on and in carpets and rugs. Many of the cleaners also have brushes which take up lint, thread and all types of coarse dirt. The dust and dirt is forced by the suction into a bag so that practically no dust is scattered about the room. As a rule the best vacuum cleaners are run by electricity or motor, although the hand cleaners which are not too heavy to be used with ease are very good.

Carpet Sweepers

Most carpet sweepers remove the surface dirt and dust on rugs and carpets. There are a few hand-power sweepers, which are in reality a combination of the sweeper and the vacuum cleaner, that suck up some of the dust as well as removing the surface dirt.

Long-handled Dust Pan

If a long-handled dust pan is used, it is not necessary for the housewife to stoop when sweeping the collected dirt into the pan. An excellent type is the one which has a lid that closes automatically as the pan is lifted. This keeps the dirt from being spilled or falling out.

Wall Brushes

Much climbing and stretching is avoided in cleaning the ceilings and walls by the use of long-handled wall brushes. The brush part may be of fine bristles which are soft, lamb's wool or loops of soft cotton twine. When such a brush is not available, the best substitute is a cotton flannel bag slipped over the bristles of the broom. Care must be taken not to scratch the walls with the bristles, that is, not to exert too much pressure on the broom.

Floor Mops

For washing a floor the ordinary mop handle with a loosely woven piece of cloth fastened in it is satisfactory. A dust mop for removing the fine particles of dust from the floors saves one from bending over to wipe up dusty patches. Some of these are constructed with soft bristles and others with loops of soft cotton twine which will reach the corners and remove the dust from them. Sometimes a soft cloth moistened slightly with liquid wax or oil is tied over the dust mop and rubbed over the floor to brighten the finish. Care needs to be taken never to apply too much wax or floor oil since they leave a surface which collects dust and dirt, and not to use oil and wax on the same floor. They will not mix.

When the floors of several rooms must be waxed, a weighted brush with short bristles is used. This rubs in the paste wax and polishes the wood. Such a brush should never be used on an oiled floor unless it is covered with a heavy piece of flannel.

Brushes for Cleaning

There are brushes adapted to the cleaning of practically every piece of household equipment. There are stiff-bristled scrub brushes for cleaning vegetables, table-tops and other surfaces and long-handled scrub brushes for scouring floors. Radiator pipes may be cleaned by the aid of a long-handled and narrow brush. A narrow brush with a flexible handle cleanses the drain pipe of the refrigerator with the aid of soap suds and hot water. Then there are narrow brushes with similar wire handles for use in cleaning out bottles, vinegar cruets, and vases. Soft bristles clean silverware, stiffer ones remove the soil from sinks, bathtubs and lavatories. Phonograph records can scarcely be cleaned without the use of soft bristles. The homemaker's hands are protected greatly by the use of brushes and the bristles are much more efficient in reaching corners and crevices than a piece of smooth cloth is.

Cooking Utensils

In buying cooking utensils the prudent homemaker considers for what they are to be used. Kettles or pans in which vegetables are to be boiled are most satisfactory if the cover rests on a

Brushes to make cleaning easier appealed so much to countrywomen that it paid brush salesmen to go from door to door, show their wares and take orders for brushes they delivered later.

In kitchens today many of the old favorites are represented, but made of several different metals, such as aluminum, stainless steel and heat-proof glass. Casseroles were gaining prominence in 1923, heralded as dish savers because food could be cooked and served in the same dish. But where is the special potato kettle so important when potatoes were served two or three times a day?

standard about an inch above the top of the utensil or if the lid rests loosely on top. This permits the water to evaporate quickly. Much food value is destroyed if large amounts of water in which the vegetables are boiled is thrown away. If cooked down, this may be served with the vegetable dish.

The ideal potato kettle is one equipped with a cover which strains the contents without danger of spilling the cooked vegetable. When this is not available, a strainer which resembles a small kettle only that it is perforated and has a long handle is satisfactory.

Cabbage and onions and all other strongly flavored food are best cooked in a flaring-sided pan so the water in which they are cooked evaporates quickly. No lid is used. Frying requires greater heat than other types of cookery so iron and aluminum utensils are best for this purpose.

The most important point in selecting the frying pan is its size. The same is true of percolators. It is impossible to make 2 cupfuls of good coffee in a large percolator. Mixing bowls are an essential piece of equipment. Those of enameled ware or other light-weight materials are satisfactory. As to shape, the deep bowl with a conical bottom is desirable since a small amount of food can be dealt with in it as well as a larger amount. In other words, the depth gives the capacity so that 8 eggs may be beaten in the bowl while the conical bottom permits the beating of 1 egg with just as much ease.

Casseroles are gaining in popularity in American homes. These bake dishes may be of china, glass, aluminum, steel or iron. If the china, earthenware and glass casseroles are used, the food is not only cooked in them but it also is served in the same dish. When the casserole is to be used in hot ovens, the lid should contain a small hole through which the boiling liquid around the food can escape as it evaporates. With a low oven the moisture can be retained so this hole is not necessary. If the lid has a hole, it may be filled with a stiff flour paste.

Glass rolling pins are proving happy additions to kitchen cabinets because they can be opened and filled with crushed ice or ice water. This makes them cold for making pastry; one of the best assurances that the pie crust will be flaky and tender is to have it cold when placed in the oven.

A set of measuring spoons and two measuring cups, one for the liquids and the other for the dry ingredients, make the housewife more certain of success with the recipes she tries. She can be sure that her measurements are accurate. Long-handled spoons with slits in the bowls are useful in mixing foods and a straight-edged knife with a flexible blade, the spatula, makes it possible to scrape all the scraps of biscuit or cooky dough from the bowl.

Women who have suffered from burned hands know that the consideration of handles is worth while when cooking utensils are being purchased. Tea kettles which have handles that stand upright and do not move are desirable. If kettles have bail handles, these should be easy to move and of a material which will not retain heat. If of wire, they should have an extra wooden holder in the center. Saucepans have either long or short handles; it is best to select those which are of non-heat conducting materials. The lips for pouring should be on both sides of the saucepan so a left-handed person can pour from the utensil with as great ease as a right-handed one.

Small, but Helpful Equipment

Appie corers, orange and lemon juice extractors, graters, vegetable cutters, potato ricers, a slicer for hard-cooked eggs, nutmeg grinders, cream ladles, pie crimpers, stainless steel paring and butcher knives, grapefruit knives and the Dunlap cream whipper are among the small pieces of kitchen equipment that are helpful.

Knife Racks

If sharp knives are kept in a table or cabinet drawer, it is easy for one to cut her fingers when getting them or some other equipment from the drawers. A rack on the kitchen wall near the kitchen table is a satisfactory way of taking care of the knives. These racks may be made of wood by taking a number of saw kerfs out of soft pine or of stiff wire coiled to resemble a pen holder rack.

Dish Drainer

It is not only less work to let the dishes dry themselves in a drainer than to dry them on a towel but it is also much more

The Dunlap cream whipper consisted of a hand rotary beater that extended through an opening in the lid to cream below in the container of glass. The lid was what caught the eyes of women who used lots of heavy cream. It held the splashes under control.

*Women who never dreamed of an electric dishwasher that really worked considered the first homemade drainers a marvelous invention. From them developed the rubber and plastic dish drainers of today.

*While women were glad to eliminate most of the drying of dishes by hand, the men and children, often called on "to wipe the dishes," rejoiced.

One of the busiest appliances in farm
kitchens was the food grinder. Its major
role was to grind beef, pork for sausage
and leftover cooked meat and chicken
for sandwiches. In addition, many
foods now chopped on a board with a
knife were put through the grinder because
it was easier than holding the food in
one hand and cutting it up with a knife
held in the other hand — nuts and celery,
for instance.

sanitary. It is almost impossible to keep the dish towel immaculate all the time.

A satisfactory drainer may be made in the home. For this an ordinary large bread or biscuit pan is used. In this rests the rack for the dishes. This is made from No. 14 wire which is bent into the proper shape for holding the dishes. This rack must fit in the pan and hold the dishes out of the water which is poured over them for scalding. The silver may be placed in a tin can with holes in the bottom or in a nest of poultry netting that resembles a small bucket.

The washed dishes are stacked in the rack and hot water poured over them. When they are dry, they are placed in the cupboard and the water in the pan is emptied. If one has a sink and drainboard, the rack may be placed on the drainboard and no pan used under it.

Wheeled Tray

The wheeled tray may be used in taking dishes and food to and fro from work table to the stove and from the kitchen to the dining room. They may be purchased at a furniture store, or a table on wheels may be used. A wheeled serving table may be made by placing wheels on an old washstand.

Food Grinders Made Useful

As a meat chopper, the food grinder is used less than it is any other way, simply because butchering time does not come more frequently. Stale bread can be ground quickly for use in puddings, scalloped dishes and other combinations. Vegetables for soup may be chopped more quickly than they can be cut. Sandwich fillings cease to worry when ground in a food grinder and they spread easily. Raisins, nuts, fruits, cocoanut and practically all dried fruits may be ground in the chopper. Peanut butter may be made in it.

Powdered sugar which contains lumps causes little delay on baking day if the grinder is near by. The cabbage, celery, onion or other vegetables for salad can be chopped quickly. Horseradish and cheese may be ground. And beaten biscuits are not difficult to make if the dough is placed through the chopper several times.

Apples may be ground so the apple sauce will cook rapidly. Instead of bothering to put cranberries through a sieve to remove the skins, they may be ground in the chopper before being cooked. Quince honey may be made with ease if the quinces are ground instead of being grated or cut. Lemons and oranges for use in marmalade may be put through the grinder. It is an economy to grind foods that must be cut or chopped for much energy and time is saved.

Narrow Shelves between Wide Ones

When cupboard or pantry space is limited, narrow shelves may be placed between the wide ones to hold cups, tiny pitchers, salt and pepper shakers, spices and other small articles.

Rolling Cloth

Instead of spending time washing the bread board after rolling out bread, cooky, biscuit and other doughs, it may be covered with a piece of heavy white duck or canvas fastened down with thumb tacks. This may be folded up and kept in a drawer when not in use. It is more sanitary than the board and it may be washed with greater ease.

Vacuum Bottles and Pitchers

The vacuum bottle has an inner container with heavy walls and a tightly fitting lid. In this the beverage is poured. The outer covering of the bottle also has a heavy wall; between it and the outer wall of the beverage container is an air space. This insulation makes it impossible for the cold or the heat of the beverage to get out into the room and for the heat or cold of the room to get into the bottle. The iced lemonade or hot coffee will retain its temperature several hours if placed in a vacuum pitcher or bottle. The pitcher differs from the bottle in that it has a spout which makes it easier to pour the beverage at the table.

Vacuum Pails

The vacuum pail is constructed like the vacuum bottle only it is much larger. It frequently holds a gallon or more. It is fine

The first cloth covers for surfaces on which pie and cookie doughs are rolled were conceived in country kitchens where pies were baked at least five or six times a week, cookies two or three times. From this beginning canvas pastry cloths evolved.

for use in taking a cold drink to the field in the hot weather or a hot one in the winter.

Electrical Appliances

Among the electrical household appliances which are helpful are toasters, ovenettes, table stoves, waffle irons, egg beaters, irons, heaters, curling irons, bottle warmers, bed warmers, fireless cookers with electrically heated discs, coffee percolators, tea pots and tea kettles.

Canning Outfits

See canning chapter.

Perhaps the simplest type of canner is the water-bath. This consists of any utensil large enough to hold several fruit jars, fitted with a lid and a false bottom which holds the jars away from the bottom of the container, protecting them from overheating and hitting together and allowing free circulation of the water underneath. These canners may be purchased or one may be made at home. The wash boiler or a small tub with a cover make excellent vessels for the water-bath. A false bottom must be made. This may be fashioned from narrow slats to form a little platform or of strong wire netting fastened on a wood frame. If this has handles which may be used in removing the cans from the water-bath, it is more convenient.

Then there is the water-seal canner which has a double walled bath and a cover which extends down into the water between the two walls, making a third wall and two jackets of water between the compartment holding the jars and the outer wall. The advantage of this canner is that it takes less water to manipulate it and since there is less, not so much fuel is required to heat it as the larger amount in the water-bath outfits.

Next to the water-bath in popularity is the steam pressure canner, which may be a pressure cooker which has been described in this chapter. A pressure canner does not differ much, if any, in construction from a pressure cooker, but it usually is much larger so more cans of food may be sterilized at the same time.

Making a Table Pad

An inexpensive pad for use in protecting the table top from hot dishes may be made from wall board. Saw this into four pieces, the size and shape depending on the table top. For a round table, saw the wall board into four pie-shaped pieces which fit together. Cover with white cotton flannel and the pad is just as satisfactory as if it were of the more costly asbestos.

Caring for Floors

If the paint, varnish or other floor finish is worn and ugly in appearance, it is an economy of time and energy to refinish it. Its care will be made so much easier if this is done. If varnish remover is applied with a brush, the old finish will soften so that it may be scraped off with a wide piece of glass or any broad spatula tool. Then the floor is cleaned and left to dry.

The next requirement is a filler. For this equal parts of turpentine and linseed oil to which sufficient Japan dryer is added to make the mixture dry overnight may be used. For soft wood floors, such as maple and pine, a little umber may be added to stain the wood. Before applying this filler to the wood, it is a good plan to apply a little on boards of the same wood as the floor, making certain that the color is right and that enough Japan dryer has been added so that the finish will dry overnight.

When the filler is applied and is dry, paste wax may be added to provide a glossy, beautiful surface, to repel the dust and dirt and to protect the wood. This is rubbed into the wood and best results are obtained if a weighted wax mop is used. A way to make a substitute mop is to fasten a brick on top of a large scrub brush and to attach a handle on this.

Waxed floors may be cleaned easily. A daily dusting with a dustless mop removes the fine particles of dust. This mop is kept clean a long time if a clean cloth is tied over it every time it is used. Liquid wax is sprinkled on the cloth about once a month to help keep the floors attractive and paste wax is added two or three times a year.

If the floor is painted, it may be waxed, but if varnished, wax is not so satisfactory. Instead of using it, a little floor oil may be sprinkled on the mop occasionally when dusting the floor.

Homemade Shower Bath

If there is no space in the house for the shower bath for summer use, it may be made on the back porch and screened off

Usually the shower was improvised by farm boys who liked a quick bath when returning home on hot, sultry evenings after active field work. Their mothers helped fix the curtains. Many boys kept a barrel filled with water to warm in the sunshine during the day from which they filled the bucket with water for the shower.

with curtains of canvas or heavy unbleached muslin. A bucket holding 4 gallons of water is needed to hold the water. A hole is cut in the bottom of this and a piece of pipe 4 inches long is soldered in this opening. Rubber tubing 4 to 6 feet long is attached to this pipe and a shower head, which may be purchased for fifteen cents, or a sprinkler from a watering can, is fastened into the end of the tube.

The bucket is raised and lowered by the use of a pulley and rope fastened with a staple to a joist in the ceiling. The end of the rope is looped over a hook in the wall. A clothespin makes a good stop-cock for the tubing.

About 2½ gallons of water are required for the shower. The person stands in a tub placed under the shower. One or two coats of white enamel make the outfit more attractive.

Making an Ironing Board Cover

A cover for the ironing board which is easily adjusted is made in the following way: hem unbleached muslin of the required length and width, allowing a turn of 4 inches on the sides. Make 8 buttonholes, 4 in each side. Then use 8 strong safety pins fastened through these holes and to 4 pieces of narrow elastic. Six inch lengths of elastic are satisfactory. This ironing board cover does not wrinkle as long as the elastic is good.

Sewing Machines

Sewing machines operated by electric motors are a great convenience in homes where electricity is available. All machines prove to their operators that good care pays. The use of good machine oil wherever there is friction is essential. If a poor grade of oil has been applied by mistake, it can be removed by the use of kerosene. Oil the machine with kerosene. Wipe off the surplus oil that forms when the machine is run a few minutes with the needle unthreaded. Then apply good oil.

If the machine needle is dull, it may be sharpened for temporary use by stitching a few inches through fine sandpaper. To keep the needle from unthreading when cloth is removed, raise it up to the highest point before taking out the cloth.

When the cloth puckers, it is a sign that the tension is too

The ironing-board covers now commercially made may equal the first ones, which were made at home, but they cannot boast of handmade buttonholes.

tight or that there is not enough pressure on the pressure foot. Very thin materials frequently need to have a layer of paper under them when being stitched.

Skipped stitches are usually the result of a bent needle, an incorrectly set needle or the use of too coarse thread. The needle will last longer if the thread is pulled backward under the pressure foot when cloth is removed. Pulling the thread forward frequently bends the needle.

Baby's Summer Nest

A convenient bed for the small baby may be made from wood and screen. The right dimensions for such a crib are 4 feet or more long, 3 feet wide and 3 feet deep. The frame is of wood and the sides and top are covered with screen. Either screen or canvas may be used for the bottom. The top is fastened on with hinges and casters under the legs make it easier to move the little bed. A mattress will make the nest soft. Baby will not only find protection from flies in this little bed, but since he cannot get out, he also is made safe from other dangers. If the wooden frame is painted and enameled white, the crib is much more attractive.

The Kitchen Stool

Much energy is saved if the housewife sits down on a high stool while ironing, washing dishes, stirring up the cake batter, paring potatoes and attending to other household duties. If a hole is made through the top of this stool through which the finger may be placed, it is easy to carry this device from one part of the room to another.

Prop for Sick Person

An ordinary kitchen chair placed back down at the head of the bed supplies a support for the pillow against which the patient may lean. This makes it much easier for an ill person to sit up in bed.

One way mothers 50 years ago protected their babies from flies, mosquitoes and other troublesome insects.

Every farm woman was the practical nurse for her family and often extended her help to neighbors in distress.

Cucumber-cool cream once was used during the summer, when the vines were generous in their yield. Women said it soothed the skin.

Cosmetics with fruit scents appealed just as they do today. Fruit-smelling shampoos and hand creams have many enthusiastic supporters. Among the popular fruit scents now are strawberry, raspberry, peach, lemon, lime and tangerine.

CHAPTER 4

GRANDMOTHER'S BEAUTY SECRETS

Cucumber Cream

To soothe an inflamed skin or to soften a dry one, cucumber cream may be used. Take 2 cucumbers that are ripe and yellow, wash thoroughly and cut in thin slices. Place in a saucepan and add barely enough cold water to cover. Simmer gently until the mass is soft and mushy. Rub through a fine sieve and strain through a cloth. To every 3 ounces of cucumber juice add 3 ounces of almond oil and ½ ounce of white wax. Heat until all the ingredients are melted. Then beat the mixture until it becomes cold, adding a few drops of tincture of benzoin during the beating.

Strawberry Lotion

For whitening the skin this lotion is excellent. Crush ripe strawberries in a saucepan to extract the juice and boil them 5 minutes, mashing them with a spoon during the cooking. Strain off the juice and cool. Measure and mix 1 part of alcohol with 2 parts of strawberry juice. Bottle and use a very little to remove tan or yellowness from the skin.

Fresh Berry Lotion

Mash ½ cupful of ripe strawberries and add the same amount of cold water. Before retiring and after the face, neck and arms have been washed, apply the strawberry mixture to the skin. When washed off in the morning, the skin will be more nearly white.

Lettuce Cream

A cream which serves for a bleach and a healing lotion is made from lettuce. Select large lettuce leaves and cover them with boiling water.   Let stand 30 minutes; then pour off the water and pound the lettuce with a potato masher.   Strain through a fine sieve.   Then melt 1 ounce of white wax, 1 ounce of spermacetti and 4 ounces of almond oil in a double boiler or over water.   The mixture should not boil, but just melt.   Remove from the stove and add drop by drop the lettuce juice, beating the mixture constantly with a fork until the cream is smooth, light and cold.

Preventing Wrinkles

If strawberries are ripe, they may be combined with cream to be used on the face to prevent wrinkles.   Mash 6 large and ripe berries and add an equal amount of heavy cream.   Pat this on the face with the finger tips, applying it liberally under the eyes and other places where wrinkles are likely to come.

Lemon Bleach

Squeeze the juice of two lemons in 1 cupful of water and wash the face with this two times daily to remove freckles.   If one wishes, the lemon juice may be stirred into as much sugar as it will hold and this is rubbed on the face.

Horseradish Bleach

Select a medium-sized horseradish root and grate very fine. Cover with fresh buttermilk and let stand overnight.   Strain through fine muslin and bottle the liquid.   Wash the face with this night and morning for a bleach.

Milk Remedies

Washing the face daily with milk helps to soften, whiten and to make the skin smooth.   Buttermilk is effective in remedying acne or removing pimples and it has a tendency to remove freckles.   Sweet cream may be used as a cure for chapped hands and lips, and for sunburn.   If the skin is broken out slightly, the addition of a little grated horseradish or flowers of sulphur to the milk is helpful.   These preparations are made immediately before being used since they do not keep well.

The acid in strawberries was the astringent, heavy cream the lubricant.

The scent of lemon pleased even if the freckles were only slightly dimmed, if at all.

Bleaches were important in the sunbonnet age, when a "lily-white" complexion was the ideal. Buttermilk functioned as a complexion aid so long as butter was churned in the home. It was used for years after the horseradish was abandoned.

For Excessive Perspiration

If a few tablespoonfuls of baking soda are placed in the bath, the water will be softened and much of the discomfort from excessive perspiration will be overcome. The baking soda may be sprinkled on the body just as talcum powder is.

Hand Astringent

For hands that are moist most of the time, frequent baths in salt water usually will check the excessive perspiration. If this fails, the hands may be washed occasionally in 1 cupful of water to which the juice of a lemon has been added.

For Hard Hands

Rub oatmeal on the hands after they have been washed. This cleanses and softens the skin. Cornmeal may be used instead of the oatmeal. A good cleanser is made by mixing 1 tablespoonful of powdered borax with 1 pint of cornmeal.

Honey for the Hands

For chapped hands rub honey on them. Put on gloves and leave the honey on all night. In the morning wash in bran water.

Bran Water

Boil a cupful of bran in a muslin bag. Put both the bran bag and the liquid in which it cooked in the wash bowl and wash the hands. When dry, rub a little honey on them. This is excellent treatment for rough, red skins.

Honey Mask

Dilute honey a little with water and rub on the face before retiring. This mask helps to prevent wrinkles and to soften the skin.

Potato Mask

For the oily skin which is subject to blackheads the potato mask is a joy. Wash the potato thoroughly and cut it in slices.

Every farm community had its beekeepers, and honey was abundant at a cost that today's food shoppers envy.

Rub these over the skin. It removes the oil, cleanses the pores and whitens the skin.

Glycerin Wash

For skin irritations, itching or redness the addition of 1 ounce of glycerin to 19 ounces of soft water makes an excellent face wash.

Oatmeal Wash

Boil 1 pint of Scotch oatmeal in 2 pints of boiling water until a clear liquid is formed. Use a double boiler for this purpose. Strain the liquid through a piece of fine muslin, boil and strain again. Add sufficient rose water to give the liquid the consistency of milk. If one wishes, a few drops of perfume may be added before the liquid is bottled.

Onion Tonic

For very thin hair, cut an onion in halves and rub the scalp with these vigorously before retiring at night. The juice of onions invigorates the roots of the hair.

Egg Shampoo

Beat 2 eggs together lightly and rub into the scalp and through the hair which has been moistened with lukewarm water. Rinse out the egg with lukewarm water to which a little melted castile soap has been added. Then rinse in two or three clear lukewarm waters.

For Dandruff

Saturate the scalp every night with sulphur water which is made by dissolving 1 ounce flowers of sulphur in 1 quart of water. Shake every now and then while the sulphur is dissolving. Let the solution stand until it settles and use only the clear liquid.

Skin Tonic

After cleansing the skin, apply a tonic to give a freshened appearance. This is made by combining 1 part witchhazel with

Obtaining soft water was no problem except in times of prolonged drought. Most families had at least one rain barrel to collect water that drained from the roof.

2 parts Florida water. If the skin is very oily, use equal parts of witchhazel and Florida water.

For Blackheads

Rub pure lard on the blackheads and let stand 5 or 10 minutes. Then wipe off gently with soft cloth and rub a cake of a mild soap, wet in water, on the surface. Wash off with warm water.

Arm and Hand Bleach

Beat 1 egg yolk until light and add 20 drops tincture of benzoin, ½ ounce glycerin, ½ ounce rose water, 1 teaspoonful olive oil and enough flour to thicken or to make a soft paste. Cover the arms with this at night and wrap them with soft cloth. Wash off in the morning and repeat the process until the skin is smooth and white.

Keeping Hair in Curl

Before doing the hair up on curlers moisten it with a mixture made by beating the white of an egg until light and adding to this ¼ cupful of cold water and 1 teaspoonful of sugar.

For Wrinkles

By combining 2 drams of butter, 2 drams of essence of turpentine and 1 dram of mastic, a cream is made which prevents wrinkles.

Almond Wash

Mash 4 ounces of sweet blanched almonds and rub until very fine and add 24 ounces of rose water. In another saucepan mix 4 drams each of white wax, castile or other pure soap and oil of almonds, 30 drops oil of lavender and 16 drops of attar of roses. Heat gently and combine the two mixtures by beating with an egg beater.   Strain.

Milk of Almonds

To soften and nourish the skin use milk of almonds. Put 2 ounces of sweet almonds, the thin shell variety usually found on the market, through a food grinder. Mash thoroughly and add 2 cupfuls of clean soft water which has been boiled and cooled. Mix and rub until a milky emulsion is made. Then strain through muslin. A few drops of perfume may be added if one wishes. Wash the face with this liquid.

Complexion Sachets

Combine 1 teaspoonful of flaxseed with an equal amount of bran and place in a tiny muslin bag. Moisten with water and apply to pimples and blackheads. Allow to remain on about 5 minutes, then remove and squeeze out the blackhead or the matter from the pimple. Pat the surface with very cold water.

Hand Wash

Combine 2 ounces glycerin, the juice of 2 lemons, 2 tablespoonfuls of water and a few drops of carbolic acid. Bottle and shake. Use on the hands after they have been washed.

After Dish Washing

Make a paste by moistening 1 cupful of cornmeal with vinegar. Use this in cleansing the hands after dish washing instead of soap. This keeps the skin soft and white.

For Oily Hair

Beat the white of an egg as stiff as possible. Rub it into the hair until the locks are wet. Let dry and then brush out.

Dry Cleaning the Hair Brush

Mix together equal amounts of salt and flour and rub through the brush. Comb out.

To Remove Onion Odor from Breath

A cupful of strong coffee will remove onion odors from the breath.

Flaxseed was a staple in every farm home. It was used mainly as a poultice.

Women who fought dishpan hands with this home-designed paste were chemists even though they did not know it. The acid in vinegar neutralized the alkali left by harsh soaps on their hands.

An elderly woman brought this beauty secret up-to-date by advising that baking soda be placed in little bags for soothing bath water.

What a temptation it must have been to whiten teeth often when berries in the strawberry patch were ripe and juicy.

Interest in weight control by selecting the correct foods was starting to blossom in 1922. The scarcity of foods during World War I put the spotlight on nutrition experts and what they had to say. The campaign on eating wisely continues to flourish.

To Soften Bath Water

Fill tiny bags of cheesecloth with crystals of sequi carbonate, using about 3 tablespoonfuls to a bag. This prevents a dry and itchy feeling that the skin sometimes has after bathing.

For Sunburn

If cucumbers are seasonable, select a ripe one and cut a slice from it. Rub this over the burned skin. This is cooling and soothing.

To Whiten Teeth

Rub crushed strawberries on the teeth before retiring.

Grandmother's Complexion Clearer

A fig paste which grandmother made to keep the complexion clear is one with a laxative effect. In addition it is good to eat. Chop 1 cupful of figs, 1 cupful of raisins and 1 ounce of senna leaves together. Add 1 cupful of water and 3 tablespoonfuls of sugar. Cook gently until a paste is made. Add $\frac{1}{4}$ teaspoonful of lemon juice and remove the mixture from the fire. Cut in 1 inch squares when cool and eat one before retiring.

About Dieting

The foods which help a thin person to gain in weight are butter, cream, whole milk, eggs and olive oil. Eggnogs are fine. Vegetables should be served with butter or rich cream sauces and an abundance of cream may be used on the dessert.

Fat persons should eat less butter, cream, bacon, pastry, cake and all kinds of sweets and starches if they wish to lose weight. A liberal use of fruits and green vegetables is desirable, but the vegetables should be served with very little, if any, butter and no cream.

Other foods which fat persons should eat very sparingly and in which thin ones may indulge are candies, ice creams, griddlecakes with syrup, breakfast cereals with cream and rich puddings. Fat persons should also avoid macaroni, rice and large quantities of biscuits and bread. Some potato may be eaten because it is filling and a slice of bread at every meal is not objectionable, especially if it is not buttered. Skim milk should be used instead of cream whenever possible and an egg for breakfast is all right. Salad dressings for fat persons should be of the boiled variety while thin folks wishing to put on weight will find the dressings with olive oil as a foundation helpful.

Since every red blood corpuscle must contain iron, foods rich in this substance help to keep one in good health and to give one rosy cheeks and red lips. Foods containing much iron are spinach, cabbage, lean beef, egg yolks, raisins, prunes and most fruits. Milk is very wholesome. Every person requires about 2 cupfuls a day, thin persons whole milk and fat ones skim milk. As a protection against scurvy, some fresh food should be included in the meals every day. Oranges, tomatoes, raw cabbage, lettuce and raw carrots are valuable for this purpose. As a rule, a tonic will not be needed in the spring if there has been an abundance of fruit, vegetables and milk in the winter diet. The use of too much fat meat should be avoided by everyone, and the fat person should eat practically none of it.

The History of Beauty Secrets

The beauty secrets in this chapter were collected during 1922 in interviews with women in what now is known as the Golden Age group. The homespun aids evolved about a century ago when ingredients to make them were available in most country homes.

After the advertising of commercial cosmetics flashed into prominence, the old-time secrets gradually disappeared. Suntan became fashionable. Country girls accepted it with an enthusiasm equal to that of their mothers and grandmothers in their efforts to avoid skins tinted by the sun.

Dermatologists certainly would question the value of and even the desirability of using many of the home remedies on all types of skin. But they reflect women's search for beauty in days when life was simpler and their creative ability to use the materials at hand.

Almost every country homemaker 50 years ago was a good practical nurse. The sick in the family, unless seriously ill, were cared for in the home. Keeping her patients well fed with nourishing foods was an ambition of most women.

CHAPTER 5

COOKING FOR THE SICK

SINCE persons who are ill frequently are not hungry, it requires skill to prepare food to cater to their appetites, as every mother knows. Cleanliness of food, dishes and tray is essential. Neat service is helpful and broken or cracked dishes are not permissible. Only an excellent quality of food simply prepared should be used. If a dish is supposed to be hot, serve it that way, not as a lukewarm combination, and if frozen desserts are on the menu, they should reach the patient without melting.

An attractive tray stimulates the appetite. Pretty dishes, artistically molded puddings, a tiny spray of flowers or ferns in a small vase, a joke or quotation from a current magazine or a fancy garnish on one of the dishes will help put the patient in a happy frame of mind so he will forget himself and eat more heartily than he otherwise would.

Children are especially appreciative when their food is served in an unique way. If oatmeal will not be eaten from a bowl, it frequently is relished if served in a flower pot. A tiny pot covered with gay crepe paper is used. In it the glass containing the oatmeal and milk or cream is set. A flower is inserted in the pot.

A banana boat is equally enticing. This consists of an empty banana skin lined with oiled paper and filled with food. Toothpicks are used for oars. A pig made from a hollow lemon with toothpicks for legs and cloves for its features delights sick children. If this is filled with a frozen ice which may be sipped through a straw, it is indeed enticing. Baskets may be fashioned from empty oranges and grapefruits lined with oiled paper. Toast hollowed out to hold scrambled eggs may represent a nest and bread cut in fancy shapes with cooky cutters and toasted usually wins approval.

The recipes given in this chapter are suitable for use in catering to the invalid's appetite. If a doctor is attending the ill person, it is advisable for the homemaker to suggest to the physician some of the dishes she wishes to prepare. This frequently is helpful to the doctor who may not have time to work out the menu as carefully as the housemother does.

Rice Water

2 tablespoonfuls rice   3 cupfuls cold water
                    ¼ teaspoonful salt

Wash the rice thoroughly. Soak 30 minutes in the cold water, heat gradually to the boiling point and let boil until soft. Strain, reheat, season with salt, and if too thick, dilute with boiling water.

Beef Juice

Cut round steak into small portions or grind in a food chopper. Place in a double boiler and add a little salt. Let stand 30 minutes and then gradually heat, keeping the meat below the boiling point. Squeeze out the juice and serve either hot or cold. One pound of meat will make about ½ cupful of the juice.

Fluffy Lemonade

Roll 1 lemon until soft and remove the juice, excluding the seeds. Add 2 tablespoonfuls of sugar, 1 cupful of water and 1 tablespoonful of crushed ice. Just before serving add ¼ teaspoonful of soda.

Toast Water

Take a thick slice of bread and cut into small cubes. Brown in the oven, sprinkle with ¼ teaspoonful of salt and add 1 cupful of hot water. Cover and let stand until cool. Strain and serve hot or cold.

Beef Tea

Wipe 1 pound of lean beef with a clean cloth moistened in water, cut in tiny cubes and place in a quart fruit jar. Add 2 cupfuls of cold water and ½ teaspoonful of salt. Then set the

The recipes in this chapter, although still used to some extent in 1923, were heirlooms handed down from one generation to the next for many years.

Boys were enthusiastic about the whistles made from the slippery elm, but they took a dim view of slippery-elm tea.

jar on the back part of the stove in a kettle of cold water and bring the water gradually to the boiling point. Strain and serve while hot. Sometimes this beef tea is frozen before being served.

Coffee with Egg

Beat the yolk of an egg until light and add to it ½ cupful of hot milk and ½ cupful of hot coffee.

Slippery-Elm Tea

Steep about 2 ounces of slippery-elm bark in 1 cupful of boiling water 30 minutes. Strain and add 3 teaspoonfuls of sugar and 1 teaspoonful of lemon juice. Serve hot or cold. If slippery-elm powder is used, dissolve 2 teaspoonfuls of it in the hot water.

Wholesome Broth

Beat 1 egg with ½ teaspoonful of sugar until the mixture is very light. Add 2 cupfuls of hot milk or boiling water and ½ teaspoonful of salt. Serve immediately.

Grandmother's Eggnog

Beat 1 egg yolk and 1 tablespoonful of sugar together until the mixture is light. Add 1 cupful of milk, 1 teaspoonful of vanilla and the stiffly beaten white of 1 egg. Pour over 2 tablespoonfuls of crushed ice and serve. If hot eggnog is desired, omit the egg white and heat the milk.

Coffee Delicious

Place 1 tablespoonful of finely ground coffee in ½ cupful of cold water and bring to the boiling point. Let stand 5 minutes, strain and add ½ cupful of hot milk. Serve at once with sugar if sweetening is desired.

Scalloped Egg

Mix 2 tablespoonfuls of cream, 2 tablespoonfuls of fine bread crumbs and ¼ teaspoonful of salt together. Butter an egg cup and place one-half the mixture in it. Break 1 egg on top of this and cover with the rest of the crumb mixture. Bake 5 minutes in a moderate oven. Garnish with strips of bread and butter or buttered toast.

Egg on Toast

Beat 1 egg slightly and add 1 tablespoonful of milk and ¼ teaspoonful of salt. Melt 1 teaspoonful of butter in a small frying pan and add the egg mixture. Cook until creamy, stirring gently. Toast a slice of bread, butter, and moisten slightly with a little warm milk. Pour the egg on the toast and serve garnished with parsley.

Invalid's Omelet

Place 2 eggs in a bowl, add ¾ teaspoonful of salt and a dash of pepper. Beat until light and fluffy and add 1 tablespoonful of milk. Melt 1 teaspoonful of butter in a small frying pan, pour in the egg and shake over the fire until the egg is set. Roll and serve on a hot plate. Garnish with bits of cooked chicken or ham or grated cheese.

Rice Treat

Pour ¼ cupful of milk in a saucepan and add an equal amount of cold boiled rice and 2 teaspoonfuls of melted butter. Heat gently. Beat the yolk of 1 egg and stir into the mixture and fold in the stiffly beaten white of the egg. Pour into a buttered and hot frying pan and brown on the bottom. Set in the oven to dry off the top and serve folded like an omelet. Garnish with bits of jelly. If the rice has not been salted, use about ½ teaspoonful of salt in this dish.

Beef Broth

Wipe 2 pounds of lean beef with a damp cloth, remove all particles of fat and skin and cut the lean meat in small pieces. Break the bones and place with the meat in the soup kettle. Add 1 teaspoonful of salt and 2 quarts of cold water. Heat gradually to the boiling point but do not boil. Remove the scum as it appears on the top. Simmer gently 4 hours, strain, cool, remove all fat and add 4 tablespoonfuls of rice, 1 stalk of celery and a

Clear, hot beef broth was one of the more-favored selections.

bayleaf and cook until the rice is soft, but do not boil. Serve hot with crackers.

Mutton Broth

Use 2 pounds of lean mutton and make in the same way as Beef Broth.

Chicken Stewed in Milk

Cut half a chicken into convenient pieces, remove the skin and put it into a fruit jar with 1 cupful of milk, a little pepper, salt and celery. Place the jar in a kettle containing water and gradually heat until the water simmers. Keep the water simmering until the chicken is tender, adding more water as it boils down. When the chicken is cooked, remove from the jar and pour the liquor around it into a pan. Thicken with a little arrowroot first placed in cold milk or a little flour. Pour the sauce over the chicken and serve hot.

Chicken Jelly

Simmer half a chicken, cut in convenient pieces, in a kettle containing 1 quart of water. During the cooking add 2 small stalks of celery, 2 tablespoonfuls of minced parsley and 1½ teaspoonfuls of salt. When the chicken is so tender that it falls in pieces, strain off the liquid and let cool. Skim off the fat. If allowed to stand overnight, this should be a clear and firm jelly.

Milk Broth

Place ½ cupful of the chicken jelly in a saucepan and add an equal amount of milk. Heat and serve hot with toast.

Oysters

Wash 1 cupful of oysters, drain, place in a pan and heat gently until the oysters are plump. Add 1 teaspoonful of butter, ½ teaspoonful of salt and a dash of pepper and serve hot on toast.

Broiled Chop

Use a mutton chop cut rather thick. Remove the skin and fat and rub the frying pan with the fat. Add the chop and heat over a hot fire. Turn constantly during the 10 minutes of cooking. Serve on a hot dish, sprinkling the chop with salt and a dash of pepper.

Broiled Steak

Use a piece of steak from the ribs or the haunch bone if possible. Heat the frying pan and rub a little piece of suet over it. Lay the steak in the pan and turn frequently during the 10 minutes it is cooking. Serve on a hot dish, sprinkling the meat with salt and a little pepper.

Beef Balls

Scrape ½ pound of lean meat until only the fiber is left. Mix the pulp with a little cream, season with salt and pepper and shape in tiny balls. Place a little butter in a hot frying pan. Roll the balls over this to take away the raw appearance, but serve very rare.

Chicken Broth

Skin the chicken, cut the meat from the bones and break up the bones. Put the meat and the bones in a kettle with 1½ quarts of cold water and 2 teaspoonfuls of salt. Simmer gently for at least 4 hours, keeping the fat skimmed off. Strain off the liquor and place in a saucepan. Add 2 teaspoonfuls of washed rice and simmer until this is tender.

Stewed Rabbit

Put a few pieces of rabbit in a fruit jar, after they have been boiled 3 minutes in water. This liquid in which it is parboiled is thrown away. Cover the meat with milk and add 1 teaspoonful of salt. Set the jar in a kettle of cold water and simmer gently until the rabbit is tender. Add more water as it cooks away.

Whenever a member of the family was "under the weather," as many a simple illness was diagnosed, the chicken coop was raided for a fine hen to convert into broth to serve with crisp toast made with homemade bread.

Baked Tomatoes

Cut the tomatoes in slices, after they have been washed and peeled, and put a layer of bread crumbs and then a layer of tomatoes in a greased baking dish. Repeat until all the tomatoes are used. Dot with butter, season with salt and bake in a moderate oven.

Tapioca Pudding

Wash and soak 1 teaspoonful of pearl tapioca overnight. Drain, place in a double boiler, add 1 cupful of milk, 1 tablespoonful of sugar and ¼ teaspoonful of salt. Cook until the mixture thickens, remove from the fire, add a few drops of vanilla and 1 egg yolk well beaten. Turn into a serving dish and cover with the stiffly beaten egg yolk in which 1 tablespoonful of sugar has been folded. Set in the oven and slowly brown the egg white. A few tablespoonfuls of chopped dates, figs, prunes or drained canned fruit may be added to the pudding just before it is removed from the stove if one wishes.

Apple Delight

Run 1 cupful of apple sauce through a fine sieve and fold in ½ cupful of stiffly whipped cream. If this is not fluffy enough, fold in the white of an egg beaten until dry. Flavor with a few drops of vanilla. The apple sauce should be sweetened or more sugar will need to be added.

Frozen Pudding

Place 1 cupful of milk in a double boiler and add 1 tablespoonful of sugar and 1 teaspoonful of cornstarch mixed together with a small portion of the milk. Stir until the mixture begins to thicken. Remove from the fire and add ¼ teaspoonful of vanilla, ⅛ teaspoonful of salt and 1 beaten egg. Stir until mixed, strain, cool and freeze. A fancy cream may be made by adding fruit or berries rubbed through a sieve.

Prune Fluff

Rub 1 cupful of cooked prunes through a sieve, add 1 tablespoonful of lemon juice and fold in 1 stiffly beaten egg white.

Frozen Pudding was one dessert the home nurse could depend on to tempt the lagging appetite of her recuperating patient.

Add 1 tablespoonful of sugar, pile on an oiled dish and set in the oven 3 minutes. Serve cold with a boiled custard or cream, plain or whipped.

Grape Jelly

Soak 1 tablespoonful of granulated gelatin in 4 tablespoonfuls of cold water and dissolve by stirring over hot water. Dissolve ½ cupful of sugar in 1 cupful of grape juice, heating this slightly. Add the gelatin and 1 tablespoonful of lemon juice and stir thoroughly. Set in a cold place until the mixture begins to harden. Then add the stiffly beaten whites of 3 eggs and beat the whole mixture until light and stiff. Serve with whipped cream or boiled custard.

Grandma's Floating Island

Heat 1 cupful of milk in a double boiler and add 1 tablespoonful of sugar, ¼ teaspoonful of cornstarch and ⅛ teaspoonful of salt which have been sifted together. Take from the fire and add 1 beaten egg yolk and stir until the mixture thickens. Add ⅛ teaspoonful of vanilla and pour into a dish. Set in a cold place. Beat the white of 1 egg until very stiff and dry and add 2 teaspoonfuls of powdered sugar. Drop this by spoonfuls on buttered paper and place in the oven two or three minutes and then place on top of the pudding in the dish.

Fruit Pudding

Use canned strawberries, raspberries or peaches. Strain 1 cupful through a coarse strainer, add ¼ cupful of sugar and ¼ teaspoonful of flavoring. Then fold in the stiffly beaten white of 1 egg. Set in a cool place and serve very cold.

Blanc Mange

Place 1 cupful of milk in a double boiler, heat, add 2 tablespoonfuls of arrowroot and 2 teaspoonfuls of sugar mixed together in a little water to form a paste. Stir until the mixture thickens, remove from the fire, add ¼ teaspoonful of vanilla and ⅛ teaspoonful of salt and pour into a mold. Let stand in a

One envelope unflavored gelatin was used in this dessert. Combine gelatin and sugar in double-boiler top, slowly add water and heat over boiling water, stirring constantly until gelatin dissolves. Stir in grape juice, which usually was homemade, and heat 5 minutes, stirring. Remove from heat, add lemon juice and chill until mixture begins to thicken. Then fold in egg whites.

Rennin tablets can be purchased in drugstores.

cold place until firm. Serve cold with whipped cream and garnished with fresh berries or candied cherries.

Junket Pudding

Dissolve ¼ rennin tablet in 1 teaspoonful of water. Dissolve 2 tablespoonfuls of sugar in 1 cupful of milk, add vanilla, a few drops, and heat the milk to body temperature. Add the rennin, turn into a wet mold and allow to remain undisturbed at room temperature until firm. Unmold and serve with sugar and cream.

Irish Moss Jelly

¼ cupful Irish moss	2 tablespoonfuls lemon or orange juice
2 figs	
1 cupful boiling water	3 tablespoonfuls sugar

Soak, pick over and wash the moss. Cut figs in strips. Add moss and figs to boiling water. Simmer about 20 minutes or until thick when dropped in a cold dish. Add lemon juice and sugar. Strain in a cold, wet mold.

The pudding, resembling blancmange, once was extremely popular in New England, where it was served with sugar and cream. Pioneers carried it to the Midwest, where it was served about 50 years ago with sliced bananas for an appealing bait. Irish moss is carrageen, a seaweed, dried, cleaned, bleached and packaged. Druggists know it as a demulcent, soothing to inflamed membranes.

INDEX

NOTES